Street Harassment as Everyday Violence

Street Harassment as Everyday Violence

Melinda A. Mills

LEXINGTON BOOKS
Lanham • Boulder • New York • London

Published by Lexington Books
An imprint of The Rowman & Littlefield Publishing Group, Inc.
4501 Forbes Boulevard, Suite 200, Lanham, Maryland 20706
www.rowman.com

86–90 Paul Street, London EC2A 4NE

British Library Cataloguing in Publication Information Available

Library of Congress Cataloging-in-Publication Data Available

ISBN 978-1-66691-237-1 (cloth)
ISBN 978-1-66691-239-5 (paperback)
ISBN 978-1-66691-238-8 (electronic)

To bell hooks, from whom I learned so much, including "talking back: thinking feminist, thinking black." Thank you for your powerful inspiration and example of creating a writer's life.
To Omar, my love. Thank you for filling our lives with light and laughter.

Contents

Introduction

As a teenage girl, I remember feeling a scary excitement when I ventured out into public by myself. The fear I felt stemmed from all of the cultural anxiety embedded in every warning I heard, urging me to be aware of my surroundings at all times; these warnings worked as cautionary tales, gesturing broadly at any real and imagined problems potential interactions with strangers might provoke. These implicit warnings intended to encourage me to engage in self-protective behaviors, to equip myself with an arsenal of strategies to socially and physically maneuver public spaces as safely as possible.

Little did I know that these warnings would persist well into my adulthood, shaping the social contours of my life, first as a girl-child and then as a woman. The excitement I felt surfaced from the glimmer of independence I felt at being trusted to take care of myself while I ran small errands for my parents. Any exhilaration I felt at the hint of such independence quickly dissipated whenever my "felt intuition"[1] sensed threats from others. While the words to describe what I sensed and experienced as threats eluded me early on, I would learn to understand them as street harassment.

My experience with street harassment almost exclusively involved managing men strangers' unwanted and unsolicited attention. Some men would say hello, while others might comment on my appearance. Others still would ask for money. The former instances illustrate that men's attempts to engage me or elicit a reaction reflect their male privilege and entitlement; in the latter case, men in economically precarious positions and in search of support could be considered harassing in their insistence or belligerence.

In the former instances, I considered men's efforts to engage me inappropriate and artificial, their words wearing a mask, thus disguising harassment as culturally expected pleasantries. Intuitively, I knew better than to believe these were everyday conversational mechanisms because I always felt uncomfortable. The harassment was lopsided and uneven, "conversations" that I did not consider as such because I did not consent to them. I found the

1

uneven exchanges with men strangers off-putting, offensive, unsettling, and uncomfortable.

As a shy, bespectacled introvert, I could easily have interpreted my unease in public through the lens of my personality, as opposed to a reflection of the broader societal level problem of patriarchy. I dreaded the moments that appeared to be "social interactions," which masked misguided motives that I came to understand as "street harassment." I enjoyed being in public, but I did not really enjoy interacting much with strangers, especially men strangers who often appeared considerably older than me.

I misunderstood my aversion to these encounters, initially attributing it to my quiet personality and displeasure at questionable, unsolicited attention. I later arrived at a different understanding of these encounters, eventually recognizing my displeasure *not* in all social interactions in public with strangers, but with street harassment. The trouble was I had so often experienced the two (street harassment and social interaction) as one and the same, especially in my early adulthood. Increasingly, strangers would attempt to engage me in what they saw as friendly conversation or what sociologist Mitch Duneier calls "sidewalk talk."[2]

Mostly, these strangers were men who asked what I found to be intrusive questions about my racial location and relationship status: "What are you?"; "Are you mixed?"; "Are you married?"; "Do you have a boyfriend? Do you want one?" I found their repertoire unimpressive and offensive, as they relied on a general set of questions that I learned to anticipate from men street harassers. Nevertheless, I resented feeling obligated to respond to these questions, and to provide both immediate *and* satisfactory answers to these men strangers.

That obligation stemmed in part from the lessons I learned as a young girl growing up in a small place, and in retrospect, from the persistence of patriarchy asserting itself in everyday ways that (socially, culturally) require women to perform emotional labor to comfort others, even at our own discomfort. At the intersection of gender socialization, cultural and familial upbringing or "good home training," I had been taught to always greet people courteously. Always.

At the points of encounter with street harassment, I engaged in internal struggles with this socialization. Did I always need to be nice to people who were not nice to me? (No, not necessarily.) Did I need to respect people who I found disrespectful of me? (Largely, yes.) Where would the pressures to internalize my socialization and cultural, familial values end, and my own empowerment begin? Why had I never been explicitly instructed to be self-protective, should a stranger say something unkind to me? Why was I expected and instructed to greet others with a hello and a smile, even at the expense of my own comfort? Had I misunderstood these expectations and instructions?

When I failed to produce accommodating answers to men who harassed me, when I failed to respond in a flattered and flattering way, and/or when I failed to respond at all, I suffered a plethora of consequences. I frequently felt trapped in the discourse of street harassment: if I responded, I would run the risk of appearing interested in such social interactions with men strangers; by extension, any engagement with men who harass would mean running the risk, I naively believed at the time, in being viewed as *that* kind of woman. Conversely, if I did not respond, I ran the risk of being perceived as arrogant or aloof. While I did not want to condone their behavior, I did not want to appear overly accommodating or friendly, nor rude and unfriendly. I did not want to endorse unflattering notions or stereotypes about the respective groups into which people placed me. In short, I did not want to be seen as "*that* kind of woman," with all of the attendant connotations proving problematic and negative. Over time, I discovered that, no matter how I moved (physically and discursively), I felt trapped: any way I responded (or not), I became *some* kind of woman.

The more I experienced street harassment, the clearer one thing became to me: I was *not* the kind of woman who enjoyed, appreciated, or felt flattered by street harassment.[3] I am not sure that many targets do. I *was* the kind of woman who spent a lot of time wondering about street harassment, thinking about how much it appeared to be a social interaction, often before quickly devolving and worsening into street harassment; I realized how much men relied on this misperception of me (and, likely, other targets) to create a false appearance of their own—as benevolent social actors simply expressing civility (as opposed to engaging in street harassment). I thought about discursive "tipping points" in social situations that potentially turn 1) a social interaction into street harassment, 2) a passerby into a target, 3) a person into a harasser, and 4) an urban public space into an inequitable one described as a "war zone."[4]

I also thought about some men's refusal to accept women's rejection of them. A paradox, but a revealing one at that. Like other women, I struggled with the aforementioned gender scripts I was expected to follow. I knew that those scripts existed to do just that—script behavior for women and for men. Among the latter, being verbally aggressive and assertive with women is one such script. Nevertheless, I wondered why men who harass women refuse to recognize that their women targets might not be flattered by their attention. (Why) do these men feel the right to ask all sorts of questions, except ones that easily might humanize everyone involved in the process: "Do you even *want* my attention?" or "Does my attention flatter you?"; "Are you comfortable with my attempt to engage you?"

Many men are not socialized to ask *these* kinds of questions to women. So often, they are encouraged to center themselves, deny their emotions and thus their humanity, and by extension, that of women. For men who learn to diminish women in attempts to assert their own dominance, they risk marginalizing women and objectifying themselves and others in the process and as a result.[5] In my experience, most men who harassed me boldly, yet incorrectly, assumed that I would welcome, enjoy and/or take kindly to their attention. Among those who harassed me, some would get furious at my (non)responses. If I was silent, they would curiously engage in behavior that most people would deem socially dissuasive, including the following: cursing me out or calling me derogatory names; accusing me of thinking I was "too good" for them; insinuating that I was a race traitor, and more. If I responded a certain way, they appeared enraged, angry at my attempts to equalize the interaction or neutralize the social situation. My efforts to minimize any impending verbal assaults often amplified them among men who harass.

At the time, I did not see my responses (or non-responses) as a stereotypically emasculating thing to do. Nevertheless, many of the men who harassed me may have experienced me in this way, viewing me as a woman who stepped out of line. Ironically, their inflammatory speech styles provided partial context for my usual reluctance to socially engage them to any degree, yet their reactions revealed a lot about their sense of place, privilege, and power, interactionally and societally. I was expected to respond in kind, or risk being called a "bitch," a "white bitch," and "stuck up" (all actual comments I heard while sitting and/or walking in public). When men verbally assaulted me, I always felt at risk. I mean, who wouldn't? If I spoke back to them, I risked being seen as a "sassy black woman," otherwise a mouthy woman who did not know her place in the world, and especially in relation to men, in this patriarchy. If I remained silent, I risked being racialized differently, with men harassers making disparaging comments in regard to my real or imagined whiteness. In those moments, I was seen as uppity and arrogant, aloofly above the whole scenario and the actors involved. It seemed that, no matter my reaction or response, I face multiple potential risks, whether social, physical, sexual, psychological, and/or emotional.

I remember thinking about the irony of my experiences with street harassment. Men who harass often used the social conventions of a conversation to make like they wanted to talk to me, but then they relied on their social power to dominate what they likely viewed as a "conversation." I could only respond if I played by their rules. Men harassers wanted my attention, yet if I asserted my agency in determining if and how to respond, I was regarded as the problem (not them nor their harassment).

Even my recognition of the problem sometimes made me feel like I was the problem, not the street harassment itself. In a social world of male privilege and patriarchal power, I continually appeared as an object to be desired, not a woman with choices to be expressed. In this appearance, I showed up as the problem, in terms of being physically and socially out of place (a woman out in public unaccompanied by a man). Furthermore, both my speech and my silence compounded that problem. How could this be? Street harassment proved to be where I would always get stuck between a rock and a hard place: between structure and agency; between silence and speech; between reticence and resistance; between risk and reward.

Having stepped out of bounds or being out of place in public, I compromised gender boundaries (based on traditional gender ideologies). By engaging men strangers, I complicated those boundaries even more, by advancing the idea that I was a woman "willing" to engage men strangers. Thus, my reactions "warranted" or "justified" me being harassed in the first place.

My recognition of this reality did little to comfort me. The more I wanted to ignore men harassers, the more they seemed to surface in my life. On the one hand, I knew I could use my experiences as data, but on the other hand, I did not want to have to deal with street harassment on a regular basis. I also did not want to normalize men's harassment in ways that I imagined they did. In my observation, men harassers normalized their harassment and their consequent verbally assaultive behavior, acting as if women targets would not find this type of aggressive behavior downright dissuasive of any further engagement.

It always puzzled me that men who harass often approach women with these occasionally (admittedly) smooth moves. However, once a woman does not respond to these disingenuous, albeit smooth moves (whether out of fear, rejection, or otherwise), some men harassers get considerably hostile. What would make such a social interaction inviting to a woman target of such harassment and hostility? Why would a woman target of harassment engage in a "conversation" with someone who so easily shifts from a "smooth operator" to verbally assaultive?

One could reasonably infer other qualities about a person (harasser) if they snap at a complete stranger for not saying hello, not offering a phone number, or otherwise not actively responding to any variety of their advances. In other words, a simple stretch of the imagination could easily lead one to connect verbally assaultive behavior to the potentiality or actuality of physically assaultive behavior. If such a continuum of gender violence exists, street harassment should be situated within it, as it reflects a range of violent behaviors and aggressions.

While I discuss and explore various fine lines in this work, I will note here that men who harass often mistake this fine line between "hello and harassment" because patriarchal logic, as a general rule, encourages men to be aggressive, assertive, and hegemonically masculine: treating women like objects is the result of the kind of socialization most men endure in this society. Harassment, then, becomes a by-product of patriarchy and sexist socialization.

Arguably, women targets of harassment may sometimes similarly mistake this fine line, simply because it can be so slippery. For example, since I was often unsure about and doubted my own perception of who or what really "counted" as harassing, I initially had a difficult time distinguishing between the two myself (is this a "hello" or harassment?). Once a benign social interaction "crossed the line" and became street harassment, I could tell (but typically only *once* it crossed the line). I came to rely upon "felt intuition"[6] to guide me through socially prickly and precarious situations.

I did not want to perceive all social interactions with men strangers as harassing, nor did I want to continue dismissing my experiences with actual harassment. I remained reluctant about, or puzzled over, how to "properly" react to social situations that blurred the line between social interactions and street harassment. The kind of aggressive behavior I encountered in men who harassed me served as some confirmation or clarification that their behavior was in fact street harassment. My growing awareness of and ability to recognize street harassment did little to minimize the actual risk involved in dealing with men who harass women.

While I could stop wondering if what I was experiencing was street harassment, I could not stop wondering how to respond to, and even further, how to solve the problem of street harassment. (I often thought to myself, "Am I being harassed? Is *this* harassment? If so, what do I *do*?!"). Aside from wishing myself invisible or invincible in those moments, I wanted some sort of interactional guidebook, on how to navigate social situations made hostile by the street harassment from men strangers.[7]

In many ways, I envision this book contributing to a conversation about street harassment, as a means of remedying the problem by first recognizing it. Because it is precisely society's failure to take seriously the (sometimes daily) imposition of street harassment that imbues value in the narratives around which this book weaves its fabric, we must recognize street harassment as such. Contrary to popular perception, street harassment is not an *individual* problem, though it is largely constructed and commonly viewed as such. Instead, this book takes, as a starting point, that street harassment is a *social* problem.

Holly Kearl, founder of the nonprofit, Stop Street Harassment, makes this point in her dedication to ending street harassment and heightening awareness of how unsafe spaces are for women. In a *Huffington Post* article, Kearl asks, "Do you remember when it was legal for a man to make sexually explicit or sexist remarks to a woman at work? I don't. . . . Do you remember when it was legal for a man to make sexually explicit or sexist remarks to a woman on the street or at a bus stop? I do. Sexual harassment in public is legal. But it shouldn't be."[8] Kearl's comments point to the way in which social interactions that targets deem to be harassing are accommodated in public spaces, and remain unregulated.

It was in these moments of being harassed, and the ones that followed, that I began to link the sense of entitlement and male privilege that men enjoy to varying degrees to their ability to aggressively express themselves in public and private, in relation to women. I was also able to contextualize their behavior in relation to the "triad of violence,"[9] in which men are socialized to perpetuate gender violence against themselves, other men, and women.

Recognizing this triad of violence did little to minimize the actual risk involved in dealing with men who harass women. However, this literature offered some vindication that street harassment is a real problem, and helped strengthen my understanding of the larger social forces guiding the behavior of men who harass, and shaping social interactions publicly and privately between them and women targets.

Seeing the larger linkages between historical and contemporary violence in society, alongside the multidimensional aspects of what appears to be some socially sanctioned violence displayed by men, situates street harassment in a broader, more meaningful context. To this end, I situate street harassment in the context of rape culture, a discussion that appears more centrally in chapter 2. I argue that rape culture accommodates street harassment, partially through the notion that women generally are men's property, physically and socially.[10]

While I did not initially see the immediate and obvious connections between street harassment and violence against women, I now see how women targets of street harassment may also be victims of other kinds of (gendered, sexualized, and racialized) violence. I focus my efforts in this book on the subject of street harassment as a form of everyday violence. I introduce the term, "web of violence" to provide insight about the connections between street harassment and other forms of violence. Recognizing this web situates and complicates, or sometimes intensifies, women's experiences of street harassment.

I build bridges between historical and contemporary society to illustrate the impact of violence on everyone. Finally, I provide excerpts from the narratives of respondents, as they directly discuss their experiences confronting and managing street harassment. I share examples of how they negotiate(d) social interactions with men who harass, to document their experiences, as well as to demonstrate their bravery and agency.

MOTIVATIONS FOR THIS RESEARCH

The experiences I had with street harassment—which began in young girl-hood and persisted through my young adulthood—largely motivated this project. I encountered street harassment long before I even knew what to call that unwanted and unsolicited attention. I continued to experience street harassment for years, and found it particularly intense and invasive when I lived in New York City and Atlanta. In fact, when I first moved to Atlanta from Queens, I optimistically (but incorrectly) imagined that I would encounter *less* (certainly not more) street harassment than I had previously encountered in New York City (and elsewhere).

Because I had experienced street harassment for many years before I began my formal investigation of the social phenomenon, I had acquired both the experiential knowledge to more readily identify it, and the social savvy to respond when it happened. I learned over time how to anticipate and/or predict it. Street harassment became such a ubiquitous part of my life. I began to normalize it, seeing it as commonplace and inevitable (within a racialized hierarchical patriarchy). This goes to show that the social structures of society impact everyone, albeit differently.

I normalized my responses to street harassment (alongside my attempts to normalize the harassment itself), by convincing myself that every similarly shy young woman would be brave enough to stand up to her street harasser(s). Then I began to think that maybe I was being something other than brave. I remember sharing stories with family, friends, coworkers, and graduate school classmates, telling them about how men would harass me on the street.

I recall repeatedly asking friends and family, "Why? Why do men (who harass) do that? What do they think is going to happen?" Rather than direct their line of inquiry at the men and their behavior, many friends and family members focused on why I chose to respond to men who harassed me. This misdirection of attention frustrated me. As with the street harassment, I became the target of attention, assessment, and attendant scrutiny. Why was I to blame for being harassed in the first place?[11]

Not only was I annoyed at the insistence of the men harassers, I also became increasingly bothered by the ways people responded to my truth-telling about my experiences with harassment. Many of these people failed to scrutinize the behavior of the men harassers, and instead opted to question me and my decisions to talk back to them. Just as a victim of rape or sexual assault often faces questions that challenge her credibility, decency, and respectability, I felt my encounters with street harassment left others challenging the legitimacy of my experiences.

This feeling of invalidation added an unanticipated layer of complexity to my negotiations with street harassment. I felt trapped in the tensions of respectability politics and punished by discourses of femininity that blame the victim rather than hold men who harass accountable. These discourses suggested that I asked for or was looking for this attention, and that by engaging men or not, I was at fault, not them.

I became more selective about who I shared my experiences with, because I found the invalidation a variation of the victimization street harassment created in my life. Writing about my experiences in this book, through auto-biographical accounts initially recorded in autoethnographic form, allows me to confront the ways that these discourses "doubly silence" street harassment victims. This "double silence"[12] often sits at the site/s of street harassment itself and then gets amplified elsewhere (whenever or wherever a target remains reticent or refuses to relate the details of the everyday violence of street harassment. Double silence creates productive tensions that draw attention to women who choose silence (over speech) as a tactic for managing street harassment, as well as any invalidation of women's experiences (including the minimization of their experiences that follows from skeptical, dubious others).

I discuss the many dimensions of this silence, when it surfaces during, as well as around discourses of or about, street harassment. Imagine the cognitive dissonance that surfaces in surviving, in one moment, the violence of street harassment. Imagine next being able to actually adequately summarize those traumatic personal experiences and articulate them, only to be silenced by people's—believing themselves to be well intended listeners—"victim blaming" or "shaming" responses. Not only, then, did I start to see how silence, during and after street harassment, proved useful. While I explore this topic more later in the book, I posit here: There is a curious silence that emerges in discussions of street harassment that also often protect the perpetrator, while shaming the victim/target.

Social worker and shame researcher, Brené Brown, makes a point about disrupting shame by disrupting silence: "Shame hates it when we reach out and tell our story. It hates having words wrapped around it—it can't survive being shared. Shame loves secrecy. The most dangerous thing to do after a shaming experience is hide or bury our story."[13] By speaking through shame, people speak through the silences as well. Throughout this book, I explore the nuances and complexities of speech and silence, as negotiated during street harassment.

Through the writing process, I am able to re-negotiate the silencing that gets compounded where street harassment and victim blaming converge. I hope that sharing my own experiences here disrupts some of the silence, while opening up space to share women's narratives about street harassment and validate our experiences.[14] I continue to encounter (primarily) gendered (but also racialized) discourses that attempt to regulate women's speech by encouraging our silences, while encouraging men's speech and discouraging their silence. I attempt to trouble or disrupt these discourses in this text. I do so in an effort to expose the extent to which rape culture[15] guides and upholds much of these problematic responses to and discourses of street harassment, and the very practice or act of street harassment itself.

Making the Personal Political

For years, I remained perplexed about why I was being targeted in public by street harassers, and was baffled by the glaring lack of social support for targets. I puzzled over these thoughts mostly privately until I was introduced to two texts that shifted the way I thought, and talked about street harassment. One visual text, the documentary film, *War Zone*,[16] inspired me to see how women could handle street harassment. At the time, I was in awe of this woman (the filmmaker) walking around asking men who harassed her to explain their behavior. I found her film and her actions audacious, bold, empowering, and inspiring.

The details of the classroom conversations that surrounded the documentary have since faded, but the energy of the empowerment I began to experience and enjoy in Dr. Layli (Phillips) Maparyan's graduate Women's Studies class, *Feminist Methodologies*, has persisted. In that space of feminist and womanist consciousness, I could see street harassment as a problem one could document, if not visually, then in other equally important ways. As a viewer of that film, I witnessed the everyday violence of street harassment, and that act of seeing empowered me to investigate and interrogate my experiences further.

If the film had not provided enough validation of my experience, Carol Brooks Gardner's book, *Passing By*, did. In her book, Gardner details the gendered experiences of public harassment. While reading Brooks' book left me feeling less alone or isolated in my experiences of street harassment, I felt disappointed that Gardner overlooked the extent to which street harassment is shaped not only by gender, but also race. The absence of much or any discussion on gendered racism further fueled my motivation for this study.

In my graduate classes, I was learning to see the complexities of identities, and I was no longer satisfied with the overgeneralization of "women" as a cohesive category. As a multiracial woman, I felt that my experiences with street harassment had as much to do with my race as my gender. Most of what I read about street harassment framed it as a gendered phenomenon, focusing on the category "woman," rather than exploring the complexities across categories; as a result, the nuances of people's intersectional identities got lost, overlooked, or altogether ignored.

Sample and Methodology

The search for this insight, information, and understanding involved interviewing women who agreed to participate in my research. Together, we discussed our experiences with street harassment, exploring several of the "slippery discourses" of street harassment. During the interviews, I asked the women to do the following: 1) define street harassment, 2) share the strategies that they employ(ed) to navigate urban public spaces, and 3) to reflect on the reasons they believe street harassment happens. In order to understand the cumulative impact of interactions that women targets of street harassment from men face, I studied their experiences, drawing comparisons to the existing literature, to sort out the similarities and differences between their narratives and ones already in print.

Having women share their experiences with street harassment differs from having ethnographers share their observations of social situations and interactions in public spaces. While both are valid and important ways of knowing, the accounts of ethnographers, or researchers conducting participant observations, even their "observant participation,"[17] should (does) not substitute for the direct accounts of the people being observed. In my research, I blend the etic and emic perspectives[18] to better understand women experiencing street harassment. To this end, I focus on the accounts women provided of their experiences navigating urban public spaces.

Collectively, the stories of women of various social locations weave together empirical and experiential knowledge stemming from our situated yet shifting locations, from our embodied social positions in society. This situated knowledge stands alongside the knowledge gained from other forms of ethnographic research, yet contrasts with this research in some important ways.

Many urban ethnographies offer insight based on participant observation, or the study of a population or place by a researcher positioned as "outsider." Arguably, another difference also stems from the social locations of women respondents and researchers as potential targets, and men ethnographers as less likely targets, of street harassment. This work contrasts with that type of ethnography in that I acknowledge my own experience with street harassment and cite this experiential knowledge as the major impetus shaping my motivation for studying this social problem and prompting me to do this research.

Conducting my ethnographic research, including qualitative interviews with twenty women, and autoethnographic work, allowed me to draw connections between people, places, and the social interactions that occur in the urban landscape of a major Southeast city. I developed more insight into women's lives and the ways we negotiate public spaces that are at once enlivening and threatening to many people. I learned different ways of seeing the social problem of street harassment. I gained a greater appreciation for the many considerations women make to keep themselves relatively safe in their attempt to minimize or reduce their risk in and heighten their enjoyment of public spaces.

In my own ethnographic research, I observed urban public spatial locations seemingly attractive to tourists and locals alike. These observations shaped my own sense of place and belonging in public, and I discuss them throughout this work. The interviews I conducted with these women shaped my interpretations of their experiences with street harassment and my own. In my analysis of these qualitative interviews, I examined the emergent themes produced in these narratives.

I wanted to know how women experienced street harassment at the intersections of their various social locations. In search of some answers, I decided to empirically investigate women's experiences with street harassment in urban public spaces. Curious about how others handled themselves in similar situations, or *if* other women found themselves in similar situations of street harassment, I conducted qualitative research with twenty women who reported being street harassed in an urban public space, and who worked, lived, or studied in the Southeast area where I conducted this research. Throughout this book, I utilize pseudonyms to protect the identities of the study participants.

This research consists of qualitative interview conversations[19] I conducted. The interview conversations lasted an average of one hour, and took place in a quiet office or conference room accessible to the participants and me. The interviews were audiotaped and later transcribed, then analyzed with grounded theory methods.

I purposefully drew a sample of white and black women to compare and contrast experiences at the intersections of gender and race. Of the twenty women respondents, ten self-identified as black, and the other ten self-identified as white. Because I had experienced street harassment as both a gendered and racialized experience, I wanted to investigate if and how other women experienced the intersections of gender and race at sites of street harassment. Did other women confront racialized and gendered street remarks? Did they experience street harassment as a racialized and gendered phenomenon? How did they respond?

At the time that I was conducting these interview conversations for my master's thesis research, I was simultaneously working on my doctoral research focused on multiracial identities. I realized that my own multiracial self-identity was shaping my experience with street harassment in ways that converged and diverged with that of my respondents.

While I begin this work with my own experiences, I center this book on that of the women I interviewed, to focus on their understandings of the everyday violence they encounter/ed. I intentionally explored the gendered and racialized aspects of street harassment, since much of my experience exposed gendered and racialized ways of being, speaking, seeing, and looking. The stories that I share in this book reveal the ways that women's experiences with street harassment converge and diverge.

Throughout this book, I discuss and reflect on my experiences with street harassment, alongside that of these women. I explore their narratives, along with the social and racial landscapes that shape social interactions that, sometimes, become street harassment. I also examine the broader social structures that enable street harassment, and that most often encourage men to assert their male privilege through these types of interactions. I attempt to complicate current understandings of street harassment by closely considering women's reactions to and negotiations with adversarial approaches by men. I do this as a way of accomplishing the following: working through the slippage between street harassment and social interactions in public; showing the messiness of the term "street harassment"; and documenting street harassment as a real social phenomenon with important, yet often dismissed or ignored connections to other forms of violence against women (or individual and institutional injustices and violence-structural racism, sexism, classism).

I also consider the ways that street harassment not only generates feelings of frustration but alienation and isolation. As I indicated earlier, I would often discuss my experiences and the horrors of street harassment with the important people in my life. Their responses sometimes made me feel like I did not have the right to respond, even if they understood that I did not deserve to be harassed in the first place.

This study allowed me to make the personal political. It illustrates how power asymmetries exist and operate across society, weaving into and informing social interactions that can go awry. This work contributes to the collective understanding of street harassment as a social problem.

Talking to women who also encountered street harassment allowed me to understand these shared experiences; it provided me with access to their interpretations of this social phenomenon, ones that not only move beyond, but actively challenge the idea of women "asking for it"[20] and men "behaving badly." The narratives they shared with me during our time together give voice to their embodied realities. I work to show the ways that this embodiment is complicated and full of contradictions that feel empowering and disempowering, exciting and scary, and more.

I center the voices of women in our interview conversations and in this text. I created and held space for them to share their stories, to counter ways that street harassment left them frequently feeling silenced, disregarded, or questioned. I wanted them to feel seen and heard, to feel lighter upon sharing their stories, to feel empowered through the acts of telling their truths.

During the interviews, women revealed the complexities of strategies they employ as they navigate urban public spaces. Centering their experiences and voices also demands that we pay attention to women as subjects, rather than as objects. Paying attention to women in this way not only diverges from the kind of attention often paid to women by men who harass, but demonstrates that women deserve to be paid attention to, in meaningful and respectful ways. Attending to women in these ways counters the devaluation, dehumanization, and objectification of women so central to street harassment.

In the process of conducting this research, I gained tremendous insight into how harassment directly and indirectly affects women. I discovered that I was not the only woman who dealt with and did not deserve nor always desire this attention. I learned how other women responded to and understood street harassment. This work illuminates our shared experiences.

My sentiments about my study of street harassment align with these words by Diana Taylor: "This study is my attempt to talk back."[21] Following Taylor, as well as the late bell hooks (from whom I learned more about "talking back, talking feminist"), I developed this project as a way to make sense of my own experiences, to engage my frustrations with street harassment, with never fully knowing when to speak up and when to stay silent in order to stay safe(r), in order to survive.

I make this point in an attempt to acknowledge the broader context of threat, danger, and disrespect in which street harassment occurs. I do so to demonstrate the complexities and considerations women make in negotiating urban public spaces. Next, I outline the contents and contours of each chapter in this book.

CHAPTER SUMMARIES

In chapter 1, I define street harassment using the literature to frame the discussion. I weave the voices of the respondents into the extent literature, to center their connotations, denotations, and understandings of street harassment. In doing so, I show how complex and multidimensional street harassment remains. I draw from our interview conversations, as a way to provide empirical data and experiential evidence of street harassment as a form of everyday violence. I make the case that street harassment remains largely unrecognized and unregulated as a social problem.

In chapter 2, I begin by acknowledging how street harassment reflects and connects to what I call the "web of violence." This web exists across time and space. It links the past to the present, and the local to the global. Understanding street harassment as a form of everyday violence, and one that links to other forms of violence against women, makes more visible this web of violence.

I also situate street harassment within the context of rape culture. I argue that, within the web of violence, a curious silence exists or emerges. This silence that surrounds violence conceals the injuries and injustices of street harassment. In discussing the dimensions of the web of violence, I introduce the term "multiplicative traumas" to acknowledge the potentially extensive list of wounds created by assaultive, offensive speech during street harassment (and other sites of violence).

In chapter 3, I begin the first of four chapters thematically organized around the concept of "danger." In this chapter, I consider controlling images of women, as they inform men who harass. I refer to this reliance upon controlling images as "dangerous ways of seeing," as reflected in the narratives of women reporting their experiences of street harassment. I discuss the difficulty women encounter who, as they try to challenge controlling images, run the risk of reinforcing them, compromising their own safety, or both.

Chapter 4 extends the theme of danger to the topic of discourses. In this chapter, I consider "discourses of danger," or the various directives, narratives, or myths that circulate about safety and danger in people and places. I take a look at how these discourses are gendered and racialized, to encourage women to invest in these discourses as self-protective measures (that are not always or ever fail-safe). I show how these discourses of danger become "dangerous discourses" that encourage women targets of street harassment to engage in victim-blaming discourses, and "dangerous ways of seeing" men who harass (through the limited lens of controlling images). I argue that this supports, rather than undoes, the web of violence created in misrecognizing people as "dangerous" problems or part of the problem (instead of solving the problem of street harassment).

In chapter 5, I continue to explore "dangerous ways of speaking." I show the nuances and complexities that women consider regarding their responses to men who harass. I demonstrate how women strategically use speech, silence, or a combination of both, to navigate street harassment. I provide examples of women using respect and civility, a sense of humor, and/or silence as equally valuable but situationally-contingent tools that facilitate their interactions with, or avoidance of, men who harass.

Finally, in chapter 6, I examine the double entendre of "dangerous ways of looking," in terms of women's appearance, and in terms of the gaze. I explore how women engage in emotional labor[22] and performative work in an effort to protect themselves by presenting themselves as respectably feminine. I consider how men who harass women, and may experience pleasure in visually consuming women, engage in "dangerous ways of looking." These actions disturb, agitate, and offend many women targets of harassment.

I also consider the technological gaze that paradoxically provides a space to report street harassment while possibly undermining the potential in arresting the problem (by focusing solely on the perpetrators, and identifying sites of violence, instead of realigning power asymmetries, dismantling rape culture, and eradicating the roots of violence by addressing and ameliorating attendant problems in society, for example).[23]

In the final analysis, I conclude by linking these various dangers to one another, showing how they get woven together in the web of violence. I end by asking what might bring an end to street harassment, if the very technologies designed to allow women to document street harassment actually intensifies the surveillance of women targets, not men who harass.

I also draw attention to the problems that these seeming solutions create, in turning the technological gaze onto men who harass, does this technology turn us into self-policing people? Or do we re-invent the street harassment wheel, with a new target—men—in sight? What are the effective ways we can address the various "dangers"—real and imagined—in society, to create more safety and less street harassment for everyone?

NOTES

1. Phillip Brian Harper, "The Evidence of Felt Intuition: Minority Experience, Everyday Life, and Critical Speculative Knowledge," *GLQ: A Journal of Lesbian and Gay Studies* 6, no. 4 (2000): 641–57.

2. Mitch Duneier. *Sidewalk.* New York: Farrar, Straus and Giroux, 1999.

3. I contrast this statement with the popular myth that some women enjoy the attention of men who harass. I contend that any such enjoyment would logically recategorize "harassment" into hellos and similar forms of communication and civility, not verbal hostility.

4. This is a nod to filmmaker, Maggie Hadleigh-West, and her film, *War Zone*, 1998.

5. Sut Jhally. *The Codes of Gender: Identity and Performance in Popular Culture.* Videorecording, 2008.

6. See Phillip Brian Harper, "The Evidence of Felt Intuition: Minority Experience, Everyday Life, and Critical Speculative Knowledge," *GLQ: A Journal of Lesbian and Gay Studies* 6, no. 4 (2000): 641–57.

7. The website, Stop Street Harassment, provides strategies for dealing with harassers. The suggested strategies include responding to and educating harassers, intervening on harassment, and/or reporting to an authority, including an employer,

police officer, or transit worker. For people who encounter street harassment, the site offers three ranges of responses ranging from nonconfrontational, to assertive confrontational, to aggressive confrontational. [See www.stopstreetharassment.org/strategies/moment/.]

8. Holly Kearl. "Street Harassment: A Real Problem that Requires Legal Regulation," *Huffington Post*, March 12, 2010b.

9. Michael Kaufmann. "The Construction of Masculinity and the Triad of Men's Violence" in *Beyond Patriarchy: Essays on Pleasure, Power, and Change*. New York: Oxford University Press, 1987.

10. Carole J. Sheffield. "Sexual Terrorism" in *Gender Violence: Interdisciplinary Perspectives (2nd Ed.)*. Edited by Laura O'Toole, Jessica Schiffman, and Margie Kiter Edwards. Pp. 111–130. New York: NYU Press, 2007.

11. Victim blaming is a common, though problematic, response that displaces accountability unto targets instead of perpetrators.

12. Blogger, Sarah Pierson Beaulieu, talks about this "double silence" in terms of birth trauma and rape trauma. (Please see http://theenlivenproject.com/category/sexual-violence/double-silence/). She argues that, in this society, people do not talk much about the traumas of birth for sexual assault and rape survivors. Because the discourses around birthing focus on pain and pleasure, but not necessarily *trauma*, it creates a potential triggering for survivors surprised that they feel *birth trauma*, as it intersects with their feelings of rape trauma.

13. Brené Brown. *The Gifts of Imperfection: Letting Go of Who You Think You're Supposed to Be and Embrace Who You Are*. Center City, MN: Hazelden, 2010: 25.

14. Just as Holly Kearl formed "Stop Street Harassment" as a way to raise awareness and gather the stories of women, this book attempts to extend that conversation, by adding more voices and stories to the discussion.

15. "It is a complex of beliefs that encourages male sexual aggression and supports violence against women. It is a society where violence is seen as sexy and sexuality as violent. In a rape culture, women perceive a continuum of threatened violence that ranges from sexual remarks to sexual touching to rape itself. A rape culture condones physical and emotional terrorism against women and presents it as the norm. In a rape culture, both men and women assume that sexual violence is a fact of life, as inevitable as death or taxes. This violence, however, is neither biologically nor divinely ordained. Much of what we accept as inevitable is in fact the expression of values and attitudes that can change." See Emilie Buchwald, Pamela R. Fletcher, and Martha Roth (Eds.). *Transforming a Rape Culture*. Minneapolis, MN: Milkweed Editions, 2005: xi.

16. Maggie Hadleigh-West. *War Zone*. Video recording. A Film Fatale, Inc./Hank Levine Film. Northampton, MA: GmbH Production, 1998.

17. See Elijah Anderson. *The Cosmopolitan Canopy: Race and Civility in Everyday Life*. New York: W.W. Norton, 2010.

18. See Conrad Phillip Kottak and Kathryn Kozaitis (2006). *On Being Different*. New York: McGraw Hill.

19. Linda Blum. *At the Breast: Ideologies of Breastfeeding and Motherhood in the Contemporary United States*. Boston: Beacon Press, 1999.

20. Kate Harding. *Asking for It: The Alarming Rise of Rape Culture—and What We Can Do About It*. Boston: Da Capo Lifetime Books, 2015.

21. Diana Taylor. *Disappearing Acts: Spectacles of Gender and Nationalism in Argentina's "Dirty War."* Durham, NC: Duke University Press, 1997: 21.

22. Arlie Hochschild. *The Managed Heart: Commercialization of Human Feeling.* Berkeley, CA: University of California Press, 2003/1983.

23. To this point, Kearl posits, "Women will never achieve equality with men until they have equal access to public places and the resources and opportunities they hold. And it seems women never will have equal access to public places until men stop harassing and assaulting them there." Kearl's points highlight the gender power asymmetries that exist in society, and that inform and shape our everyday interactions. (see Holly Kearl. "Street Harassment: A Real Problem that Requires Legal Regulation," *Huffington Post*, March 12, 2010b).

Chapter 1

Defining Street Harassment

What *is* street harassment and how does one know when one is being harassed and/or harassing? Can a target of harassment become a perpetrator of harassment in reaction to or retaliation of being targeted? What does street harassment look, feel, or sound like, and who decides? How will people know to take street harassment seriously if they do not know how to recognize it, name it, or contest it? How will people take it seriously, if women, as the typical targets of harassment, are often seen as "telling stories" (telling lies) versus telling truths, or more powerfully, "telling to live"?[1] What does "telling to live" mean in contrast to the common view that casts women victims of street harassment as "telling lies"?

In this work, I explore these questions in order to understand how patriarchy and rape culture create the space for street harassment. Many women find their authority often challenged or undermined in a patriarchy, and their credibility specifically questioned within the rape culture that prevails amidst or alongside misogyny. As a result, women who speak truth about how they experience various forms of violence are often viewed as "telling stories." Managing misogyny, or a hatred of women, often entails managing violence that gets expressed in a patriarchy, largely for the purpose of putting (and keeping) women "in their place." The stories that women targets of street harassment tell operate as an intervention to said violence, functioning as a means of "telling to live," and facilitating the potential to heal from the traumas caused by or stemming from street harassment.[2]

This work attempts to address that lacuna created by the lack of scholarly literature on street harassment. By drawing on the narratives of women who experience/d street harassment, I build on the small but significant body of work on street harassment, to further collective understanding. The work of Holly Kearl[3] proves powerful as the author, who has individually experienced street harassment, makes the personal political. In addition to three published books, Kearl created a nonprofit organization that shares the name of one of said books: Stop Street Harassment (SSH)[4] The attendant website provides ample resources including a blog, advice, resources, support, and more. The statistics presented on the site stem from a SSH survey:

> In 2014, SSH commissioned a 2,000-person national survey in the USA with surveying firm GfK. The survey found that 65% of all women had experienced street harassment. Among all women, 23% had been sexually touched, 20% had been followed, and 9% had been forced to do something sexual. Among men, 25% had been street harassed (a higher percentage of LGBT-identified men than heterosexual men reported this) and their most common form of harassment was homophobic or transphobic slurs (9%).

In contemporary society, as I argued earlier, street harassment remains largely unregulated or unrecognized, socially and legally, as a social problem. Street harassment is not recognized as a crime or an issue related to spatial injustice (with gendered, raced, classed, and sexualized intersections and implications).

This work troubles the limited ways of seeing and understanding violence, by showing how street harassment is a commonplace kind of interactional violence or spatial injustice that adversely impacts its targets, and its perpetrators. A national survey of women (612) conducted in 2000 found the following:

> [A]lmost all women had experienced street harassment: 87 percent of American women between the ages of 18–64 had been harassed by a male stranger; and over one half of them experienced "extreme" harassment including being touched, grabbed, rubbed, brushed or followed by a strange man on the street or other public place. Shattering the myth that street harassment is an urban problem, the survey found that women in all areas experienced it: 90 percent in rural areas, 88 percent in suburban areas, and 87 percent in urban areas. Sadly, 84 percent of women "consider changing their behavior to avoid street harassment."[5]

According to Kearl's data, street harassment is commonplace and ubiquitous.

Another nonprofit organization, Girls for Gender Equity (GGE), addresses issues of gender violence, failed compliance with federal legislation (*Title IX*) that ostensibly offers protection from said violence, and other dimensions of gender inequity. Their efforts to address street harassment and focus on equal rights legislation and its implementation are also detailed in the book, *Hey Shorty!*[6] Within that text, the authors introduce readers to the term, "street sexual harassment,"[7] which adds nuance to existing terms like "public harassment"[8] and "street harassment."[9]

While the book (*Hey Shorty!*) focuses on young girls' and women's experiences with violence in a variety of settings, other books (including Carol Brooks Gardner's book, *Passing By*) focus more squarely on adult women's experiences. These texts speak to a continuity in experience with street harassment across decades and generations. They gesture at the ubiquity of this social problem as one that lingers, even as attention to street harassment as a social problem grows.

In Bowman's work, "Street Harassment and the Ghettoization of Women," she focuses on the dilemma created by the protection of free speech, and the slippage between that and hate speech that arguably constitutes much of the discourse of (or embedded in) street harassment. Her discussion of the difficulty of regulating speech in public spaces dovetails with that of Smith et al. In the latter case, their work attempts to ensure that the legislation designated to protect access to equal education provides a protective atmosphere to young girls and women. Kearl makes a similar argument, advocating for legal recognition and regulation of street harassment.[10]

Feminist legal scholars have debated the regulation of speech in public, pointing to the ways that public or street harassment could constitute a crime in its assaultive character ("fighting words"). Laura Nielsen makes this point in her work, *License to Harass*. She considers how threatening street harassment is to its targets, and how unregulated offensive public speech remains commonplace and reflective of racist and sexist systems of oppression. She documents how threatening this everyday language is and explores people's legal consciousness regarding their rights about protection from offensive public speech.

Nielsen and other scholars recognize the near impossibility of this regulation, citing the infringement on the harasser's right to free speech. Just as the law protects such speech, the law ostensibly protects perpetrators in many ways.[11] By diminishing the significance of street harassment, this social problem continues to compromise civility in urban public spaces. As Nielsen argues, the questionable effectiveness of the legislation and regulation of street harassment suggests intentionality, with regards to its lack of punishment of perpetrators. Her work offers a critique of both street harassment and society's response to it.

Is the lack of regulation of offensive public speech simply a refusal to recognize street harassment as a social problem, or to respond to it with negative sanctions? Does this refusal to regulate street harassment reflect an intention to replicate power asymmetries in public life, as they exist in private life as well? Drawing parallels between perpetrators of violence specific to street harassment and to other forms of sexual violence acknowledges the "blurred lines" that also exist between free speech and offensive public speech; I discuss this more in considering the slippage between "hello" and "harassment." I also explore the productive tensions between speech and silence, to consider how women rely on both as strategies to navigate street harassment. I turn next to a discussion of some of the literature that helped identify and name the problem of offensive public speech and verbally assaultive behavior.

In her book, *Passing By: Gender and Public Harassment*, Carol Brooks Gardner writes, "I often write as if I alone have discovered public harassment. It *is* true that I have named it.[12] Many colleagues have written about the phenomenon of marked incivility in the street and about streets and public places as sites for more brutal behavior."[13] With this observation, Gardner notes the way that sociologists have likely studied incivility, but perhaps without much of a gendered lens or analytical framework.

While this elevates Gardner's initial contribution to the literature, it obscures the existing literature that attempted to show incivility by way of the "ghettoization of women" in public spaces. Enter Cynthia Grant Bowman. While Gardner makes claims about naming "public harassment," Bowman writes about "street harassment" in her work.[14] When taken together, the two offer enriched understandings of public and street harassment. Both can be credited for establishing a platform upon which to build research and debates about street harassment. Their contributions help us name and begin to identify a different "problem that has no name"[15]: the problem of street harassment.

In part, this problem of street harassment reflects the problem of a patriarchal society that draws loud silences around violence against women, and conjures up screams of resistance that so often fall on deaf ears. Naming street harassment as a problem troubles the silence that surrounds violence against women, draws attention to the ways that violence weaves a web into the fabric of social life, and extends outward to affect us all, indirectly, if not directly. Naming street harassment as a social problem connects the problem of violence that hides in plain sight (and that people attempt to tuck neatly away) in the home, in schools, at work, in any other setting, out into the public. Naming street harassment is a way of "airing dirty laundry" publicly, by linking all of the various forms of violence together, to illustrate how it shows up on the street, in plain sight, and still manages to get (mis)read as a conversation, not as a violent or aggressive kind of interaction.

In this chapter, I name street harassment as a social problem, in order for it to be continually recognized as such. It is important that it be distinguished from enjoyable everyday interactions, or the ways people inhabit and interact in public spaces that show or display civility, connection, recognition, and respect. I name street harassment in an effort to show how violence that exists everywhere gets expressed in these everyday interactions, which allows us to look specifically at public spaces, while wondering what goes on behind closed doors. I name street harassment to recognize its targets, and create the space for those targets to produce their own meanings and understandings of what social interactions that they believe "count" as street harassment. I weave some of the women respondents' definitions of street harassment with that presented in the existing literature.

In her work, Gardner defines "public places" as follows:

[T]hose sites and contexts that our society understands to be open to all; our characteristic behavior and appearance for public places do and are meant to vary from those for private dwellings. Communication in public places is characteristically appearance dependent; that is, the individual relies on her or his estimation of another's discernible, visible form of a clue to what is, for the context, significant identity, and the individual understands that others will judge her or him in the same way.[16]

Her discussion here offers suggestions about why street harassment masks its own appearance to be mistaken as an everyday social interaction. In her investigation, Gardner found that public harassment includes a range of behaviors that interrupt the communication between individuals in these public places.

Gardner defines public harassment as including the following: "pinching, slapping, hitting, shouted remarks, vulgarity, insults, sly innuendo, ogling, and stalking. Public harassment is on a continuum of possible events, beginning when customary civility among strangers is abrogated and ending with the transition to violent crime: assault, rape, or murder."[17] Gardner's description of a *transition* to violent crime suggests that whatever precedes said violent crime (verbal assaults in the case of street harassment) is neither violent nor criminal, yet legal scholars might argue otherwise. Some of my respondents certainly did.

For example, Julie, a white working-class lesbian, said, "Street harassment is making people uncomfortable; it can be violence, or just catcalls, intimidation." Julie went on to describe her experiences and expressed her concern about her potential vulnerability in relation to men harassers' potential violence toward or harm of her. She imagined ways to empower herself, but spoke honestly about the disparity she imagined between her ability to defend herself and the relative threat to her safety and well-being.

Julie had what might be described as a fear of this *transition* to violent crime, as Gardner describes above, but also understood the act/s of street harassment as a form of violence (irrespective of whether or not more or intensified violence followed). This contrasts with other respondents who saw street harassment as a part of everyday life. As Nikki Jones argues, young girls and women engage society by recognizing "violence as the backdrop of everyday life."[18] As such, street harassment is an everyday violence that young girls and women face in urban areas. I elaborate on the extent to which this everyday violence links public expressions of violence, such as street harassment, to private expressions of violence, such as sexual assault.

The assaultive and offensive capacity of street harassment provides partial explanation for what motivates feminist scholars, activists, and justice workers to insist on the legal regulation of street harassment[19] (also called "excitable speech,"[20] or "offensive public speech.)"[21] These and other scholars make the case that policing speech in public would be a messy battle. But would it prove to be a necessary one, in order to achieve spatial justice and equity in this society?

As Olivia, a black working-class respondent noted, street harassment compromises women's ability to enjoy public spaces free of harm: "Street harassment is situations where an individual is receiving unwarranted sexual advances that can be perceived as a threat to their personal space. . . . To me, safety isn't just direct bodily harm, but emotional, that personal space that you sort of uphold, um, where it may not be threatening, but some people aren't comfortable having exchanges with people that they don't know. So, so, physical, emotional, and social safety then." Olivia's comments add dimension to the ways people feel safe, explaining how street harassment shortchanges and interferes with those feelings of safety and comfort. (Street harassment is "a stranger saying something that is unwanted or unwelcome when I am walking down the street.")

Olivia's understanding of street harassment underscores the potential or imagined (not imaginary) threat that men who harass pose to their (typically women) targets. Because men who harass often fail to recognize themselves as harassers or their action as harassing, they are likely to fail to see themselves as threatening. Yet, as women targets such as Olivia describe, men harassers do pose a threat, and their harassment is threatening in this very potentiality and its actuality. In some ways, then, the threat is always already present, signified by the street harassment itself, then heightened or magnified by the way in which the men continue to harass (or de-escalated by men's diminishment of harassment).

Olivia's comments echoed my earlier thoughts about my own social and physical discomfort moving through public spaces when I was a young woman. Olivia's definition and explanation show that she conceptualized street harassment in relation to safety, not simply in terms of harm or injury. Her comments suggest a "triad of safety" exists, perhaps as a counterpoint to the "triad of violence."[22] The triad of *safety* recognizes people's needs or desire to feel physical, emotional, and social safety, dimensions of which street harassment compromises.

Other respondents offered definitions in alignment with Olivia's. Martha, another black heterosexual working-class woman noted, "I define street harassment as a stranger saying something that is unwanted or unwelcome when I am walking down the street." Red, a middle-class black bisexual woman, defined street harassment in this way: "It's basically a man trying to get your attention by any means, whether it's 'Psst, psst,' or "Hey, hey, 'red'"; or somebody blowing their horn at you, while you're walking down the street." Mickie, a heterosexual middle-class black woman, had this exchange during our interview conversation:

> Mickie: "When typically any male that is trying to talk to you, and you *don't* want to talk to them, they start making negative comments about your body, about who they think you are now that you don't wanna talk to them."
> Author: "What sorts of negative comments do they make?"
> Mickie: "Well, you're not that pretty anyway, or I didn't really want to talk to you."

Mickie's comments illustrate how men who harass often do so in a retaliatory way; the men appear angry, perhaps, because they have been socially slighted or altogether rejected by their targets; they fail to recognize their (mis)behavior as even more reason for women *not* to reciprocate attention.

In addition to having street harassment threaten people's safety and compromise their comfort level, Snow, a heterosexual working-class white woman respondent, explained, "It's an intrusion to this personal space. It's a breeching of the interaction on the street. Something that goes not according to the rules." Another heterosexual working-class white woman respondent, Sarah, echoed and agreed with Snow's point, noting how intrusive and invasive street harassment feels. Sarah described street harassment as including or constituted by the following:

> Anything where anyone is intruding on another person. Also, like saying anything to me. If someone looks as though they don't want to talk to you, or they're minding their own business, and someone else intrudes on that, I think that in itself is harassment. And it doesn't have to be negative, like, "You've got a big butt." or anything. I think when someone says, "Hey, good looking!," that's harassment to me.

Sarah's definition of street harassment had many dimensions, such that "there are different types but I don't think one's worse than the other. I mean I consider them all to be negative." Rather than ranking or differentiating between milder or more extreme forms of street harassment, Sarah regarded any kind of unsolicited street remarks as harassment.

While Sarah could accommodate gestures of civility, or engage strangers in the ritualized form of civil inattention (where "if you have eye contact, then it's different, if you're allowing for that person to say something because you have their eye contact"), she was not at all accommodating of the imposition that stemmed from unsolicited street remarks ("but like if you're not paying attention, and we do that on purpose in many occasions, then I think someone saying anything I guess."). When asked if she finds any attention from men who harass positive or neutral, rather than negative, Sarah offered, "I guess there are different types (of harassment) but I don't think one's worse than the other. I mean I consider them all to be negative. . . . I don't generally find any of them (men's comments) positive, because if somebody does compliment me, I still don't find it positive because they don't know me and it's just like, all they're saying is what they can see on my outside layer and so they're going to be, 'Oh, you're beautiful,' like, 'You don't know me. Just don't.'" Sarah's disinterest in men's comments suggests that she sees their remarks as disingenuous and unnecessary, superficial even. That men strangers comment on her appearance reflects the ways in which women are always already their bodies, which illustrates the extent to which they experience objectification. Through society, and often during street harassment, they become spectacles, put under surveillance, objectified and scrutinized, as well as assessed by others for their pleasure.

Despite some of the respondents describing street harassment as threatening, imposing, and compromising to their safety, well-being and enjoyment of public spaces, street harassment continues to be deemed relatively *unthreatening* and unproblematic in society:

> Women . . . can currently experience shouted insults, determined trailing, and pinches and grabs by strange men and be fairly certain that no one—not the perpetrator and probably no official—will think anything of note has happened. Thus, public harassment is a sort of civic denial, the study of how, why, and with what effects this harassment exists for women and men.[23]

Thus, public harassment disrupts the dominant discourse about civility and instead points to the way that "crime is taken to be a reality."[24] Gardner's point underscores how infrequently violence against women is taken seriously. If and when violence against women occurs, we may or may not recognize it as such, and more often than not, we choose not to regulate or respond to it. Gardner's point reminds us that in a patriarchy, women must confront the reality of crime, typically from positions of relative vulnerability and lack of legal protection. Women's social locations as varied by race and class also differentially shape experiences with patriarchal protections and the lack thereof.

This vulnerability and lack of legal protection exists as a contradiction in a patriarchy, where women are rhetorically acknowledged as deserving of men's protection. Nevertheless, we hear from women targets of street harassment that they felt anything but protected by men during such encounters.

Women's bodies have always operated as "public texts" that men can read and choose (or neglect to protect) as they so desire.[25] Susie, a black heterosexual middle-class woman in my study, defined street harassment as this: "anyone that says something to me that upsets me or makes me feel uncomfortable." When asked to provide examples, Susie mentioned that she gets told very sexualized things because she is bow-legged; men perceive her "body as evidence"[26] of her "hypersexuality." While she did not initially see this part of her body as flawed, she came to reinterpret this because of the perpetual and continual reminder, via the various highly sexual street remarks men made about her.

Men presumed her to be sexually skilled as a result of her bow-legged body; perhaps this also relates to the hypersexualization of brown and black women's bodies. Black women in particular have been constructed as hypersexual and animalistic.[27] These controlling images of black women's bodies suggest an always already availability that problematizes the kinds of interactions that black women report having with others. These images of black women present its own set of challenges in everyday interactions, and can be particularly problematic to negotiate in tenuous moments such as street harassment.

Across time and space, black feminist scholars note, black women's bodies have been put on display.[28] Historian Karla Holloway contends:

> Identity matters when private personhood is made public. In a public sphere, where gender or race reign through the force of social construct, historical pattern, and even constitutional authority, social narratives are shaped within the nation's body politic. . . . It is my argument that there are some bodies that will and can ordinarily disappear into the normative, that are not vulnerable to the socialized identity scripts that ensnare public narratives. White male heterosexuals are the unspecified norm against which alternative bodies find themselves publicly visible.[29]

Holloway's work pays attention to the publicity and visibility of black women's bodies, and the extent to which their bodily autonomy and personal privacy were compromised and denied by the colonizing and patriarchal white male gaze.

Holloway's work links to that of Patricia Hill Collins, who argues that black women are constructed as always already hypersexual objects:

> African Americans and Black culture are highly visible within the American movies, music, sports, dance, and fashion that help shape contemporary ideologies of race, gender, sexuality, and class in a global context. Sexual

spectacles travel, and they matter. Historical context disappears, leaving seemingly free-floating images in its wake that become the new vocabulary that joins
quite disparate entities.[30]

Collins continues to discuss how African Americans are curiously positioned
within national discussions and debates about sexual politics, yet persistently
show up in terms of the problematic imagery.

In this context, then, we can situate some of the black women respondents'
experiences with street harassment. That Susie is sexualized by black men
harassers should come as little surprise then, given the history of constructing
black women's bodies as spectacular ones.[31] Consider what Karla Holloway
writes on the matter:

> Spectacularity, a hyperpublic notice, exists in direct relationship to ethnicity and
> gender. In the United States, this has traditionally meant that blacks and women
> find themselves noticeable in public ways that scan and sculpt perspectives
> regarding their private personhood. In this national script, the bodies of women
> and blacks are always and already public.[32]

Perhaps no less surprising, or the more confounding part, is Susie's silence,
which seems the residue of the historical legacy of gendered racism (think
Sarah Baartman, Henrietta Lacks, and more).[33] Susie briefly explained her
frustration with street harassment when she noted, "Usually I just stay quiet
because I always say to myself, 'They have the freedom to say whatever they
want to say, and I just have the freedom to not respond.'" Susie's comments
remain striking, in that she clearly expresses, in the comfort of the interview
conversation, the price some women pay for being in public.

That Susie feels silenced and sexualized during street harassment illustrates the importance of taking street harassment seriously. Her comments
also reveal the messiness in regulating speech, in order to offer her and other
targets of harassment some minimal social and legal protection. I engage
these tensions between speech and silence throughout this work, and consider
their dynamics as women work to negotiate street harassment.

What Susie describes relates to the disciplinary mechanism of street
harassment, which silence women. Her comments reveal her acceptance, or
tolerance, of this requirement for women. Some women, who would rather
reject the gendered expectations that socially support women's silence, may
feel unsafe being vocal during street harassment.

Many women consider the pros and cons of speech and silence, including
the risks to employing discursive speech practices during street harassment.
A strange and curious paradox often surfaces for women who think that
speaking back to strangers during street harassment might feel empowering;

oftentimes, finding and using one's voice in such moments actually creates a backlash that some women report feeling disempowered during street harassment.

Susie's experiences reveal this contradiction and the complexity around speech and silence. It is important to recognize that she, as do other women, felt compelled to protect herself rather than challenge such norms. Thus, the feminist notion of "finding your voice" is not singularly or universally empowering or emboldening, especially not when women's voices encourage and fuel men's violence against women. In this work, I explore the shifting significance and meanings attached to speech and silence, as it plays out during street harassment.

Susie's comments also serve as a powerful reminder of the way black women, in her example, continue to struggle for bodily autonomy, as well as full citizenship and freedom (a struggle more generally pursued by women). Street harassment certainly compromises such rights and freedom. Throughout this book, I demonstrate how white and black women continue to struggle for their right (to be in public and private, safely and securely, in speech or in silence).

Productive tensions exist in the debate about street harassment, in regards to free versus offensive speech.[34] Susie draws attention to that debate, in her recognition of the ways that men are a protected group, and the ways that women can attempt to protect themselves from men harassers in public through silence. In her work, Audre Lorde wrote, "Your silence will not protect you."[35] But in Susie's case, does it? As I discuss in later chapters, silence often proves both protective and/or problematic at once.

Finally, Amy, a middle-class white heterosexual woman, defined street harassment in this way: "I would say being in a public space, literally on the street, and having men make noises, or words, or gestures specifically for me, towards me, in relation to how I look and I'd say the motivation is to, I want to say like (children) tease but it's some stronger word, like whistling or calling out but it's not, well, no I think sometimes it can be to flatter me, but I also think it can be specifically to get a reaction from me." Amy's comments suggest that her *reaction* means more to men harassers than her *feelings*. That men harassers do not always actually speak *to* her, but *at* her, or with noises, not always words, suggests the extent to which men who harass may not consider the impact of their actions on their women targets. Their primary concern may be the reaction, as Amy implies.

Provoking a reaction differs from respectfully engaging a woman stranger in a conversation in a public place. Again, this is partially what differentiates a social interaction from street harassment (as I discuss later). In sum, street harassment includes the persistent attempts by men to get women's attention, behavior deemed threatening, intimidating, invasive, evaluative, intrusive, and unwanted; and unsolicited; but also neutral and civil.

An Unregulated Crime?:
Street Harassment as Normalized Violence

Just as Gardner suggests that street remarks and harassment go unregulated as a crime against women, others suggest that variations of violence against women go similarly unpunished. Not only does rape often go unpunished, it is commonly not recognized as a crime. On Pinterest a few years ago, the following sign offered this powerful observation: "Rape is the most common crime on college campuses in the U.S."

As noted throughout this work, much of the "silence of violence" or the "silence that surrounds violence" against women begins to explain why these acts are not taken seriously, not regarded as crimes, and may be diminished or disregarded as serious offenses or at all injurious to women victims. The silence that surrounds violence also reflects, as the above quote from Susie illustrates, how women targets of violence (including street harassment, sexual assault, stalking, and/or rape), feel silenced.

Joy James also addresses this issue of the illegibility of criminality in her work, *Resisting State Violence.* In considering the historical context of sexual assault, harassment, and rape, James draws attention to the disparate ways violence could be seen and unseen. The danger in the persistent double standard, or different ways of (not) seeing violence, meant that some groups were seen as always already violent (black men) which left white men's violent unseen. By extension, and in relation to this seen and unseen violence, black women were always already hypersexual (Jezebels). "In brief, jezebels couldn't be raped."[36] This notion constructed black women as invulnerable to threat, and incapable of violating; these constructions legitimated and accommodated violence directed at black women, while enabling violence among its perpetrators.

James notes:

African American men . . . were identified as rapists; defined as inherently promiscuous, African American women could not be violated because they were said to be without virtue. A white man could not desire a brute or likely join in coalition with someone considered to be a sexual object. During the era of lynching, voluntary sexual associations between black males and white females were constructed as rape, and were punishable by death (of the African American involved). Wells and others argued that the mythology of black sexual pathology that motivated lynching functioned as the apologia for rape in a society where actual and alleged assaults against whites were prosecuted while convictions in cases of sexual violence against black women were rare.[37]

This discussion encourages us to consider how street harassment reflects the intersections of sexism and racism in historical and contemporary contexts.

Danielle McGuire centers her work on the historical context that supported street and public harassment of black women during the burgeoning civil rights movements of the mid-1900s.[38] Turning her analytical lens on this historical moment allows us to tack current practices and social behavior in contemporary society to previous behavior throughout history. As McGuire discusses, the legacy of racism and sexism remains evidenced in the mis/ treatment of black women who suffered harassment simply for being themselves. The harassment of women of various social locations persists, and invites us to consider ways to ending this inequity, especially as evidence exists to suggest that, as a society, we remain reluctant to regulate street harassment or recognize it as problematic.

The intersecting points raised in the work of these scholars (Bowman, Gardner, James, Kearl, and McGuire)[39] raise interesting and nagging questions about crime (especially as it relates to public harassment), prompting one to ask, "Is street harassment a crime?" If so, how does such harassment get regulated, particularly given how *unregulated* such harassment has been in the past? If rape is not regarded or hardly recognized as a crime, why would street harassment be?[40] (That street harassment is so hard to define also complicates the process of regulating it and deeming it criminal behavior.) What would it take for violence against women, in its various form, to be legally and socially recognized as offensive, if not criminal?

Feminist legal scholar, Cynthia Bowman, entertains these questions when she posits:

> A recurrent theme of feminist jurisprudence is that the law fails to take seriously events which affect women's lives. The law trivializes or simply ignores events that have a profound effect upon women's consciousness, physical well-being, and freedom. Until relatively recently, for example, no term even existed to describe what is now universally called "sexual harassment," although the phenomenon itself was well known to women.[41]

Arguably, "no term even existed" because violence against women is and has been normalized and naturalized.[42] While efforts to name street harassment has led to the creation of the term (which now exists), efforts to do more than name the social problem remain minimal. Street harassment may no longer be a "problem that has no name," but its problematic practice and presence in society persists. Street harassment may, in fact, be encouraged, because it reproduces the kinds of power asymmetries that reinforce racist and sexist domination and privilege.[43]

The normalization of violence against women reflects rape culture in the United States specifically, and global patriarchy more generally. Rape culture reflects broad patterns of sexualized violence that often gets reframed as "sexy violence."[44] When this violence is not sexualized, it is often trivialized, diminished, or ignored. That violence against women largely goes unnoticed and unpunished illustrates the presence of rape culture.

That women expend energy trying to avoid, minimize, or deal in/directly with the violence that rape culture supports and encourages marks just a part of the problem. In the following chapter, I address in more depth what rape culture has to do with street harassment, including why neither street harassment nor rape is taken very seriously legally or socially in the United States (or globally, for that matter).

The existing literature explores the normalization of street harassment through its denial as a problem: "Street harassment is a phenomenon that has not generally been viewed by academics, judges, or legislators as a problem requiring legal redress, either because these mostly male observers have not noticed the behavior or because they have considered it trivial and thus not within the proper scope of the law."[45]

Scholars argue that white male privilege impedes men's ability to see sexism as a problem in its many manifestations.[46] This would begin to explain why white men manage to abuse their privilege and power, by sexually assaulting women, and not having to face negative sanctions or punishments. In fact, we could argue that society supports, if not encourages, such violence, from past historical moments up to the present. Researchers illustrate the importance of feminist legal scholars, activists, and public policy experts in shaping legislation to formalize public protection of women's rights.[47]

Another way of understanding the normalization (and minimization) of violence is to consider the literary concept of "forwarding."[48] This literary technique known as "forwarding" allows readers of a text to create distance between themselves and what the text describes. In a similar fashion, anyone who dismisses the empirical evidence of violence as an everyday occurrence is practicing "forwarding."

Furthermore, violence in the United States impacts everyone, so responding to the epidemic of violence by distancing or denying its prevalence seems to exacerbate its already dangerous potential. Ignoring the extent to which violence disrupts and diminishes the quality of our lives also reflects another dangerous dimension of the normalization process.

Certainly, we see examples of the normalization of violence, as discussed below, in much of the ethnographic work conducted by men researchers. Thus, if scholar ethnographers cannot or choose not to properly document the problem of street harassment as it may or may not unfold before their own eyes, and the legal system also "fails to see" street harassment as a problem, then why would (or should) ordinary citizens be held to a higher standard of civility or responsibility? It only seems likely that society will largely continue to disregard street harassment as a crime, much less regard it as a serious social problem.

Sometimes, the problem of street harassment gets intensified by its ostensible invisibility and illegibility. Let me explain the paradox. If street harassment is a "problem that has no name," the ways in which scholars describe (or not) social phenomena frames readers' ability to interpret social data. As illustrated in the following example, when such social interactions between men and women strangers are framed as "verbal entanglement" instead of "street harassment," readers may accept the information as presented (without question, contestation, or a different interpretation).

Some men in public may attempt to "verbally entangle" some women in conversations.[49] Depending on the ways the women react or respond to these "verbal entanglements," the men may intensify their attention to the women, escalating the interaction to harassment by degree of hostility, antagonism, or anger directed at the target/s. In this case, street harassment reflects the public arena in which the harassment occurs, and the stage in which such "interactional vandalism"[50] plays out.

While the possibility certainly exists in which social interactions are more playful and reciprocal (key ingredients to a mutually enjoyable and civil experience), a greater possibility exists that these social interactions will be lopsided and imbalanced, experienced as an imposition, an unwanted conversation or a nuisance. Yet, many men ethnographers neglect to describe social situations in this way. Notably, many men ethnographers have described such social interactions as anything *but* street harassment.

In some cases, some describe situations that sound like street harassment as interactions that occur under the "cosmopolitan canopy."[51] While the thick description of the city provides insight into specific cityscapes, work that reinterprets or reframes street harassment as benign social interaction between strangers can normalize these tenuous situations. Work that veils a social problem such as street harassment under the guise of civil interaction (or civil inattention) partially explains how the problem of street harassment hides in plain sight, in society and in scholarship (such as ethnographies).

The way scholars write about or edit out accounts of street harassment partially explains its illegibility and invisibility as an everyday occurrence, and violence at that. At other times, the illegibility of street harassment may account for its invisibility, and therefore its normalization. The illegibility may partially be the result of social interactions that look like *civility* to an observer of those interactions, but that may be experienced (as evidenced in the reporting of street harassment) as *incivility* to individuals within those interactions.

This partially explains the lack of literature on street harassment as it presents situations that some would describe in vastly different ways. In other words, street harassment hides in plain sight, in many ethnographic accounts of urban landscapes, and in those very landscapes themselves. Curiously, most scholars purposefully studying street harassment challenge its illegibility and invisibility in society, by drawing attention to this problem. However, one is left to wonder if anyone in addition to targets of street harassment literally see it and socially recognize it as a problem.

The work of Nikki Jones offers up one example of how attending to gender, race, and class makes street harassment more visible to urban ethnographers studying social life.[52] Jones illustrates how young girls and women learn how to navigate urban public spaces as safely as they possibly can, surviving by adopting the "code of the street."[53] Her work can be read as a point of contrast to that of Anderson.[54]

I argue that one might read passages of *The Cosmopolitan Canopy* as examples of street harassment, despite Anderson's failure to name the interaction as such. Anderson provides one such example, when he describes a sixty-something older black man who does this:

> [L]ooks down at the floor, then up to study the passersby, stares vacantly into space, and pans the runway again. He sees various people wearing shorts and a halter . . . The man is transfixed. He studies her every move. Finally, their eyes meet and lock. She's even with him now, about to pass by. He looks her up and down, struck by her display. As she passes, he demonstratively turns his head. Both know what has just happened. Some onlookers know, too. All are attracted to this instant. Then, as suddenly as this show began, it is over . . .[55]

As a feminist woman ethnographer and a target of street harassment, I read this passage with puzzlement, and wonder, "*What* has just happened? What kind of 'show' is he talking about or referring to?" I can only speculatively conclude that Anderson has just normalized street harassment, though I cannot be sure. Nor can I be sure that something other than the performance staged by urban dwellers, for their own and/or others' pleasure has happened. My own embodied knowledge encourages me to read this passage and wonder, given the way Anderson describes the interactional dynamic, if street harassment is "what has just happened."

Yet, Anderson's emphasis on the older man's behavior, behavior which seems like ogling and objectification of women, seems more about the man's enjoyment and visual pleasure (enjoyment of her striking display). Why is it normalized as a part of city life? What would the older man say if the younger woman checked him on "studying her every move" or on his being "transfixed"? What feminist interventions might we offer here, to disrupt the discussion of the display of bodies and pleasantries in public spaces that allow street harassment to hide in plain sight? Can we safely and comfortably accommodate social or visual (nonverbal) interactions between strangers predicated upon the pleasure of seeing and being seen?

Instead of deflecting attention away from moments that sound like street harassment, I turn more fully throughout this work toward the topic of street harassment as a social problem. One of the key contributions I hope to make in this work is adding evidence to support the recognition of street harassment as a social, not individual, problem. I investigate and interrogate social interactions through a feminist lens, to gather more information about my own and other women's experiences with street harassment. Illustrating the normalization of violence underscores the importance of this work, and the ways in which violence adversely shapes our everyday lives and interactions with one another. This also requires us to acknowledge the interconnectedness of violence, as the assortment of weak and strong ties in social groups and networks that link us directly and indirectly to one another.

While I focus in this book on gender violence that targets women, I must acknowledge the extent to which men are more often the "typical targets" of men's violence. In order to illustrate this point, I develop a discussion in the following chapter on the web of violence that imbricates us all in this society. Next, I discuss the sample and methods employed in this research. I follow that by addressing the dilemma described above, as related to acknowledging the difficulty of studying social interactions including the fine line between "hello and street harassment."

FROM "HELLO" TO "HARASSMENT": SLIPPERY DISCOURSES OF STREET HARASSMENT

According to many of my respondents, street harassment often begins benevolently, in what appears to be a conversation. Sometimes this benevolence is mutually agreed upon, and sometimes not. Benevolence becomes contestable when men harassers "cross the (ill-defined) line" but continue to see themselves as carrying on a conversation, not as becoming harassing.

What are the "blurred lines" that exist between hello and harassment, or between everyday speech acts and everyday violence (street harassment being one form); between consensual casual conversation in public spaces and street harassment as an unwanted and unsolicited imposition of interaction; and the blurred lines between the verbally assaultive character of street harassment and more obviously physical types of assaults?

The "gray area" or "blurred lines" between everyday social interaction and everyday violence exists in the form of street harassment. These terms, "gray area," and "blurred lines," refer to the language that emerges in a rape culture. Specifically, the terms suggest a certain ambiguity regarding the line between sex and rape. Here, I use them to suggest that similar blurred lines may exist regarding the distinction between social interaction and street harassment. To explore these blurred lines, I consider the benefits of paralleling street injustice and sexual violence. To that end, I situate street harassment in the context of rape culture, as a way of emphasizing the everyday occurrence of this violence.

Some of the women respondents in my study drew very firm boundaries around social interactions with strangers in urban public spaces, and thus had a very clear understanding of street harassment as an act that crosses "the line," moving from appropriate or acceptable to unacceptable interaction. This "line" could also be understood as distinguishing between the harasser's "right" to free speech, and the target's right to not be harassed; the line is also about the potentially productive tension between free speech and hate speech or offensive speech.

"The line" between social interaction and street harassment may differ for every target, varying on the basis of personal and social boundaries, individual histories with violence, and knowledge of navigating urban public spaces (being "streetwise"). This line may in fact be "the line in the sand,"[56] one that can be drawn and eroded in a moment's notice. In such cases, the shifting tides of social interactions suggest that women targets have much to consider and negotiate if street harassment can wash away a woman's boundaries, and quickly seep into what starts as a social interaction.

Other women targets of harassment sometimes find it hard to define the shift from social interaction to street harassment, or from "everyday speech" to "interactional vandalism" or street harassment. Men who harass may conveniently frame their harassment as conversational, to normalize it, and get away with it. They can choose to see their behavior as an imposition or an entitlement. Often, male privilege and heteronormativity impede men's ability to gauge when this shift occurs. After all, the codes of gender[57] encourage men to be dominant, aggressive, and assertive. This code includes verbal engagement between men and women, and begins to explain why many men fail to see their behavior as harassment.

The codes of gender meet the code of the street to produce potentially tense sites of social interaction. Jones[58] builds on Anderson's[59] work, by showing the particular set of tensions that young girls experience when navigating urban public spaces. As people attempt to respect the codes of gender and the code of the street, they may end up harming others or being harmed, in their efforts to protect themselves, and their street credibility, reputation, and status.

This harm often plays out during social interactions that shift from that to street harassment, or what Mitch Duneier describes as "interactional vandalism."[60] The shift between a benevolent or normative social interaction and what Duneier describes as "interactional vandalism" is an important one because it marks the difference between a conversation and harassment. What Duneier calls interactional vandalism others might call street harassment. Is the distinction an important one? (It depends on whom you ask.)

The distinction between "interactional vandalism" and street harassment may seem a trivial point, but it reflects a larger matter. The line between a hello and harassment reflects yet another "gray area" where one person's definition of the situation considers it a conversation, and another considers it street harassment. Because of the gray area between a hello and harassment, and due to the limited empirical evidence in the broader literature, the study of street harassment has yet to address these blurred lines, or "slippery discourses."

However, scholars have attended to these nuances in research on sexual harassment, so I will borrow from this literature to illustrate its importance and relevance here. For example, scholars distinguish between varying degrees of sexualized language and behavior, explaining that some sexualized behavior pushes the boundary lines of acceptable behavior; when accompanied with laughter, or framed as humor, this behavior is condoned.[61] Thus, variations in harassment, such as sexual banter, razzing, heckling, and hassling muddy interpretations of harassment, creating even more shades of gray, or blurred lines.

While no surprise to scholars who posit, "What constitutes harassment is hard to say,"[62] my respondents could not come to any one conclusion about what constitutes street harassment. However, they each had their own ideas about where they drew the line between benevolent conversation and harassment, or unsolicited, unwanted remarks and attention. Each respondent had a different threshold, noted what they perceived as harassing behavior, and provided examples from their personal lives during the interview conversations, to illustrate or support their definition.

The respondents' definitions then help counter or clarify some of the existing inconsistency in definitions of sexual and street harassment with the former being categorized into two types: quid pro quo and hostile work environment;[63] and the latter remaining largely (legally) unregulated, partially due to the degree of variation of such harassment, and the multiple interpretations as well. This variation in interpretation of intention and action makes messy, blurry, and fuzzy this thing called "harassment."

Part of what complicates the task of defining and regulating street harassment relates the generalized confusion (for some) about where talking (and the right to free speech) ends and harassment (as a kind of offensive or hate speech) begins and a reluctance or refusal to regulate speech because individuals do not want to have their rights infringed upon. As stated earlier, the rights of the harasser/speaker seem to get offered more protection than the harassed/listener/responder in most cases).[64]

It is important to consider how street harassment tacks onto rape and rape culture in fundamental ways. Street harassment appears to produce similar kinds of blurred lines between interaction and "interactional vandalism," and often crosses the line in ways that people seldom speak about, punish, or disrupt. In this way, street harassment might benefit from the language of consent and sexual agency advocacy intended to challenge rape culture.

Making consent a requirement for conversations in urban public spaces would sour the spontaneity that makes such spaces fun to inhabit. However, the idea of consent is a promising one, in that it highlights how so much of what people (harassers) consider social interaction others (targets) consider harassment. If the idea of consent circulates in ways that parallel consent for sexual activity, imagine how this would change public discourses, and the kinds of interactions strangers had in public spaces. To borrow from this sex-positive, anti-rape language, imagine if people willingly or enthusiastically consented to conversations in public? What if people were encouraged to "just say no," or learned that "no means no," in ways that mimic rape-reduction programming? What would the public response look or sound like?

The Blurred Lines between an Initial "Yes" and an Eventual "No"

In many ways, parallels between rape and street harassment exist. In the latter case, a woman may initially respond to, or even initiate, social interactions with strangers on the street, just as she may choose to initiate sexual advances with strangers (or familiar others). At what point can a woman walk away from a conversation that discomforts her, without fearing that she will be harassed or harmed, socially or sexually?

In both cases (of rape and street harassment), when things go awry because of the man's aggression and insistence, a woman is often deemed responsible. She is often denied her agency and the choice to cease participation in a conversation or flirtation. The (il)logic of rape and street harassment suggests that women "want it," or otherwise invite this attention.

I argue that women have a variety of definitions and working understandings of street harassment. Most, if not all, of them challenge or refute this notion that they willingly participate in conversations with men strangers or desired their (uninvited and unwanted) attention. I contend that, in a rape culture, women are perceived as always already inviting (attention or otherwise). This perception connects to the ways women targets of violence are deemed responsible for this violence.

In cases of rape, street harassment, or other forms of violence, women are held accountable for the violence that is directed at them. (Notably, the passive voice of the sentence even protects perpetrators, as this language conceals the actor/s involved.) Shifting to an active voice would recognize the responsibility of the perpetrators in various forms of gender-based violence (the forms of interactional vandalism, street harassment, sexual assault, and rape).

Perhaps the important distinction rests in the motivation, but interpreting such motives among strangers seems an impossible challenge. Just as a woman might initiate sexual advances or sex with men, she might also initiate a conversation. This does not mean that she "wants" to be taken advantage of, either by rape or street harassment.

Because society views women who take initiative as provocative at best, women who assert their agency risk ruining their reputations. They also risk having others' judgments imposed on them. I discuss the ways that women consider these impositions, and make considerations to minimize the adverse impact of these judgments.

Just as in similar forms of violence (such as rape), there is a blurry gray area where the shift occurs, from consensual conversation (or other behavior) to harassment. When women find themselves in these shifting situations where this shift occurs, what are they to do, when the proverbial shift from an (initial) "yes" to an (eventual) "no" occurs but is ignored? Why does street harassment constantly seem like an unhappy marriage of two vastly different perspectives: the man harasser's view of reality that the interaction is conversational, and the woman target's view of reality is that the interaction is harassment?[65]

These "blurred lines" can cause quite a stir, as they are negotiated and/or clarified for everyone involved.[66] As I suggested earlier, this clarification may dampen the improvised quality of social interactions in urban public spaces; however, such clarity would also prove useful in minimizing the moments that targets find harassing, and that harassers misread or misinterpret as "innocent" interactions.

Often the blurred lines reflect both productive and problematic tensions. These blurred lines exist in a variety of settings and extend the reach of violence often directed at women and perpetrated by men. "Violence is situated interaction."[67] That women resist acting or reacting violently shows the extent to which women want to minimize their own role in the violence. This is not to say that women who respond to harassment are never violent or harassing but that they may respond in ways that differ from the person initiating the

harassment. In this way, responding or reacting to harassment remains qualitatively different than initiating harassment. The same could be argued about
other types of violence: initiating differs from reacting to it.

An increasing number of authors are investigating these distinctions in
their work.[68] Distinguishing between an initiated violence and a violent
response that stems from a self-protective impulse, or defensive posture,
seems as important as differentiating between a "hello and harassment." From
the outside, or to outsiders of these experiences or moments, the violence and
interaction respectively seem the same. To insiders, the differences or distinctions are important.

This scenario reflects the fuzzy distinctions between street harassment and
any number of other possibilities. Lerum notes the "common use of sexual
innuendos and puns, references to sex toys and specific sex acts" and the
general acceptability of sexual banter that exists.[69] Lerum argues that some
men rely on this "fairly broad" category of behaviors to entice and entangle
women, to toe the line between sexual innuendo and socially inappropriate
or harassing behavior; she explicitly exposes the gendered power differential
that exists and shapes one's reactions and responses to a breach of appropriate behavior.

"Interactional vandalism"[70] can occur when some men ignore the implicit
rules of civil inattention and give a little too much attention to some women.
It is also possible for social interactional play to occur, in which a casual
conversation unfolds. Such a conversation allows all involved to enjoy the
lighter side of a social exchange, or to engage in reciprocal gestures (such as
choosing to be mutually humorous or pleasant). In cases where a man wants
to appear witty, clever, attractive to a woman, or likewise, he may engage in
this interactional play, to inspire a woman to respond accordingly, rather than
for her to perceive the interaction as undesirable.

In terms of street harassment, men harassers and women targets have to
rely on interactional cues that suggest a social interaction is benevolent. How
do women react when those (potentially playful) interactions sour, to the
extent that they (the interactions and/or the women) become violent in verbal
or other ways?

Rather than simply being playful and blurring the boundary (blurred lines)
of appropriate behavior, the man stranger who makes sexual innuendos or
speaks in sexually charged ways can easily appear to be presuming much
about a woman (her perceived promiscuity, availability, and interest). These
(mis)perceptions might be offensive and off-putting to her.

In the absence of mutual interest in the interactions, a man's sexually
aggressive speech, perceived as a precursor to desired action (for sexual
intimacy), would understandably put some women at unease and make them

feel discomfort or nervous about the unfolding situation and the pending, unpredictable action of the man stranger.

There are various settings in which people may see sexualized interactions in positive and/or negative lights. Given that many workplaces accommodate these sexualized interactions, which employees can experience as harassment or camaraderie, the same could be said about the kinds of comments generated during street harassment. How do people clarify the "blurred lines" between casual conversation or camaraderie, and harassment? How can people otherwise effectively determine the difference between playful, casual interactions, and more malicious or assaultive ones?

This dilemma of "drawing the line" between fun and harm, play or malice, reflects the emotional work that targets of harassment must engage in, as a means of making a distinction [so that the targets might respond "appropriately" or manage their in/accessibility, by not being too uptight (it's just a conversation), or too friendly (when it's harassment)].

In her work on sexual harassment, "The Line in the Sand," Lora Lempert[71] describes the ways abuse disrupts social interactions:

> In conventional interactions, the actions of the participants are understood as flowing from the definition of the situation and from conventional actions embedded in routine realities. Most aspects of interaction are taken for granted. These assumptions were the routine schema within which abused women began interpreting the abuse. But abuse, whether it is physical, psychological, and/or emotional, is not a conventional interaction. Abuse is problematic. It dramatically ruptures the taken for granted flow of interaction.[72]

Her work facilitates some recognition that street harassment, as a kind of everyday violence, can arguably extend from various expressions of abuse in other settings and social interactions. This violence gets picked up to some degree in the work of Duneier and others. I begin the following chapter by exploring the web of violence that exists in this society. Then I explore some of the ideological and discursive parallels that exist between street harassment and rape, to explain how women are devalued, discredited, or dismissed as illegitimate victims of the violence perpetrated against them in a patriarchy.

NOTES

1. The Latina Feminist Group. *Telling to Live: Latina Feminist Testimonios.* Durham, NC: Duke University Press, 2001.

2. Women respondents had ample space to "tell stories" through the process of being interviewed. They were invited to share their experiences encountering street harassment, and engage in truth-telling about their experiences with everyday

violence. For many of them, the telling of their survival strategies applies to both street harassment and to the broader society. In this way, many "tell to live" in order to alleviate some of the stress associated with enduring everyday violence.

3. Holly Kearl. *50 Stories of Stopping Street Harassers*. New York: Praeger, 2013; Holly Kearl. *Stop Street Harassment: Making Public Places Safe and Welcoming for Women*. New York: Praeger, 2010a.

4. Please visit: https://stopstreetharassment.org

5. Holly Kearl. *Stop Street Harassment: Making Public Places Safe and Welcoming for Women*. New York: Praeger, 2010a: 3.

6. Joanne Smith, Meghan Huppuch, and Mandy Van Deven. *Hey Shorty! A Guide to Combating Sexual Harassment and Violence in Schools and on the Street*. New York: The Feminist Press at CUNY, 2011.

7. Joanne Smith, Meghan Huppuch, and Mandy Van Deven. 2011: 51.

8. Carol Brooks Gardner. *Passing By: Gender and Public Harassment*. Berkeley, CA: University of California Press, 1995.

9. Cynthia Grant Bowman. "Street Harassment and the Informal Ghettoization of Women" in *Harvard Law Review 106(3)*: 517–581, January 1993.

10. Holly Kearl. "Street Harassment: A Real Problem that Requires Legal Regulation," *Huffington Post*, March 12, 2010b.

11. Janell Hobson. *Body as Evidence: Mediating Race, Globalizing Gender*. Albany, NY: SUNY, 2012.

12. In claiming to name the problem, Gardner takes ownership of the social problem, making it both her personal trouble and society's social issues. This undermines others' efforts to acknowledge the societal, not individual, roots of the problem.

13. Cynthia Grant Bowman. "Street Harassment and the Informal Ghettoization of Women" in *Harvard Law Review 106(3)*: 517–581, January 1993: x.

14. Cynthia Grant Bowman. January 1993.

15. See Betty Friedan. *The Feminine Mystique*. New York: Penguin Books, 2010.

16. Carol Brooks Gardner. *Passing By: Gender and Public Harassment*. Berkeley, CA: University of California Press, 1995: 3.

17. Carol Brooks Gardner. 1995: 4.

18. Nikki Jones. *Between Good and Ghetto: African American Girls and Inner-City Violence*. Piscataway, NJ: Rutgers University Press, 2008.

19. See Holly Kearl. *50 Stories of Stopping Street Harassers*. New York: Praeger, 2013; Holly Kearl. *Stop Street Harassment: Making Public Places Safe and Welcoming for Women*. New York: Praeger, 2010a; Holly Kearl. "Street Harassment: A Real Problem that Requires Legal Regulation," *Huffington Post*, March 12, 2010b; Cynthia Grant Bowman. "Street Harassment and the Informal Ghettoization of Women" in *Harvard Law Review 106(3)*: 517–581, January 1993.

20. Judith Butler. *Excitable Speech: A Politics of the Performative*. New York: Routledge, 1997.

21. Laura Nielsen. *License to Harass: Law, Hierarchy, and Offensive Public Speech*. Princeton, NJ: Princeton University Press, 2006.

22. Michael Kaufmann. "The Construction of Masculinity and the Triad of Men's Violence" in *Beyond Patriarchy: Essays on Pleasure, Power, and Change*. New York: Oxford University Press, 1987.

23. Carol Brooks Gardner. *Passing By: Gender and Public Harassment*. Berkeley, CA: University of California Press, 1995: 4.

24. Carol Brooks Gardner. 1995: 3.

25. I should note that "protection" can be interpreted as paternalistic and patriarchal but also perhaps caring, which highlight its double-edged sword quality. The notion that women *need* to be protected particularly by men underscores this paternalism, and reveals inconsistency in patriarchal ideology in moments when men neglect or fail to protect women, by directly harming, hurting, or killing women.

26. Janell Hobson. *Body as Evidence: Mediating Race, Globalizing Gender.* Albany, NY: SUNY, 2012.

27. Janell Hobson. 2012; Patricia Hill Collins. *Black Sexual Politics: African Americans, Gender, and the New Racism*. New York: Routledge, 2005; Karla Holloway. *Private Bodies, Public Texts: Race, Gender, and a Cultural Bioethics*. Durham, NC: Duke, 2011.

28. Patricia Hill Collins. 2005.

29. Karla Holloway. 2011: 14.

30. Patricia Hill Collins. 2005: 42.

31. Patricia Hill Collins. 2005; Karla Holloway. 2011.

32. Karla Holloway. *Private Bodies, Public Texts: Race, Gender, and a Cultural Bioethics*. Durham, NC: Duke, 2011: 15.

33. Patricia Hill Collins. 2005; Janell Hobson. 2012; Karla Holloway. 2011.

34. Cynthia Grant Bowman. "Street Harassment and the Informal Ghettoization of Women" in *Harvard Law Review 106(3)*: 517–581, January 1993; Judith Butler. *Excitable Speech: A Politics of the Performative*. New York: Routledge, 1997; Laura Nielsen. *License to Harass: Law, Hierarchy, and Offensive Public Speech*. Princeton, NJ: Princeton University Press, 2006.

35. Audre Lorde. *The Cancer Journals*. San Francisco: Aunt Lute, 1980.

36. Patricia Hill Collins. *Black Sexual Politics: African Americans, Gender, and the New Racism*. New York: Routledge, 2005: 66.

37. Joy James. *Resisting State Violence: Radicalism, Gender, and Race in U.S. Culture*. Minneapolis, MN: University of Minnesota Press, 1996: 134.

38. Danielle McGuire. *At the Dark End of the Street: Black Women, Rape, and Resistance.* New York: Vintage, 2011.

39. Cynthia Grant Bowman. "Street Harassment and the Informal Ghettoization of Women" in *Harvard Law Review 106(3)*: 517–581, January 1993; Carol Brooks Gardner. *Passing By: Gender and Public Harassment*. Berkeley, CA: University of California Press, 1995; Joy James. *Resisting State Violence: Radicalism, Gender, and Race in U.S. Culture*. Minneapolis, MN: University of Minnesota Press, 1996; Holly Kearl. *50 Stories of Stopping Street Harassers*. New York: Praeger, 2013; Holly Kearl. *Stop Street Harassment: Making Public Places Safe and Welcoming for Women*. New York: Praeger, 2010a; Holly Kearl. "Street Harassment: A Real Problem that Requires Legal Regulation," *Huffington Post*, March 12, 2010b; Danielle

McGuire. *At the Dark End of the Street: Black Women, Rape, and Resistance.* New York: Vintage, 2011.

40. Cynthia Grant Bowman. "Street Harassment and the Informal Ghettoization of Women" in *Harvard Law Review 106(3)*: 517–581, January 1993.

41. Cynthia Grant Bowman. January 1993: 518.

42. See the website, "Force: Upsetting Rape Culture" at the following address: https://upsettingrapeculture.com/.

43. Eduardo Bonilla Silva. *Racism without Racists: Color-Blind Racism and the Persistence of Racial Inequality in America.* Lanham, MD: Rowman & Littlefield, 2017; Peggy McIntosh. "White Privilege and Male Privilege: A Personal Account of Coming to See Correspondences through Work in Women's Studies." Working Paper 189. Wellesley College Center for Research on Women, Wellesley, MA, 1998.

44. See Emilie Buchwald, Pamela R. Fletcher, and Martha Roth (Eds.). *Transforming a Rape Culture.* Minneapolis, MN: Milkweed Editions, 2005.

45. Cynthia Grant Bowman. January 1993: 519.

46. See Peggy McIntosh. 1998.

47. Cynthia Grant Bowman. January 1993; Holly Kearl. 2013; Laura Nielsen. *License to Harass: Law, Hierarchy, and Offensive Public Speech.* Princeton, NJ: Princeton University Press, 2006.

48. Patricia Connolly-Shaffer. "Staging Cross-Border (Reading) Alliances: Feminist Polyvocal Testimonials at Work." Published Dissertation Available online: http://conservancy.umn.edu/bitstream/141437/1/ConnollyShaffer_umn_0130E_13269.pdf., 2012.

49. Mitch Duneier. *Sidewalk.* New York: Farrar, Straus and Giroux, 1999.

50. Mitch Duneier. 1999.

51. See Elijah Anderson. *The Cosmopolitan Canopy: Race and Civility in Everyday Life.* New York: W.W. Norton, 2010.

52. Nikki Jones. *Between Good and Ghetto: African American Girls and Inner-City Violence.* Piscataway, NJ: Rutgers University Press, 2008.

53. This discussion highlights how numerous the considerations are in terms of the spatial practices that people engage in when occupying and traversing urban public space, and the maneuvering and code switching that they must undergo in order to safely and seamlessly navigate the streets to create a façade of ease and effortlessness that masquerades the complexity of thought, choices, and decision making each urbanite must undergo.

54. Elijah Anderson. *Code of the Street: Decency, Violence, and the Moral Life of the Inner City.* New York: W.W. Norton, 1999

55. Elijah Anderson. 2010: 95.

56. To borrow a line from Lora Bex Lempert. "The Line in the Sand: Definitional Dialogues in Abusive Relationships." *Studies in Symbolic Interaction*, 18, 1995.

57. Sut Jhally. *The Codes of Gender: Identity and Performance in Popular Culture.* Videorecording, 2008.

58. Nikki Jones. 2008.

59. Elijah Anderson. 1999.

60. Mitch Duneier. *Sidewalk.* New York: Farrar, Straus and Giroux, 1999.

61. Kari Lerum. "Sexuality, Power, and Camaraderie in Service Work." *Gender and Society 18(6)*: 756–77, 2004.

62. Terry L. Leap & Larry R. Smeltzer. "Racial Remarks in the Workplace: Humor or Harassment." *Harvard Business Review*. 62(6), 74–78, 1984: 14.

63. Audrey Cohan, Mary Ann Hergenrother, Yolanda M. Johnson, Laurie S. Mandel, and Janice Sawyer. *Sexual Harassment and Sexual Abuse: A Handbook for Teachers and Administrators*. Thousand Oaks, CA: Corwin Press, Inc., 1996.

64. Judith Butler. *Precarious Life: The Powers of Mourning and Violence.* New York: Verso, 2006. Laura Nielsen. *License to Harass: Law, Hierarchy, and Offensive Public Speech*. Princeton, NJ: Princeton University Press, 2006.

65. I borrow from Jessie Bernard (1982) here and her discussion of "his and her" marriages.

66. This reference to "blurred lines" picks up the current controversy surrounding Robin Thicke's song of the same title. The controversy draws out the tensions between multiple interpretations of the song—that on the one hand, the song is entertaining and fun, and on the other, that the song supports or promotes rape culture. Opponents of the song take issue with such lyrics as this: "I know you want it." And "What rhymes with hug me?"

67. Lora Bex Lempert. "The Line in the Sand: Definitional Dialogues in Abusive Relationships." *Studies in Symbolic Interaction*, 18, 1995: 164.

68. Meda Chesney-Lind and Nikki Jones (Eds.). *Fighting for Girls: New Perspectives on Gender and Violence.* Albany, NJ: SUNY, 2010; Sharon Lamb (Ed.) (1999). *New Versions of Victims: Feminists Struggle with the Concept*. New York: New York University Press.

69. Kari Lerum. "Sexuality, Power, and Camaraderie in Service Work." *Gender & Society 18(6)*: 761, 2004.

70. Mitch Duneier. *Sidewalk.* New York: Farrar, Straus and Giroux, 1999.

71. Lora Bex Lempert. 1995.

72. Lora Bex Lempert. 1995: 159.

Chapter 2

Recognizing the Web of Violence and Reckoning with Rape Culture

THE WEB OF VIOLENCE

The study of street harassment facilitates its very recognition as a *social problem*—and a persistent and pervasive one at that. My initial investigation focused singularly on this problem. However, after further inquiry, I began to see violence as foundational to this society. Following this observation, I noticed information to this point widely evidenced in the literature:

> The United States, it has been said, has a history but not a tradition of domestic violence. A history, because violence has been frequent, voluminous, almost commonplace in our past. But not precisely a tradition, for two reasons: First, our violence lacks both an ideological and a geographical center; it lacks cohesion; it has been too various, diffuse, and spontaneous to be forged into a single, sustained, inveterate hatred shared by entire social classes. Second, we have a remarkable lack of memory where violence is concerned and have left most of our excesses a part of our buried history.[1]

Violence has many victims, including both targets and perpetrators. In this way, it gestures at the web of violence that entangles everyone in this society. Within the web of violence, various forms of violence thread together, yet their connections to each other and to historical society, are not always already legible or immediately recognizable.

In addition to the dearth of scholarly literature on women's experiences with street harassment, a curious omission exists around men's experiences as well. This gap in the literature suggests that society ignores the ways in which men are adversely impacted (objectified and dehumanized) by their harassment of others (with women the most typically targeted. Many men have also been targets of harassment, so they likely experience objectification and dehumanization through these encounters and interactions as well.

In fact, people across the gender spectrum are differentially affected by violence, directly and/or indirectly.[2] Global and local culture facilitates—and disrupts—people's interconnectedness to one another. This interconnectedness (and lack thereof, specifically) can result in an internalization and perpetuation of violence, which results in victimization for targets of such violence.

The triad of violence[3] has, in recent years, undergone a critical transformation, spinning itself into a more extensive web of violence where everyone becomes potentially or actually violent and/or vulnerable to violence. Recent discussions of the impact in certain urban public spaces have prompted me to consider the complex web of violence that has historically existed in this country and that persists in contemporary society. This web invites us to consider the connections between various forms of gender violence, in urban public spaces, and in the broader society. Seeing how street harassment connects to other forms of violence brings the web of violence into focus.

The web of violence also takes into consideration people's violent reactions, whether equally aggressive in response, or understandably self-defensive and self-protective. Taking this a step further also involves linking *public* expressions of gender violence (street harassment) to *private* expressions of gender violence (intimate partner violence; domestic violence; or relational violence), which the imbrications and interconnections between the public and private further supporting the "web of violence." I explore the connections (and contentious dissolutions) between the "public" and "private" later, alongside the curious "silence that surrounds violence," in all of its various degrees, expressions, and forms.

Recognizing this web of violence also entails seeing how people perpetuate and navigate this web. This research specifically explores how women get caught in this web of violence, during moments of street harassment. How do women respond to men harassers, given the extent to which they may be facing violence in a variety of other ways and settings in their everyday lives? This work considers the web of violence that informs men harassers' behavior as well. To my earlier point, this web also frames how we construct or view people as in/vulnerable, and as potential or always already victims or perpetrators.[4]

Complicating our ways of seeing people through intersectional lens allows us to see the complexity in the web of violence. In the several years since the inception of my formal investigation of street harassment, many policies and patterns of policing violence have emerged with dubious success, and questionable focus on constructing black and brown men as threatening. While it may be the case that men are often the perpetrators of street harassment of women in public spaces, increasingly they are also the targets of harassment from other men (typically those with more formal power and authority).

The recent implementation of the "Stop and Frisk" policy in New York City began to draw a light on this very problem hidden in plain sight. Complaints and reports about the policy and its utility called into question its equity and efficiency. Not only were particular groups of people showing up as "problems" in public spaces, but the tactics employed during these stops revealed a sort of harassment, or "racial profiling" and gender policing that incriminated brown and black men.[5]

Notably, media attention generated enough interest in and concern about the implementation of "Stop and Frisk" to warrant an investigation about its legality. On August 12, 2013, the policy was deemed unconstitutional, as it infringed on and violated human rights.[6] As the policing of brown and black (men's) bodies endures, the overturning of these policies implores us to think about how harassment of one kind links to other kinds. The very policy makes it possible to monitor harassment, but curiously becomes a vehicle for it as well. It becomes more difficult to discuss in relation to institutional practices that are ostensibly harassing.

The attention that the policy garnered draws our attention to the extent to which some groups of people in (urban) public spaces provoke suspicions and connote "danger," or a potential threat to the civility and safety of these spaces. But if arguably innocent people are being unfairly stopped and frisked for "walking while black (or brown)" and being men,[7] how do we construct notions of safety and danger, especially in response to such a policy and the problematic practices of "preserving" safety? How safe do public spaces feel, primarily for men of color, who get "stopped and frisked" so often for no legitimate reasons, other than looking "suspicious"?

The above questions point to various ways of looking that prove dangerous for people in public spaces. Understanding their experiences help us understand the related but different experiences of women who encounter street harassment by men in urban public spaces. Developing a "triad of safety" might counter the adversities experience within the "triad of violence," by creating mechanisms to ensure equitable and experiential access to safety in this society.

The kinds of street harassment that some men endure, alongside any minimization of the impact of such experiences, parallel what women targets frequently face. The offensive public speech[8] often embedded in street harassment is frequently disregarded or diminished, much like that of the harassment many men (particularly of color) face vis-á-vis the aforementioned problematic practices (among others). I make this point to illustrate how the triad of violence gets woven into a web of violence, thereby making the minimization of the problem of street harassment all the more nefarious.

Because street harassment does not register as a crime, in the public imagination, it is viewed as an occasional inconvenience, something that runs interference, but nothing more than mundane. As an everyday violence, street harassment is so nebulous and shape-shifting, that it is sometimes hard to identify, and even more difficult to regulate, as a result. If regulating behavior that is harassment proves a challenge, so too does regulating the speech acts that so frequently constitute speech harassment.

The web of violence announces itself in this way, making clear the connections between various institutional and individual forces (and sources) of violence, and the imposition of the violence onto our lives. The more sobering reality strikes when thoughts of such violence are contested, if it is even acknowledged, or ignored (or diminished) if it is acknowledged. While I do not elaborate on the connections between these types of harassment, they are clearly supporting systems of violence that become increasingly hard to police, and difficult to dismantle. This is especially so when the accountability structures in place offer little surveillance to those charged with the very task of surveillance. (In other words, "Who monitors this?")

SITUATING STREET HARASSMENT IN THE CONTEXT OF RAPE CULTURE

Here, I posit that street harassment is situated within rape culture. Increasingly, scholars,[9] grassroots advocates and activists, practitioners, and professionals direct their attention toward, and introduce various interventions to address, the kinds of violence that exist in our everyday lives.[10] They also attend to the complexities and contradictions of violence, offering ways to recognize, minimize, and resolve violence.

Examples of this work stem in part from organizations such as Girls for Gender Equity (GGE), and individuals such as Tarana Burke, the founder of the #MeToo Movement.[11] Organizations like GGE and the movement have mobilized individual and collective efforts around the world to challenge and dismantle rape culture.[12] These efforts include a desire to enrich the lives of girls and women through education and empowerment. More specifically, Burke advocates a theory of "empowerment through empathy." The work of the movement involves the following:

[C]hanging the way the world thinks and talks about sexual violence, consent and body autonomy. Tarana has used her platform to share her long standing belief that healing is not a destination, but a journey. This philosophy has inspired millions of survivors who previously had to live in isolation to deal with the pain, shame and trauma of their experience.

Alongside this statement, visitors to the website[13] can locate ample information to learn about the proliferation of violence, understand various related concepts, and find resources to guide their own healing journey.

Situating street harassment within the context of rape culture helps to clarify the connections between the two, while showing the extent to which parallels exist and operate as evidence of everyday violence in our lives. Rape culture makes space for street harassment to exist and persist, and to go unregulated and get disregarded legally and socially:

> In a rape culture, people are surrounded with images, language, laws, and other everyday phenomena that validate and perpetuate, rape. Rape culture includes jokes, TV, music, advertising, legal jargon, laws, words and imagery, that make violence against women and sexual coercion seem so normal that people believe that rape is inevitable. Rather than viewing the culture of rape as a problem to change, people in a rape culture think about the persistence of rape as "just the way things are."[14]

Scholarship on the rape culture that exists in the United States highlights the pervasiveness of disrespect, devaluation, and dehumanization directed toward (or of) women in this country; rape culture reflects a normalized violence against women, as evidenced in the rates of domestic violence, relationship violence, sexual assault, and sexual abuse in this country.[15]

In various countries, violence against women gets expressed through feminicide, or the murder of women; female infanticide, or the murder of girl babies; and the "disappearance" of women viewed as "out of place" for their political activism or vocal opposition to social and/or economic positions or conditions they deem unjust.[16]

The trouble with street harassment, much like the trouble with rape (beyond existence or occurrence), lies partially in the difficulty of definition. Unlike rape, which has definitive legal definitions, street harassment does not.[17] While definitions of rape vary by type and from state to state, they still exist; they frame our collective consciousness about what behavior constitutes the crime.

Conversely, no such definition of street harassment legally exists, or may even be possible, given its variability. This absence also frames our collective consciousness about what behavior constitutes street harassment. The absence of a singular definition (or even multiple ones) of street harassment complicates its study and underscores the importance of efforts to understand this social phenomenon and problem.

By situating street harassment in a rape culture, people may be better able to understand target's experiences with street harassment as a reflection of the culture of this society. The women I interviewed offered narratives that helped me to deepen my understanding of the richness and fullness of their experiences, and the complexities and contradictions embedded in their negotiations with street harassment. They also expanded my vision regarding the web of violence, facilitating my ability to see some connections between street harassment and other forms of violence (that I had not previously been attentive to but should have been). The strategies that women employ to navigate social interactions in urban public spaces provide some insight into their inner, private lives as well. The interviews I conducted revealed some of the tenuous interactions that women had with men in various settings, at the site(s) of street harassment and beyond.

Recognizing and Reckoning with Rape Culture

The study enabled my efforts to more fully comprehend the freedoms and fears women face in negotiating urban public spaces (the specific focus of my research), and in this country in general. As various authors note, many of the discourses about where danger exists for women distorts the reality of where danger resides, and further endangers women's well-being. Take, for example, the comments of Jill Filipovic, a contributor to *Yes Means Yes!* (an anthology dedicated to dismantling rape culture and promoting female sexual power and agency):[18]

> Unlike other forms of assault or even murder, rape is both a crime and a tool of social control. The stranger-rape narrative is crucial in using the threat of sexual assault to keep women afraid, and to punish women who step out of the traditionally female private sphere and into the traditionally male-dominated public one. Portraying rape as something that happens outside of a woman's home enforces the idea that women are safe in the domestic realm and at risk if they go out. . . . There exists a long history of conflating female exodus from the home with female sexual availability—for quite a long time, the "public woman" was a prostitute. The defining feature of the "common woman" sex worker was "not the exchange of money, not even multiple sexual partners, but the public and indiscriminate availability of a woman's body." Public and outspoken women today are routinely called "whores" as a way of discrediting them. Street harassment remains a widespread method of reminding women that they have less of a right to move through public space than men do. And rape serves as the ultimate punishment for women who move through public space without patriarchal covering.

Acknowledging women's fears helps people see that women feel fear, and of what women remain fearful. "While the threat of rape has hardly kept women indoors, it does keep women fearful."[19]

In thinking through, and threading together, these discourses of rape and "stranger danger" to other gendered discourses, people can begin to explore the discourses produced of and within the experiences of street harassment. In many ways, street harassment plays off of the notion of "stranger danger." Arguably, it supports and/or strengthens that myth.

At the same time, Filipovic's suggestion that women's fears of rape have failed to keep them home obscures the reality that homes are not necessarily safe spaces for women. Many women face violence of various kinds in their homes; some experience sexual assault and violence in their homes, by un/familiar perpetrators. According to the National Institute of Justice, "About 85 to 90 percent of sexual assaults reported by college women are perpetrated by someone known to the victim; about half occur on a date."[20] Frequently, these assaults happen at a party or social gathering.

> Half of all student victims do not define the incident as "rape." This is especially true when no weapon was used, there is no obvious physical injury, and alcohol was involved—factors commonly associated with campus acquaintance rape. This is one reason rape and other sexual assaults on campus are not well reported.[21]

These statistics underscore the linkages of violence across various sites, which helps deconstruct notions of safe and dangerous spaces, if not people. This also shows how the circulation of myths and discourses about safety and danger impacts our perceptions and realities. Along the way, almost everyone gets (in/directly) implicated in this web of violence that persists into the present.

The implicit threat of harm, harassment, and violence frames the way women learn to think about their presence in public spaces. Discourses about gender have traditionally suggested that a woman's place is in the home, thereby making a woman in public "out of place."[22] The fear of encountering violence in public can dissuade some women from inhabiting public spaces much; they may understandably, but falsely, believe that minimizing their time in public minimizes their risk of violence.

Based on the available statistics, this decision does not necessarily protect women from violence in the public or private sphere, nor in the curved space in between. That is, traditional gender discourses attempt to diminish the ever-present threat of violence that many women face in the domestic sphere. Within the private sphere, and as noted above, most often women face this violence at the hands of male loved ones or acquaintances.[23]

Gender discourses discipline women's behavior, but seldom do they do the same disciplinary work, to the same degree, on men. The regulation of women's bodies and behavior is no accidental or unintended consequence of these discourses. Gender discourses are designed as disciplinary mechanisms of social control. Arguably, they work to primarily regulate (and limit, more specifically) women's behavior, while generally granting men more freedom and autonomy. Myths that distort where dangers lie for women then work to dissuade, or scare them away from public participation; these myths also putatively protect men from the harm they do unto women.

As a result, rape culture creates illusions about women's safety, by supporting myths about the threat of danger, and where risks reside. For example, myths about "stranger danger"[24] mask clear and present dangers to women that stem from intimate partner violence. Couples in all sorts of configurations can face and perpetuate intimate partner violence. However, within this work, I am focusing on heterosexual intimate partner violence. While this decision risks upholding heteronormativity, it fosters a specific understanding of some of the social tensions that exist between men and women, that play out amidst power asymmetries in various settings.

This admittedly heteronormative frame also allows space to challenge the idea that women face the threat of harm and violence largely or exclusively from men whom they do *not* know, especially as evidence exists to the contrary. Consider these CDC statistics: "About 1 in 4 women and nearly 1 in 10 men have experienced contact sexual violence, physical violence, and/or stalking by an intimate partner during their lifetime and reported some form of IPV [intimate partner violence]-related impact."[25] Notably, that some men experience similar sorts of violence offers a more nuanced portrait of the extent of the problem in society.

Often when women share uncomfortable truths about this (or any) violence against them, they are seen as saying things that/to disparage men. Seldom are they seen as holding perpetrators of violence accountable for their actions. Instead, in these instances, they are viewed as "telling lies" (v. "telling to live"). Individually and/or collectively, their testimonies become disputable accounts of the "truth." Instead of being applauded for revealing difficult truths, they are often viewed as "telling stories." That is, women in these situations are seen as fictionalizing reality or generating lies in order to disparage men.

Women are consequently characterized—and demonized—for (implicitly) generating the details as they go, or fabricating falsehoods, rather than relating the facts of the everyday violence that they encounter and experience in their lives. As a result, these women are regarded with suspicion, or even scorn. Their difficult truths inspire reactions of doubt, rather than compassionate concern. Just as women rape victims are often blamed for the crimes committed against them, so too are women targets of street harassment. In both circumstances, (which are not mutually exclusive), women victims are commonly viewed as "inviting" such attention.

The Silence Surrounding Violence and the Violence of Silence

Consider how discourses of street harassment reflect gendered discourses that proscribe how men and women are supposed to act. These gendered discourses minimize attention toward men's participation in violence, because men are expected to be violent. Men who vocalize opposition to or simply question violence risk having their own masculinity and manhood questioned.

This begins to explain the silences embedded in such discourses. The discourses around men's violence are further laden with silences so as to legally and socially protect men. If men do not speak of their violence, they do not implicate themselves. In the context of street harassment, men who harass hold in tension their speech acts and later, their silence or reticence, which disregards or obscures their participation in such behavior. Alternately, some women remain silent during street harassment, but afterward, speak out about its impact on their daily lives.

When perpetrators of violence, men can utilize silence to protect themselves. In the context of the triad of violence, silence surrounds violence, shrouding it from full view, even as it exists within and extends beyond this society. The silence that surrounds men's violence does little to disrupt or dismantle its occurrence. Instead, this silence often works to deny or diminish the persistent and pervasive problem of violence.

The silence that surrounds women's victimization from violence does little to disrupt or dismantle interlocking systems of oppression that disadvantage or disprivilege women.[26] When taken together, these silences allow us to see how they surround violence. Otherwise stated, sometimes the silence that surrounds violence supports it.

The silence that surrounds violence attempts to minimize, instead of magnify, attention to the web of violence. It supports the presence and persistence of the web of violence in society. This web of violence is historical and contemporary, multidimensional and cyclical.

We see this occur when we draw connections between street harassment and rape culture. The two also connect in the sense that both are forms of violence that typically target women, and so often get dismissed, diminished, and normalized in society. In part, this dismissal, diminishment, and normalization occur through the discourses that people produce about violence. As mentioned earlier, silence frequently frames, and paradoxically, permeate these discourses.

While everyone gets implicated in the web of violence, women face particular threats of violence. Every day, women around the world negotiate various forms of violence, including rape, sexual assault, abuses, (cyber) stalking, workplace harassment, and/or more.[27] I consider how these forms of violence inform street harassment, since the threat of violence, in both its potentiality and actuality, shape the contours of women's lives.

I explore the everyday ways that women get caught in and potentially disrupt this web of violence, in their responses to street harassment. This work attempts to connect the past to the present, to acknowledge how the historical residue of racism and sexism shapes contemporary social relations that reflect patterns of violence deeply rooted in this society.

The Denial of Violence (Or How Denial Silences, Shames and Blames Victims)

Amidst evidence of the incidence and prevalence of violence, some people still deny the impact of violence on women's lives. According to some studies, the majority of women report experiencing some form of harassment in their lives,[28] and 1 in 4 women report attempted or completed rape in their lives.[29] The aforementioned impulse toward denial also neglects to acknowledge how violence also impacts the perpetrators, or that violence compromises people's collective experiences, not singularly or simply the quality of people's individual lives.

The specific denial of the occurrence and impact of violence on women's lives can be understood as a form of victim blaming which operates as a "dangerous discourse." Take, for example, Daphne Patai, who describes the "Sexual Harassment Industry," (SHI) as one that implicitly "manufactures" victims, or offers "training in victimhood." She contends, "I can think of no other areas in life in which putative sufferers require so much help in order to recognize the damage supposedly inflicted on them and have come to depend on such careful instruction in how to script the accounts of their victimhood."[30] Patai sees the SHI as one that constructs "woman as victim" where "people need to learn how to identify the injuries they suffer . . . Clearly, most of us cannot be counted on to understand that every tacky little episode of sexual (or gender) innuendo may really be a grave example of victimization."[31]

Patai's comments reveal and reflect rape culture and suggest an internalization of sexist patriarchy. That women "learn" to become victims, and victims are "putative sufferers" suggests that accounts of victimization are often, if not always, overstated, exaggerated, or altogether false. While possible, her claims feel overgeneralized, and risk invalidating the experiences of victims who do not make embellishments or speak in hyperbolic terms about the harassment they face.

The use of "putative" also suggests that victims have no way of accurately gauging their pain, as if some objective measurement of pain exists to qualify or disqualify victims accordingly. Here it might be useful to turn to Karla

Holloway, who writes about the difficulty of quantifying pain: "Imagine, for example, the common scenario at the doctor's office: 'Are you in any pain today? What is the level—from 1 to 10—of your pain?' The questions do not allow for the complex of heartache, the pain of one's spirit. What number might one assign to that?"[32] These points prove important. They get echoed by feminist debates about epistemologies: How do we "know" what we cannot see? How can we prove injury or harm in its invisibility? How can we measure pain or make it legible, recognizable, quantifiable even?

Increasingly, researchers are drawing attention to the adverse impacts of the minimization of pain. Scholars find evidence that historically marginalized groups of people persistently have their pain minimized in medical settings.[33] If physical or physiological pain is not registered or respected in such settings, what of the pain felt in public spaces? What price, individually and collectively, do people pay when the pain that they incur comes at a cost, literally and figuratively to their lives (when pain is often understood as imagined rather than real)?

There are no easy answers to these questions, nor to the ones about why street harassment, and other forms of violence, are not consistently regarded as such; there is no easy answer to the question of why women's experiences cannot be accepted as truth, rather than regarded with doubt. Patai's skepticism of the Sexual Harassment Industry begs the questions, "Are women expected to accommodate pain, in some futile attempt to show our invulnerability? Are women supposed to refute or minimize any injury stemming from harassment?"

Does Patai's dismissive gesture toward "putative sufferers" operate as an additional injury or source of pain, thereby intensifying the initial injuries victims suffer at the hands of others? To connect Holloway's point to Patai's, one must wonder how victims of trauma would enumerate their suffering. What number would victims assign? Why does Patai fail to recognize how trauma and pain produce dissociation and other responses, ones that sometimes requires the help of others (though not for the purposes of recognizing "the damage supposedly inflicted" but the actual damage that violence against women creates)? What if victims *do* need others' help in labeling their experience, not in feeling or knowing but *speaking* as a victim who can *become* a survivor through that process?

To understand Patai's suspicions of the SHI, we might follow feminist scholar, Cherrie Moraga, who warned us not to "rank oppression" but rather to understand how we are all oppressed.[34] By dismissing the experiences of "putative sufferers," Patai advances the notion that victims learn to identify their injuries, rather than simply experience them. The learning implies a kind of "coaching" rather than clarity about the injustices that victims face.

Patai's discussion problematically demonstrates the uphill battle gender justice scholars, advocates, and activists face. What do we know about the ways perpetrators *learn* to be perpetrators? There are important parallels here that Patai neglects to consider. Her discussion begs the question, "What is really the problem: various forms of harassment or the ways in which women learn to recognize and name their experiences?"[35]

Again, feminist scholarship would suggest that the power in naming our experiences might minimize some of the pain caused by oppressive conditions of our society. Turning Patai's contentious comments on their head facilitates an understanding of how rape culture, violence against women, and street harassment in particular here, get normalized. Who is to say that what she considers "every tacky little episode of sexual (or gender) innuendo" may in fact feel like "a grave example of victimization"[36] to a target of harassment (or some other form of violence)? Why should targets of harassment deny these "little episodes," particularly if the cumulative effect of "microaggressions"[37] is a persistent hostile space that compromises the quality of their lives? Why should targets *not* make a big deal about harassment, rather than risk being seen as making a big deal about nothing? Why are women who name the problems they face considered the problem rather than the problem itself?

The language that Patai deploys treads along the line of "victim blaming" and explains why targets of harassment *should* talk about the everyday slights, street remarks, and evaluations they encounter in public spaces. This proves particularly important in terms of documenting the frequency and regularity of these experiences (and the impact of their cumulative effect). Doing so disrupts society's impulse to normalize street harassment and misperceive it as everyday social interactions rather than everyday violence.

The suggestion that women learn to be victims obscures the devastating effects and in/direct impact of violence on people's everyday lives.[38] For victims, violence disrupts a sense of safety and infringes on feelings of personal freedom and a sense of bodily autonomy. For perpetrators, it requires an allegiance to enacting violence as an expression and/or in support of hegemonic, and toxic, masculinity.

This violence is further compounded by the silence that Patai seems to suggest, a silence that stifles and mutes out individual and collective evidence of experiences with everyday violence. Silence that surrounds violence works to support it, instead of supporting victims or survivors in speaking their truth. Breaking silences by sharing narratives of surviving violence along a spectrum (in ways so clearly huge or, alternately, so seemingly tiny that may appear to others to be trivial) all prove a part of interrupting, instead of normalizing, violence. Arguably, victims of violence should feel encouraged and emboldened to break their silences rather than break under the weight of holding their tongues or holding onto their truth. Releasing it reflects one way for women to share their experiences, to encourage an improved response and a more formal and systemic one at that.

Who *would* people report street harassment to, and would officials take these reports seriously? Patterned evidence in how harassment cases in the workplace, as one example, are handled indicate that a miniscule number of said cases are decided in favor of the victim.[39] What would make authorities more seriously consider street harassment that may be trickier to prove (given that it occurs in public spaces between strangers)?

People who report street harassment to the police often find their concerns are met with indifference or even confusion from authorities. Websites like "Hollaback!" encourage targets of street harassment to document the location of the violation, or the site(s) of spatial and intersectional injustice (see http://www.ihollaback.org). Aside from these grassroots efforts, formal mechanisms of reporting and recording street harassment incidence remains relatively nonexistent.

Amidst the aforementioned efforts to offer information and kinds of intervention to the social problem, skeptics of street harassment posit: "There is a suspicious circularity to the shape of some sexual harassment cases. They begin and end with the worldview promoted by the Sexual Harassment Industry. Once one is caught in this vicious cycle, escape is difficult."[40]

Many people do not report their victimization from violence, for fear of re-victimization, further trauma, and more. Nevertheless, people like Patai advance this notion that women learn the language of victimhood through the SHI.[41] Arguably, women *do* learn the language of victimization, to the degree that it does the following: heightens their awareness of their experiences; puts a name to the violence that they experience; counters some of the alienation and isolation that they feel in response; and draws attention to how commonplace occurrences such as street harassment remain.

Is there space to imagine a process that moves beyond women as victims to envision them as survivors and potentially—perhaps ultimately—as thrivers? Acknowledging the difficulty of speaking truth to power and/or standing in their power facilitates a recognition of women's agency. The suggestion that women feign or exaggerate injury advances the aforementioned notion that women cannot accurately understand, and thus convey, pain that they experience.

Advancing the notion that many women launch false accusations against men perpetrators of violence obscures the likelihood that, for every "alleged" harasser or perpetrator imagined, *actual* harassers and perpetrators of violence exist. While there is no justice in false accusations, there is also no justice in a perpetrator of harassment, rape, sexual assault, or likewise, eluding punishment. This is a particularly important point, given the high rates of recidivism evidenced in the literature.[42]

(Surviving the) Silence of Violence

Scholars and survivors alike often speak of the silence that surrounds violence against women, and discuss the process of "surviving the silence of violence." This "silence of violence"[43] takes on many troublesome dimensions. Targets of violence often feel victimized by the crimes committed against them, crimes that objectify and dehumanize them, that deny their humanity.

For any number of (often complicated) reasons, women victims of violence do not report crimes committed against them. One might interpret this as a failure of society, not the individual. Their apprehension and/or refusal to formally report victimization becomes another kind of silence, one that might protect the victim in the short term, but protects the perpetrator in the long run. In instances of street harassment, no mechanism of punishment exists for the person who harasses, aside from informal reactions that operate as negative social sanctions.

A large part of what keeps the web of violence intact is the silence that surrounds this violence. Often, there is also a silence *within* this violence: this happens when targets of violence feel trapped not only in the violence itself (in the moment of its occurrence), but also as a result of the manner in which we talk about (or refuse to talk about) street harassment as everyday violence. Attempts to deny or minimize street harassment fuel and further this silence.

Not only do victims experience violence, but they also may experience potential re-victimization if they are not silent about the violence they experience. They are catapulted into the process of what I call "surviving the silence of violence." This is a circuitous process intended to support and uphold the web of violence that is this society in the following way: everyone is adversely affected by violence in/directly, yet most victims of violence are silenced by victim-blaming discourses that work to hold them accountable for other people's actions.

For victims, staying silent about the violence they experience can feel like another form of violence and victimization; it can amplify their initial experience with violence and has been linked to diminished or poorer health.[44] Shame breeds on silence, so speaking about experiences that cause shame (often experiences with violence create feelings of shame) can quickly evaporate negative feelings.[45]

American culture and society support this silence of violence. This means that victims need not simply survive the *actual* incidence of violence (primary violence); they must also endure the ripple effects of such violence. The secondary, tertiary, and additional layers of violence they face may stem from any linguistic or *discursive* violence pertaining to yet ignoring or minimizing their experiences with primary forms of violence. Add to this as well the symbolic violence that is consistently working to limit—literally and figuratively—women's mobility in society.[46]

Experiencing an incidence of violence and then any ripple effects from that, as it interfaces with other forms of violence, reflects its interconnectedness (I discuss this more momentarily, in terms of multiplicative trauma.) This also reflects the web of violence, and acknowledges the many layers of violence that people experience directly (as primary violence) and indirectly (discursively, as a secondary violence). This is not to suggest that the secondary violence is less traumatic.

My point is intended to show how violence is *compounded* by our attention or inattention to it, on micro and macro levels (and is compounded by other attendant forms of violence). It also illustrates that people can face the *same* kind of violence and/or different kinds of violence (in multiple settings). They experience violence on a scale (from "never" to "seldom" to "several times" within a time period [hour, day, week, month, year]).

Sometimes, silence is expected, if not demanded, of targets or victims of violence, as numerous accounts detail.[47] This contrasts with a silence full of empathy, when words fail people who do not know what to say in response to a victim's disclosure of enduring violence. In the former, victims of violence sometimes discover the affronting actions of harassers or perpetrators of violence who insist that they must stay silent in order to survive.[48]

Survivors manage the silence that surrounds them if/when no one intervenes on their behalf; the silence that many survivors of violence may find solace in, until they have the strength and courage to share their truths,[49] should they so choose.[50] Asking women to remain silent when they are trying to find their voice and come to terms with their victimization denies women the very vocality that often ensures their survival in a patriarchy. This vocality counters much of the vulnerability and invisibility women feel. As I show later, this vocality can also curiously intensify the vulnerability and liability of being women in a misogynistic society.

As the above illustrates, victims of violence are often charged with managing a self-silencing during incidence(s) of violence (as a survival strategy), and afterward (as a form of concealment). In the latter case, victims of violence may not experience disclosure as an alleviation of pain; rather, what might otherwise be empowering can actually amplify the pain and alienation victims feel if they encounter invalidation of their experiences. Sometimes, disclosure can be re-traumatizing.[51] Brené Brown argues that people must earn the right to hear our stories.[52]

Jaclyn Friedman addresses this re-victimization, arguing that sexual harassment is typically handled in much the same way as street harassment, through nonresponsive inaction: the victim or target of the harassment speaks up to report an incident; she (typically a she) is re-victimized through various discursive acts of shaming and blaming.[53] The perpetrators seldom experience the same sort of scrutiny, socially or behaviorally, and thus "get off" with their harassment.[54] Men who harass often fail to acknowledge their actions as inappropriate or painful for others.[55]

A paradox emerges in street harassment, where targets of harassment are seen as the problem, as opposed to the perpetrator (or the larger culture, for that matter). The targets of harassment are expected to remain silent during and about their experiences, as if such silencing remedies the problem. When victims or targets are encouraged to voice their concerns, to demand change, those who uphold rape culture react to these demands with hostility and/or disdain. Collective efforts are required and necessary, in order to challenge and dismantle the rape culture present in the United States.

Speaking out about violence is risky business. Talking back to perpetrators of violence requires a kind of bravery and courage.[56] Nevertheless, many of the women in my sample chose to do so as one way, among others, they attempted to safely navigate urban public spaces. The women share their strategies for doing so, in ways that appear to reject and/or reinforce rape culture and the set of assumptions so often imposed on women in public. Choosing to talk back to street harassment can be seen as a "dangerous discourse," a topic I turn to in chapter 5. Demanding change agitates the status quo, and can intensify the very violence some people are trying to minimize, as they expose the reality of their everyday lives.

Multiplicative Trauma

"Multiplicative trauma" conceptually acknowledges that victims can be victimized again and again, in various ways, at various sites of victimization, and across the life course. As discussed earlier, there are layers to any singular traumatic event, though this implies that an event is discrete, has pronounced parameters, and punctuates a moment in time, rather than expands across time and space, in its duration and its aftermath. It is important to recognize that each "singular" traumatic event potentially connects to other traumatic event(s), reminding us of the web of violence that exists in this society and its expansive impact on our lives.[57]

"Multiplicative trauma" results from one experience of trauma connecting to another (or others); the combination of those incidents of violence likely lead to complex-PTSD (or post-traumatic stress disorder). Multiplicative trauma can result from people encountering or experiencing a primary incident, and then a secondary event of the same kind, or a different kind.

Arguably, exposure to similar events over time causes harm to the victim, as does exposure to varied events of violence. In the former case, an individual may regularly and repeatedly experience everyday violence, such as street harassment, while never experiencing other forms of violence. In the latter case, victims may experience violence in multiple locations, over the course of a day, week, month, or year, as well as over the life course.

Often, society reluctantly accommodates victims of violence. As victims work on managing any feelings of shame and social stigma, they may also be affronted by societal tendencies toward victim blaming. The potential for victims to encounter victim blaming exists on a scale (from "not at all" to "sometimes" to "often"). Thus, a victim may never experience victim blaming. Alternately, they may encounter victim blaming frequently, possibly every time they share their experiences with violence. Victims may experience victim blaming at one time, but from multiple people. Any and all of the possible combinations of ways victims of violence experience victim blaming can cause multiplicative trauma.

A victim can be re-victimized every time she is blamed for crimes committed against her. She may also potentially be re-victimized any time she experiences violent crime in her lifetime. This illustrates the pervasiveness of victimization that the web of violence creates. The term, "multiplicative trauma," facilitates recognition of the often *cumulative* and *compounded* victimization from various forms of (or some combination of everyday and/or extreme) violence.

Multiplicative trauma can stem from the adverse or unsupportive responses victims receive with regard to their experiences; when victimized are affronted by any silencing, diminishing, or dismissive responses upon or after reporting said victimization, and/or when they are not recognized or respectfully treated as a victim of violence, these responses and misrecognition combine with the initial trauma(s), compounding and likely worsening the situation.

In the case of street harassment, women can experience one kind of trauma as targets of such verbal assault. That trauma can then be amplified and/or multiplied by 1) any and all other types or incidences of violence women face (in past, present, and future tense), as well as 2) any injurious or traumatizing discourses produced about the targets' experiences with violence (whether the target "deserved" or "asked for it").

Men who harass women express a wide range of behaviors that illustrate the existence/prevalence of male privilege and the sense of entitlement guided by that privilege. This privilege enables and emboldens men who harass to engage women intrusively. Again, these invasive forms of interaction reverberate in a rape culture.

When men react aggressively and with hostility to women who reject them during (and because of) street harassment, many of these men act in ways that could also be "triggering" to some women.[58] For survivors of sexual assault, street harassment can link to harassment in other settings such as the home, workplace, school, public accommodation or various public spaces and places. I would also argue that for survivors of other kinds of related traumas, including racial assaults and microaggressions,[59] street harassment can also be triggering.

The concept of "multiplicative trauma" then helps us understand the often ongoing assaults that people face in an unjust world. Seeing street harassment as a reflection and perpetuation of that enables a deeper understanding of the kinds of trauma wounds that people have, and the ways in which people can worsen these wounds with "just words" or help people to heal these wounds with *just* words.

Not only does this illustrate and support the web of violence, but it shows how dangerous and damaging street harassment can be, especially when it triggers memories of other abuses and/or precipitates future violations. Often, people are encouraged to see these abuses and violations as separate and distinct forms of behavior. In actuality, however, they link up to one another in the web of violence.

Furthermore, we see how people, including some targets/victims, normalize street harassment by diminishing the significance and impact of it on themselves and society. (This offers partial explanation of why violence against women occurs, gets normalized, and remains largely unrecognized as a social problem.) Street harassment disrupts the quality of social life, and further tears at the social fabric of urban public spaces. Recognizing street harassment in and of itself, as well as in relation to other forms of violence and injustice would begin to wear away at the web of violence.

Contextualizing street harassment within rape culture arguably facilitates some recognition of how the former is a form of violence threaded to other forms of violence and into society. Such recognition would also include registering the deleterious impact of street harassment on those involved. Women might more easily see the connections between their encounters with street harassment and past, present or future experience with other forms of violence.

Ideally, they might also see that these connections are not their fault, but rather reflect patriarchal power asymmetries informed by intergenerational and intersectional injustice, including gendered racism. Perhaps seeing these broader connections might also motivate women to report these injustices, rather than feeling like they "asked for it" somehow deserve the unwanted attention, or have to endure everyday violence. One must wonder if women would be emboldened by such heightened awareness of inequalities and systemic injustice or feel more disempowered than ever.

An attendant problem to the aforementioned absence of an official mechanism for reporting and measuring street harassment is the minimal social support then for any multiplicative trauma that women targets of street harassment experience. Multiplicative trauma may emerge in relation to repeated victimizations (through recurrent street harassment) and related victimization (other forms of violence and harm).

Multiplicative trauma recognizes the various traumas that occur in a web of violence, where victims of violence often face layers of trauma, not singular traumatic events, and/or face violence in/directly. I use the following terms to refer to the indirect exposure to the everyday violence of street harassment: "approximated victimization," "victimization by proxy," or "vicarious victimization." Laura Gray-Rosendale provides a powerful example of this in *College Girl*:

> At heart, our narratives are never really about just one person's story. Since traumas are experienced communally, our stories are always shared ones, impacting (and continually revising) every other life and story they touch. Oftentimes, too, the construction of trauma narratives themselves is not possible without communal involvement.[60]

That is, for every crime, for every injustice, there are many victims, not just the one(s) legally recognized as such, even as these victims experience, or are denied, justice.

Participants in my study described how impactful the act of witnessing other women being harassed by men proved to be to them. Imagine the experience of this witnessing, as it weaves together with one's own direct experiences with street harassment. What is the cumulative effect or impact of this witnessing, beyond the power of the collective truth-telling? Is there a trauma in witnessing, as there is a trauma in telling and re-telling, or even surviving? Alongside Laurie Vickroy, Eden Wales Freedman suggests as much, in her work, *Reading Testimony, Witnessing Trauma*. She offers a way of seeing trauma as a "psychological, cultural, and sociopolitical phenomenon."[61]

During one of my interview conversations with respondents, Regina, a black woman participant, noted that she observed how men harass women: "It is kind of irritating to me just to see [men who harass], because you can feel when someone is staring at you, but I like to watch men watching women walk down the street and the women don't know it because their backs are turned, because I think what they do is disrespectful. So, I can only imagine." Here, this woman feels a sense of solidarity with another woman whom she observes being ogled and objectified by a man harasser. As a result, she develops disdain for him and other men who harass.

This witnessing also serves as a cautionary tale to women (that they may be the next victim, if not previously victimized). Amidst the sisterly solidarity and camaraderie,[62] is there also a shared agony or sense of defeat in watching one another as women being mistreated by men who harass? Do women targets of street harassment who witness and observe other women being harassed experience what scholars call "secondary trauma"?[63] Perhaps women in these circumstances feel less isolated in the injuries that street harassment can produce, knowing or seeing that it can happen to other women, sometimes right in front of them.

Witnessing does seem to equip some women with strategies for moving around such harassment. This example illustrates the extent of people's interconnectedness, and the way society implicates everyone in the doing of this web of violence and of victimization. As lives are imbricated, everyone must play a part in undoing violence, working to ameliorate conditions that broadly impact people's well-being.

CONCLUSION

Throughout this work, I explore this practice of surviving the silence of violence. Silence can also be a dangerous discourse, in ways that men who harass find similar agitating. I recognize silence as a form of resistance or an informed choice that survivors of violence often make in order to be self-protective. I also explore silence as a form of power, as in the case of a refusal to speak about the importance of a topic.

In cases of violence against women, there is a silence that veils the significance, if not occurrence, of violence. The people with the most power and privilege to speak out about violence against women often neglect to see its direct impact on women, and indirect impact on men. The silence that surrounds violence thus operates on a rhetorical or discursive and institutional level, as well as an individual one. In this book, I explore the conditions in which silence supports survivors (and facilitates a victim's very survival), as well as the conditions in which silence supports and condones more violence. This work maintains a meditation on the matter of how self-protective silence can be.

Because so many victims of sexual violence feel silenced, or feel a sense of shame when they have been victimized by others,[64] I draw parallels between those silencing acts and the ways women targets of street harassment are made to feel when they are harassed. The parallels should further clarify the connections between rape culture and street harassment, since both instances fault the (typically women) targets of violence. In these ways, rape culture accommodates and supports street harassment.

Next, I discuss how controlling images shape people's perceptions and behavior during street harassment. Then, I consider how discourses about safety and danger circulate to dissuade women from entering or being in public spaces. I also consider how discourses shape speech acts, to encourage or discourage women from responding to street harassment.

NOTES

1. See Richard Hofstadter's, "Reflections on Violence in the United States." Available here: thebaffler.com/ancestors/reflections-violence-united-states. Published July 2015.

2. For example, transgender people increasingly face transphobic harassment. See "Violence Against Trans and Non-Binary People" at the following website: vawnet. org/sc/serving-trans-and-non-binary-survivors-domestic-and-sexual-violence/ violence-against-trans-and.

3. See Michael Kaufmann. "The Construction of Masculinity and the Triad of Men's Violence" in *Beyond Patriarchy: Essays on Pleasure, Power, and Change.* New York: Oxford University Press, 1987.

4. See Judith Butler, *Precarious Life: The Powers of Mourning and Violence.* New York: Verso, 2006.

5. Michelle Alexander. *The New Jim Crow: Mass Incarceration in the Age of Colorblindness.* New York: New Press, 2012.

6. The "Stop and Frisk" policy practiced in NYC is one such example, eventually found to be unconstitutional. See www.nyclu.org/en/stop-and-frisk-data.

7. See www.stopandfrisk.com.

8. See Laura Nielsen. *License to Harass: Law, Hierarchy, and Offensive Public Speech.* Princeton, NJ: Princeton University Press, 2006.

9. See Laura L. O'Toole, Jessica R. Schiffman, and Rosemary Sullivan (Eds.). *Gender Violence: Interdisciplinary Perspectives (3rd Ed.).* New York: NYU Press, 2020; Nikki Jones. *Between Good and Ghetto: African American Girls and Inner-City Violence.* Piscataway, NJ: Rutgers University Press, 2008.

10. See Laura Gray-Rosendale, *Me Too, Feminist Theory, and Surviving Sexual Violence in the Academy.* Lanham, MD: Lexington Press, 2022.

11. See metoomvmt.org/get-to-know-us/tarana-burke-founder/.

12. GGE aims to eradicate the "gender, race, and sexual oppression" where women live. They do so in order to acknowledge the ways that some people use spaces to harass young girls and women. For more, see Joanne Smith, Meghan Huppuch, and Mandy Van Deven. *Hey Shorty! A Guide to Combating Sexual Harassment and Violence in Schools and on the Street.* New York: The Feminist Press at CUNY, 2011: 11.

13. See metoomvmt.org/.

14. See the website, "Force: Upsetting Rape Culture" at the following address: upsettingrapeculture.com/.

15. See Emilie Buchwald, Pamela R. Fletcher, and Martha Roth (Eds.). *Transforming a Rape Culture.* Minneapolis, MN: Milkweed Editions, 2005.

16. Rosa-Linda Fregoso. "Toward a Planetary Civil Society" in *Mexicana Encounters: The Making of Social Identities on the Borderlands.* Edited by Rosa-Linda Fregoso. Pp. 1–29. Berkeley, CA: University of California Press, 2003a; Diana Taylor. *Disappearing Acts: Spectacles of Gender and Nationalism in Argentina's "Dirty War."* Durham, NC: Duke University Press, 1997; Barbara Sutton. *Bodies in Crisis: Culture, Violence, and Women's Resistance in Neoliberal Argentina.* Piscataway, NJ: Rutgers University Press, 2010; Julie Zeilinger. *A Little F'ed Up: Why Feminism Is Not a Dirty Word.* New York: Seal Press, 2012.

17. Carol Brooks Gardner. *Passing By: Gender and Public Harassment.* Berkeley, CA: University of California Press, 1995; Terry L. Leap & Larry R. Smeltzer "Racial Remarks in the Workplace: Humor or Harassment." *Harvard Business Review.* 62(6), 74–78, 1984.

18. Jill Filipovic. "Offensive Feminism: The Conservative Gender Norms That Perpetuate Rape Culture, and How Feminists Can Fight Back." In *Yes Means Yes!: Visions of Female Sexual Power and a World Without Rape.* Edited by Jaclyn Friedman, 2008: 22–3.

19. Jill Filipovic. 2008: 23.

20. See National Institute of Justice, "Most Victims Know Their Attacker." Available here: nij.ojp.gov/topics/articles/most-victims-know-their-attacker. Accessed on April 20, 2022. Published on September 30, 2008.

21. See National Institute of Justice. 2008.

22. See Rachna Sethi's, "'Out of Place' Women: Exploring Gendered Spatiality in Delhi." *Journal of Postcolonial Writing,* Vol 54(3): 398–420. Special Issue: Delhi: New Writings on the Megacity, 2018.

23. See National Institute of Justice. 2008.

24. Jill Filipovic. 2008.

25. Centers for Disease Control (National Center for Injury Prevention and Control, Division of Violence Prevention). "Fast Facts: Preventing Intimate Partner Violence." Available online: www.cdc.gov/violenceprevention/intimatepartnerviolence/fastfact.html. Accessed April 20, 2022. Page last reviewed: November 2, 2021.

26. Patricia Hill Collins. *Black Feminist Thought: Knowledge, Consciousness, and the Politics of Empowerment.* New York: Routledge, 2008; Melissa Harris-Perry. *Sister Citizen: Shame, Stereotypes, and Black Women in America.* New Haven, CT: Yale University Press, 2011.

27. See Emilie Buchwald, Pamela R. Fletcher, and Martha Roth (Eds.). *Transforming a Rape Culture.* Minneapolis, MN: Milkweed Editions, 2005; Jaclyn Friedman and Jessica Valenti. *Yes Means Yes!: Visions of Female Sexual Power and a World Without Rape.* Berkeley, CA: Seal Press, 2008; Laura L. O'Toole, Jessica R. Schiffman, and Rosemary Sullivan (Eds.). *Gender Violence: Interdisciplinary Perspectives (3rd Ed.).* New York: NYU Press, 2020.

28. Holly Kearl. *Stop Street Harassment: Making Public Places Safe and Welcoming for Women*. New York: Praeger, 2010a.

29. See Emilie Buchwald, Pamela R. Fletcher, and Martha Roth (Eds.). *Transforming a Rape Culture*. Minneapolis, MN: Milkweed Editions, 2005.

30. Daphne Patai. *Heterophobia: Sexual Harassment and the Future of Feminism*. New York: Rowman & Littlefield, 2000: 274.

31. Daphne Patai. 2000: 274.

32. Karla Holloway. *Private Bodies, Public Texts: Race, Gender, and a Cultural Bioethics*. Durham, NC: Duke, 2011: 13.

33. See Kelly M. Hoffman, Sophie Trawalter, Jordan R. Axt, & M. Norman Oliver. "Racial Bias in Pain Assessment and Treatment Recommendations, and False Beliefs About Biological Differences Between Blacks and Whites." *Proceedings of the National Academy of Sciences of the United States of America*, 113(16), 2016: 4296–4301. doi.org/10.1073/pnas.1516047113

34. Cherrie Moraga. "La Guera" in *This Bridge Called My Back*. Pp. 27–34. New York: Kitchen Table: Women of Color Press, 1983.

35. As I mentioned earlier, many of the women in my sample discounted their experiences as street harassment. They remained uncertain about what experiences counted as street harassment. Their lack of clarity did not mean a lack of experiences, or a lack of understanding. Instead, it reflects a difference in language, not in awareness. These women were clear that they were receiving unwanted attention. To learn that there is a name for this behavior is not teaching women that they are victims, but identifying the problem of harassment. Feminist research often hopes to raise consciousness, but that does not default into coaching women about their oppression. Instead, such research endeavors hope to engage women and heighten awareness of their everyday realities. This research also actively aims to challenge the myths that women fabricate their victimization. Just as "fiction is made up of complexity," so too do truths have their "multiple, even contradictory, meanings" (Holloway 2011: 12).

36. Daphne Patai. *Heterophobia: Sexual Harassment and the Future of Feminism*. New York: Rowman & Littlefield, 2000: 274.

37. Derald Sue. *Microaggressions in Everyday Life: Race, Gender, and Sexual Orientation*. New York: Wiley, 2010.

38. Certainly, women who feel that they are *not* oppressed by the violence in their lives should not be convinced that they have some sort of false consciousness about their realities. Because women have been socialized to see the structure of society as natural and not oppression, gender justice proponents might argue that their responsibility involves heightening women's awareness of how this oppression plays out in the world. Street harassment serves as one example, though many exist in this patriarchy.

39. See General Accounting Office Report GAO 20–654. "Workplace Sexual Harassment: Experts Suggest Expanding Data Collection to Improve Understanding of Prevalence and Costs." September 2020.

40. Daphne Patai. *Heterophobia: Sexual Harassment and the Future of Feminism*. New York: Rowman & Littlefield, 2000: 275.

41. Patai's implication here is dangerous, in its suggestion that women are "not really" victims of violence, but rather coached (or coerced/forced?) into being perpetual victims in the SHI.

42. This begs the questions, Can the same patterns be observed among the men who harass women? Are they habitual harassers akin to, or as well as, "recidivist rapists"?

43. See William Gay. "Supplanting Linguistic Violence" in *Gender Violence*: *Interdisciplinary Perspectives (2nd Ed.)*. Edited by Laura O'Toole, Jessica Schiffman, and Margie Kiter Edwards. Pp. 435–442. New York: NYU Press, 2007.

44. See Brené Brown. *Daring Greatly: How the Courage to Be Vulnerable Transforms the Way We Live, Love, Parent, and Lead.* New York: Avery, 2015; Brené Brown. *The Gifts of Imperfection: Letting Go of Who You Think You're Supposed to Be and Embrace Who You Are.* Center City, MN: Hazelden, 2010.

45. Brené Brown. 2010.

46. Pierre Bourdieu and Loic J. Wacquant. *An Invitation to Reflexive Sociology.* Chicago: University of Chicago Press, 1992.

47. See Charlotte Pierce-Baker. *Surviving the Silence: Black Women's Stories of Rape.* New York: W.W. Norton and Company, 1998; Laura Gray-Rosendale. *College Girl.* Albany, NY: SUNY Press, 2013.

48. Laura Gray-Rosendale. 2013: 28.

49. See Ruth Nicole Brown. *Hear Our Truths: The Creative Potential of Black Girlhood.* Champaign, IL: University of Illinois Press, 2013.

50. See Chanel Miller. *Know My Name: A Memoir.* New York: Penguin, 2020.

51. Charlotte Pierce-Baker. *Surviving the Silence: Black Women's Stories of Rape.* New York: W.W. Norton and Company, 1998.

52. See Brené Brown, *Daring Greatly: How the Courage to Be Vulnerable Transforms the Way We Live, Love, Parent, and Lead.* New York: Avery, 2015.

53. Jaclyn Friedman. *What You Really Really Want: The Smart Girl's Shame-Free Guide to Sex and Safety.* Berkeley, CA: Seal Press, 2011.

54. Robert Jensen, *Getting Off: Pornography and the End of Masculinity.* Boston: South End Press, 2007.

55. Joanne Smith, Meghan Huppuch, and Mandy Van Deven. *Hey Shorty! A Guide to Combating Sexual Harassment and Violence in Schools and on the Street.* New York: The Feminist Press at CUNY, 2011: 63.

56. See bell hooks. *Talking Back: Thinking Feminist, Thinking Black (2nd Ed).* New York: Routledge.

57. For an alternate view, see Sarah Pierson Beaulieu. *The Enliven Project.* Available online: theenlivenproject.com/category/sexual-violence/double-silence/. Accessed on March 30, 2022. Published 2014.

58. "Triggers" are reminders or things that evoke emotionally charged reactions in survivors. Triggers essentially and potentially re-traumatize survivors.

59. Derald Sue. *Microaggressions in Everyday Life: Race, Gender, and Sexual Orientation.* New York: Wiley, 2010; Terry L. Leap & Larry R. Smeltzer "Racial Remarks in the Workplace: Humor or Harassment." *Harvard Business Review.* 62(6), 74–78, 1984.

60. Laura Gray-Rosendale. *College Girl.* Albany, NY: SUNY Press, 2013:214.

61. Eden Wales Freedman. *Reading Testimony, Witnessing Trauma: Confronting Race, Gender, and Violence in American Literature.* Jackson, MI: University of Mississippi Press, 2020: 4.

62. Kari Lerum. "Sexuality, Power, and Camaraderie in Service Work." *Gender and Society 18(6)*: 756–77, 2004.

63. Sharon Lamb (Ed.). *New Versions of Victims: Feminists Struggle with the Concept.* New York: New York University Press, 1999.

64. See Brené Brown, *Daring Greatly: How the Courage to Be Vulnerable Transforms the Way We Live, Love, Parent, and Lead.* New York: Avery, 2015; Brené Brown, *The Gifts of Imperfection: Letting Go of Who You Think You're Supposed to Be and Embrace Who You Are.* Center City, MN: Hazelden, 2010; Melissa Harris-Perry. *Sister Citizen: Shame, Stereotypes, and Black Women in America.* New Haven, CT: Yale University Press, 2011.

Chapter 3

Considering Controlling Images, or "Dangerous Ways of (Not) Seeing"

DIFFERENT WAYS OF SEEING

Thinking about the web of violence woven into this society requires much consideration of the continued significance of interlocking oppressions from historical moments to the present. In contemporary society, the system of social stratification gives some social groups more power and privilege than others.

In this chapter, I take a look at how these interlocking oppressions persist, and often get expressed or experienced on a micro level. Social interactions between strangers reflect a lot about the broader social patterns of privilege and power (and the lack thereof) that play out among groups differentially positioned within this inequitable society.

To examine how street harassment supports, and has been supported by, a set of imagery and ideologies about various social groups, I center the theme, "dangerous ways of seeing." To this end, I explore how people are encouraged to see themselves and one another; in particular, scholars have argued, historically marginalized groups have been viewed through a myopic lens, with stereotypical images created in a "slanted room"[1] to be circulated in media and society.

Recognizing multiple or interlocking oppressions includes the recognition of groups of people often misrecognized (or ignored) in society. This investigation attempts to make visible the ways that people are constructed as and simultaneously confront social problems. When people are only seen through a distorted lens, the result can reflect "dangerous ways of seeing."

As noted earlier, one dangerous way of seeing street harassment is by not seeing it. Ignoring the problem of street harassment facilitates its continuation, or fails to fully intervene. Alternately, many people who understand street harassment as a problem see it as a solely gendered phenomenon. Such a view limits our collective understanding of how gender and race, as well as sexism and racism, operate together, to shape people's experiences with street harassment differently. That is, the various social locations that people occupy can create different kinds of experiences with harassment. As the result of gendered racism, some women have not been (and are not) seen as potential and/or actual victims of violence, including street harassment.

This work explores the similarities and differences in white and black women's experiences as targets of street harassment, and the different ways society views women within these two racial groups. My research makes visible the reality of black women's harassment in public spaces in the face of the following: "Historically research on gender and sexual harassment has excluded women of color."[2] I attempt to address this exclusion and advance the existing understandings of street harassment as women experience it.

In the previous chapter, I worked to show how discourses of danger exist to socially control people. Discursive practices operate as a form of social control, which reflects their disciplinary potential; it speaks to the way people are constructed as dangerous or endangered, as safe or unsafe, as vulnerable or threatening, seldom some combination of the aforementioned. To this point, Donna Haraway offers, "Vision can be good for avoiding binary oppositions."[3] This idea proves useful in exploring society's collective vision of different groups of people. This vision is shaped by powerful social forces, and can become myopic when left unchecked or unregulated.

Troubling "discourses of danger" requires a critical intervention and discursive analysis, as bodies can be powerful and vulnerable, dangerous and endangered at once. How do we see people's bodies as belonging to singular and static (and often stereotypical) categories or social locations? Where did we cultivate these ways of seeing, and when do these visions of ourselves and others become "dangerous ways of seeing"?

Arguably, all bodies endure social control through the various discourses and "controlling images"[4] that circulate about various groups. This social control reflects the persuasive power of imagery that circulates to inform, and perhaps cloud, our vision. I credit Donna Haraway for her work on "vision," but I center this chapter around the work of Patricia Hill Collins.[5] Both scholars prompt us to think about our existing ways of seeing, and ask us to move "toward a new vision" of society. What would make such a vision possible, even likely? Haraway continues,

"Being" is much more problematic and contingent. Also, one cannot relocate in any possible vantage point without being accountable for that movement. Vision is *always* a question of the power to see—and perhaps of the violence implicit in our visualizing practices. . . . Vision requires instruments of vision; an optics is a politics of positioning. Instruments of vision mediate standpoints; there is no immediate vision from the standpoint of the subjugated.[6]

Haraway's work underscores the importance of feminist standpoint episte-mology, or different ways of knowing. People's subject positions inform their vision and perspectives.[7]

Different ways of knowing remain iterative to different ways of seeing. Haraway draws attention to claims of objectivity, in order to show that vision can be impeded by such a stance. Instead, she encourages an acknowledgment of positionality, so that people can show what they can see from where they stand. Her work is useful in thinking about how situated knowledge stems from and guides women through their experiences with street harassment.

In my study, women were offered the opportunity to discuss their point of view, from their standpoint.[8] Doing so recognizes that women are dif-ferentially located in social structures that inform and shape situated knowl-edge. Women, therefore, not as a universal or coherent category, can offer up a plethora of perspectives given these various standpoints. This situated knowledge differs then from claims of objectivity and truth made by people speaking for themselves and others.

By extension, the claims of objectivity and truth obscure the existence of multiple realities, multiple perspectives. Feminist objectivity accommodates this multiplicity. It insists on disrupting the notion of a singular truth, a top-down model of truth, and instead urges a truth-telling from one's stand-point. This results in multiple, perhaps conflicting realities, yet acknowledges that there is no singular vision. Instead, it invites us "toward a new vision."[9]

Becoming "answerable for what we learn how to see" means challenging ways of seeing that remain problematic, a hidden vision of sorts (a hiding of intention in the injurious ways of seeing oneself and others): it also means not privileging one way of seeing over others.[10] "There is good reason to believe vision is better from below the brilliant space platforms of the powerful." Haraway remains suspicious of this privileging of a singular vision, or one way of seeing. Instead, she encourages "situated and embodied knowledges" so that people may consider a wide variety of perspectives amidst power asymmetries.[11] Following Haraway, my work calls for new epistemologies and new ways of seeing.

"Dangerous Ways of Seeing": Considering Gender

What are the ways in which we are trained to see women and men in our society, through a two-and-only-two gender binary? Where do we learn to see people in such limited ways? What are the negative consequences of gender constructions that place women in a "vulnerable" category in need of "protection," and men in an "invulnerable" ("violent" or "troublesome") category, designated as "protectors" of women?

Gendered discourses tend to reinforce the gender/sex binary, as a two-and-only-two category system.[12] These gendered discourses tend to describe and construct women as weak, submissive, quiet, gentle, caring, nurturing, kind, compassionate, emotional, and so on. Men are constructed as rational, dispassionate, strong, athletic, competitive, and so on.

Within the category "woman," discourses produce further divisions and distinctions. These distinctions are drawn along moral lines, and appear as mutually exclusive categories of "good" and "bad" girl varieties. Far more complexity and contradiction exist within these distinctions, yet we can point to ways that these discourses remain "dangerous."

Conducting interview conversations with women provided me with access to insight and information about how women perceive themselves and others in the context of street harassment, and in society. Many of the women I spoke with discussed the gender imperative that framed women's behavior in terms of respectability. Respondents relied on the idea of "respectable femininity" to assess their own and others' experiences with street harassment. Because traditional gender expectations encourage women to be respectable, women may learn to see themselves in reference to this quality of respectability.

"Respectably" feminine women enter public spaces with others, not alone. When women show up in public by themselves, they risk their respectable femininity. They also deny men the opportunity to enact their own performance of hegemonic masculinity, a performance that intends to assert authority, control, and dominance over women. This, in part, explains why men harass women, as women in public are marked as disreputable and therefore unrespectable, or undeserving of respect (from anyone).

When my respondents spoke about these gendered requirements and their own gendered performances, they had to sometimes attempt to close the gap between the ideal respectably feminine woman and themselves, since all of them experienced street harassment in urban public spaces. That is, some women who ventured out into the city embraced this idea that they might face repercussions for being a woman in public, particularly in cities. They prepared themselves for street harassment, anticipating it on the basis of previous experience.

Arguably, street harassment is the price women pay for being in public. Encountering street harassment motivated many of the women respondents to personalize these interactions, and falsely believe that they acted in ways that provoked or invited the harassment. Some women wondered what they had done to "deserve" the undesired attention that street harassers directed at them. Others considered how being harassed made them look. Some reflected on how street harassment made them feel in general, and about themselves. "What does it say about me that men harass me when I'm in public?"

Street harassment becomes a vehicle for women targets to question themselves, rather than the harassers. The dilemma in this way of seeing relates to women seeing themselves as "deserving" of or provoking this negative attention. For the women who had internalized the respectable femininity requirement, they wanted to see themselves as decent people who happened to be harassed.

While many women saw street harassment as a normalized part of life in urban public spaces, they often solidified the connection between men and harassment. This way of seeing meant that women who show up in public compromise their respectability, and men who show up in public are always already harassers. Aren't these dangerous ways of seeing people?

The cult of true womanhood encourages women to be polite, docile, and respectful of others.[13] Women should ideally practice and perform respectable femininity.[14] Yet, a woman who is polite by being responsive to others may actually jeopardize her respectability, if she responds to and engages with her harasser.

A paradox emerges for the woman who responds to her harasser, *in order* to be polite. That is, in trying to be polite and practice respectable femininity, a woman can compromise said respectability, in her efforts to be civil to and respectful of all others (this includes men harassers). This begs the question, "Do or should respectable women respond to men harassers?" Yes and no.

When a woman responds to her harasser, she potentially disrupts the way we see her and the harasser. If she engages courteously, she may simply affirm the ways we see women as caring, nurturing, and considerate of others (putting others ahead of themselves). If she engages angrily or furiously, she complicates her appearance to herself and others. If she engages a harasser in any capacity, she may appear to lack judgment or decorum herself, by "deigning" to talk to someone disrespectful of her. How might a woman who talks back to men harassers express and/or recuperate her respectability?

Because respectable femininity imposes a particular kind of subjectivity on women, understanding how women contest or disrupt these gendered expectations remains relevant and important in the study of street harassment. Since most men rely on traditional notions of respectable femininity, and often express surprise or shock at women who assert themselves in public when responding to street remarks or harassment, examining the role of ideology on subjectivity remains central.

What seems clear relates men's reliance on this notion of respectable femininity to categorize women by sorting them into these crude dichotomies and oppositional binaries of "good" (Madonna) or "bad" (whore). This categorization then arguably influences both the ways in which men harass women, as well as how women respond in relation to their self-concept and understanding of their own subjectivities).

Placing women into the "bad" category might allow men who harass to sexually objectify women differently—they might view women as "good" or decent—thus, respectability politics shapes social interactions in decidedly distinct ways. In either case, men who harass women tend to ignore the extent to which women do not welcome or invite this unsolicited attention. Many men ignore the extent to which women possess the power and human agency to challenge these notions of respectable or legitimate femininity. By responding to men's advances during street harassment, women disrupt notions of hegemonic femininity and assert power that they otherwise might surrender to the male harasser.

The good girl/bad girl construction also works to suggest, "bad things do not happen to good girls."[15] This line of thinking oversimplifies women's gender and sexuality, falsely constructing women as sexually pure or not. The dichotomy ignores the fluidity and collapses the complexity of sexuality, by presenting women as belonging to one of presumably only two, mutually exclusive, categories.

These dichotomous ways of categorizing women remain inadequate (or insufficient), and prove to be "dangerous ways of seeing" women, gender and sexuality, for a number of reasons (including the perpetuation of sexism). Denying women their agency, or limiting the various ways they might otherwise choose to express their gendered, sexualized, and autonomous selves reflects the mechanism of social control in these discourses, as employed through "dangerous ways of seeing" women (and men).

We further complicate these dangerous ways of seeing women, when we perpetually sexualize, objectify, and even infantilize women (by suggesting that women need men escorts when in public). Feminist scholars continue to argue that the many ways of seeing women reflect capitalist society's tendency to package up, market, and make women available for consumption in a variety of desirable ways. These dangerous ways of seeing women as always already available for consumption offer partial explanation for the kinds of interactional vandalism and street harassment that occurs on an everyday basis.

[A]ny image of a sexy woman that is sold, no matter the content, will encourage men to view women and sexual pleasure as commodities to be bought, sold, gotten for free, or stolen—that is, raped. But the fact that many men don't respect women ought not to keep other men and women from exploring their sexuality through nonsexist images.[16]

Rape culture enables the contradiction of celebrating and denigrating a woman's sexiness. Media and society encourage both the male gaze[17] and the "pornographic gaze."[18] They inform our ways of seeing, in patterns and forms that I consider "dangerous ways of seeing."

This imagery shapes our ways of seeing ourselves, as well as others. When this imagery influences the way men harassers see women, it is not surprising that street harassment "seems ambiguous in this regard, complex and difficult to classify in terms of social celebration or degradation."[19]

The "good/bad girl" ways of seeing women infantilizes, oversimplifies, and intends to control women, by suggesting that there are proper and respectable ways of being. Encouraging girls and women to be "good" discourages "bad" behavior, but begs the question: "Good" and "bad" on whose terms, and for whose benefit?

Researchers suggest that the "good girl/bad girl" binary denies girls and women the space to live complex lives, speak uncomfortable truths about their lives, and to "resist this good girl ideal."[20] Evidence exists that such resistance comes with a price, the penalty girls and women pay for rejecting passivity and carving out life on their own terms.

The very expectation of goodness is supposed to encourage the desired behavior, though not necessarily for women's benefit. The dynamic of discipline and control, as largely defined by men, regulates women's behavior, and shows some of the shortcomings of this gendered dichotomy and disciplinary binary.

By ostensibly rewarding "good girl" behavior, and punishing "bad girl" behavior, society reinforces the value of the dichotomy, and underscores the importance of drawing these distinctions.[21] Women who show up in public trouble this dichotomy, their female bodies producing tensions related to respectability.

Yet, these notions of "respectability" are also racialized. As Jones[22] and others illustrate in their work,[23] race also informs understandings about respectability, and therefore complicates this "good girl/bad girl" binary. Because of gendered racism,[24] women of various racial groups are perceived in particular ways.

In my study, I interviewed 20 women, 10 of whom reported a white racial identity, and 10 a black racial identity. I chose to look at the lives of women in these two racial groups, in part because of the city demographics where I conducted the research and as importantly, to consider and examine the similarities and differences in women's experiences at the intersection of gender and race. Of the literature on street harassment, few focus on and explore these intersections.

This chapter considers some of the ways the women I interviewed reported on their experiences, including their consciousness about the gendered and racialized aspects of street harassment. The discussion below helps to contextualize how racialized and gendered controlling images shape, and sometimes intensify, the experience of street harassment.

Young black girls frequently witness a wide variation of violation. As a result, they are constantly negotiating this violence in their everyday lives, walking the line between "good and ghetto."[25]

> The need to avoid or overcome dangers throughout their adolescence presents a uniquely gendered challenge for girls who grow up in distressed inner-city neighborhoods. As a system of accountability, gender reflects widely held beliefs, or normative expectations, about the "attitudes and activities appropriate for one's sex category." During interactions and encounters with others, children and adults evaluate themselves and others in light of these normative gender expectations in ways that reinforce or challenge beliefs about the natural qualities of boys and girls, and especially the essential differences between the two (West and Zimmerman 1987, 127; West and Fenstermaker 1995). Generally, women and girls who are able to mirror normative expectations of femininity during their interactions with others—for example, by assuming a passive demeanor and presenting an appearance that does not significantly deviate from the standards of mainstream culture or local preferences—are evaluated by adults (e.g., family members, teachers, counselors) and by peers as appropriately feminine girls or *good* girls. Meanwhile, girls or women who seem to violate perceived gender boundaries by embracing stereotypically masculine behaviors (e.g., strength, independence, and an outwardly aggressive demeanor) often are disparagingly categorized as "unnaturally strong" (Collins 2004, 193–199).[26]

Patricia Hill Collins furthers our understanding of the complexities surrounding our social locations, and the intersections of these positions. She discusses the manner in which the matrix of domination distorts ways of seeing others, and ourselves. She describes the purpose and process of society creating "controlling images," or negative images that control the represented group. Collins argues,

> Race, class, and gender oppression could not continue without powerful ideological justification for their existence. . . . As part of a generalized ideology of domination, these controlling images of Black womanhood take on special meaning because the authority to define these symbols is a major instrument of power. In order to exercise power, elite white men and their representatives must

be in a position to manipulate appropriate symbols concerning Black women. They may do so by exploiting already existing symbols, or they may create new ones relevant to their needs (Patterson 1982). Hazel Carby suggests that the objective of stereotypes is "not to reflect or represent a reality but to function as a disguise, or mystification, of objective social relations" (1987, 22). These controlling images are designed to make racism, sexism, and poverty appear to be natural, normal, and an inevitable part of everyday life.[27]

Just as controlling images naturalize and normalize these interlocking oppressions, street harassment does as well. Street harassment often supports these controlling images, and thus the disciplinary mechanisms of this social control.

Controlling images thus inform the "dangerous ways of seeing," in the case of street harassment, men who internalize or utilize controlling images as a reference point may see women as such, and interact accordingly. If these controlling images are racist, sexist, and classist, then the interactions that rely on these images are likely to reflect similar patterns and broader systems of oppression.

One might ask, "Do similar mechanisms of social control operate for men? Do men experience a similar set of social pressures regarding their gendered performance of masculinity during street harassment?" While controlling images of men also exist, the control or regulation of them differs in relation to the kinds of power and privilege men can access (or not). The controlling images circulating about women are arguably much more nefarious and dangerous, especially to women. Collins argues:

> Portraying African-American women as stereotypical mammies, matriarchs, welfare recipients, and hot mommas has been essential to the political economy of domination fostering Black women's oppression. Challenging these controlling images has long been a core theme in Black feminist thought. . . . Even when the political and economic conditions that originally generated controlling images disappear, such images prove remarkably tenacious because they not only keep Black women oppressed but are key in maintaining interlocking systems of race, class, and gender oppression. The status of African-American women as outsiders or strangers becomes the point from which other groups define their normality.[28]

Controlling images of black women have also been updated to include the following: divas, freaks, gold diggers, dykes, gangsta bitches, earth mothers, sister saviors, baby mamas, big girls, and so on.[29] These stereotypical ways of seeing black women build upon these existing controlling images of black women: the asexual mammy; the hypersexual Jezebel; the emasculating, powerful, independent matriarch; the black bitch; the black lady; and the welfare queen.[30]

Several black women respondents reported being respectful of others, including men who harass them. They say hello to everyone, as one respondent put it, "to beat them to the punch. Just to let them know, I see you; I acknowledge you. I'm going on my way." Despite these efforts at recognition of others (including men harassers), some of the same women confronted men's harassment, and men's use of controlling images to interact with them.

One respondent, Red, shared this example of being called a 'bitch":

> I mean I've had situations where guys will, you know, [say], "F—k you, bitch," and obviously showing anger but it's just like, how can I respond to them because it may cause, I already don't want to be in this situation, but it may cause something else to get out of hand. "Well, f—k you," [the male harasser might say]. "Well, f—k you, too." But other than that, I just try to stay calm and free of drama. You wanna make remarks; that's fine. It is kind of irritating to me just to see, because you can feel when someone is staring at you, but I like to watch men watching women walk down the street and the women don't know it because their backs are turned, because I think what they do is disrespectful. So I can only imagine.

Red's comments illustrate that she observes how men who harass treat her, as well as other women. She notes their aggression and assaultive behavior during these interactions, and mentions, in comments that echo Samantha's, a similar feeling of disgust at being looked at, at *feeling* being looked at. This is a small but significant point; it advances ideas about the strategies (including "felt intuition"[31]) that women employ to navigate urban public spaces and to survive social life. That she *feels* men making a spectacle of her allows her an awareness that arguably keeps her safer than if she lacked this sensation and awareness.

The respondent's comments also show how women in public fall under the male gaze, much to their own displeasure and disapproval. The dilemma in having this opposition to being visually consumed is not feeling comfortable and safe enough to challenge men who harass women in this way.

Women targets of street harassment rely on discursive speech practices and silence to challenge and counter the controlling images that men who harass perpetuate or impose on them. I will note here, however, that in choosing not to respond, Red (and other black women respondents) challenge the controlling images of black women as loud, sassy, or emasculating. She notes,

> I usually just try to ignore it and keep walking or keep going about my business because I don't want to encourage it; I don't want to reject it, because I know what it's like to be rejected, I think, but it's something that I've never figured out

how to deal with. . . . I don't want to damage someone else's self-esteem. . . . I want to reject it because I don't want to deal with it, but I don't want to damage someone else's self-esteem.

Despite being called a "bitch," or facing similarly abrasive, offensive public speech,[32] Red responds to men who harass by not responding, by opting to respect, rather than reject, them. Her example shows how powerful and purposeful silence can prove.

Another black woman respondent, Olivia, shared a complex example of how she confronted the controlling image of "the black bitch."[33] While once hanging out,

[T]his guy was trying to pick me up I guess, and um, and he was saying that he saw me walking down the street, and he said something about, something that implied sex; it was a slang, but I didn't know it, because I'm not very good at slang, and I was like, "Excuse me. What did you say?" And he was like, "Let me get in those skins," or something like that, more than I would know. And I was like, "Excuse you." And I went all on this thing about, "What would make you think that I would want to sleep with you just because you approach me on this street? Nowhere in what you see implies that I am looking for five dollars for two minutes of your time." And then he was like, "Bitch!"

Olivia then describes how her military (men) friends intervened on her behalf, asking the harasser, "Who you calling a 'bitch'?" And the guy would be like, "Oh, is that your girl?" And they'd be like, "Oh, that's not my girl; that's my baby sister. So, what are you doing? Why are you calling her a 'bitch'?"

Notably, the intervention and assistance of men friends helped Olivia diffuse an otherwise escalating hostile situation of harassment, since her unreciprocated attention[34] and direct confrontation with the man angered him to the point of him disrespecting her. It is interesting that the man harasser is willing to back down if Olivia is "someone else's property." In this way, the man harasser becomes curiously (and problematically) more considerate of the men intervening on Olivia's behalf; the harasser does not seem willing to disrespect the men, but he willingly disrespects Olivia.

The controlling images of black women as "the black bitch" and as emasculating suggest some of the ways in which this man might have seen Olivia. Her account also illustrates why relying on controlling images can prove to be a "dangerous way of seeing" black women, given the assaultive and offensive speech of the man harasser. It also becomes more evidence of misogynoir, or the hatred of black women.[35]

Olivia also explained that, on another occasion, other men called her a "bitch." "These guys . . . tried to hit on me, and I just said thanks, and basically I'm not interested because I'm dating somebody. And kept going and he said. . . . 'That's the problem with white bitches, you know? Just because they sleep with a white guy, they think they're white.' And at the time, my hair was, it was this long. . . . And, so, he said, 'She just thinks that because she's got all of that long hair and white guys want her, and then he called me a 'white bitch.'"

This accusation from men harassers of "white bitch" partially reflects how she, as a black woman, gets antagonistically re-racialized as white because of her interracial relationship with a white man. This relationship, coupled with her hair, speech, voice, or other characteristics that people misread as her "acting white," may produce feelings of resentment and rejection from men who harass her. These black men may have been able to preserve their masculinities and identities by calling her a "white bitch," presumably two categorically undesirable qualities for the black men to desire in women.

During our interview conversation, I shared with Olivia that I, too, had been called a "white bitch" by a man harasser. I was surprised and disappointed to hear other examples of some men using this term to refer to brown and black women. As a multiracial woman, I wrestled with the term, in part because it seemed so hostile, but more importantly, accusatory. I learned interesting lessons about the perception of race and gender, the persuasion of controlling images on those perceptions, and the presumption of loyalty.

Both Olivia and I were regarded as such because we failed to follow the informal rules of racial kinship. Perhaps we were falling outside of the parameters of controlling images of black women, both of us through our social relationships with white people, and/or our perceived proximity to whiteness.[36]

In comparison to Olivia's example of facing harassment that operated as interracial regulation, Samantha, a white woman in the sample, noted that she felt harassed when she and her black male partner were in public together. Notably, though, she was never called a "bitch" or a "white bitch," which is consistent with the narratives of most of the other white women in the sample, and contrary to other black women respondents. Speculatively, Samantha's whiteness, and attendant white privilege,[37] may have protected her from the same harsh criticism that Olivia faced, even as they both endured hostility from men who disapproved of their interracial connections or relationships.

The contrasting ways that black and white women respectively experience street harassment reveals the different controlling images that apply to women of various racial groups. I mention this example here, to briefly contrast the experiences of respondents in my sample. Later in this chapter, I discuss more of the controlling images specific to white women, and resume my discussion of controlling images of black women here.

While both black- and white-identified women reported experiencing unwanted touches or sexual assault from men during street harassment, some black women shared examples of men touching specific body parts, including their breasts and buttocks. For instance, Mickie, a black middle-class heterosexual woman, expressed some frustration over the lack of regulation of intrusive incidents of street harassment: "I do remember when I have been touched before and . . . this guy goosed me (grabbed my behind) and I just turned around and started swinging/elbowing him. I was just like, 'Why would you do something like that?'" Mickie continued to describe other incidents where men violated her personal space, and harassed her at once. In the context of the controlling image of black women as "the hypersexual Jezebel," men who harass black women may be relying on this notion of the women's hypersexuality.[38]

In fending off the physical intrusions of men who harass, black women appear to be the "emasculating, powerful independent matriarch" mentioned above, while white women who do the same fail to give a convincing performance of femininity, and their risk compromising it (or being read as masculine as well). For example, Olivia shared this experience she had in which a man intruded on her personal space:

> Some guys, they're not trying to touch you, but they're going to reach out like they're going to touch you, to get your attention. I don't like that either. . . . Then they'll tell you, "Oh, I wasn't trying to touch you. I was just trying to get your attention." "Hmmm, don't reach out for me, because that's scary." Um, and I don't entertain anything they have to say.

Olivia noted that, upon realizing that she has interpreted their attempts to touch her as horrifying, the men offered what she considered disingenuous apologies to the women, possibly to appear considerate of her feelings, even after negatively provoking them in the first place.

The men often mistakenly asserted their male privilege and found that many women have different triggers, in part based on previous personal traumas and experiences with abuse. The cumulative impact of these experiences combines to form multiplicative traumas. The combination and accumulation of traumatic experiences can provoke women to have certain rejecting reactions and adverse consequences to men who harass. By unintentionally crossing that line of comfortable social distance between themselves and the women they attempted to entangle,[39] men can agitate women's feelings and fear, resulting in that energy being directed at the men.

In a sense, street harassment can become a new trauma, especially given how frequent and commonplace it remains for some women. Over time, the accumulation of these incidents can begin to look like or form the multiplicative traumas I mentioned above. The increasing incidence of street harassment thus creates its own web of violence and forms the basis of multiplicative trauma, stemming in part from the verbal aggression and offensive public speech women experience, as well as the physical and sexual assaults some women targets endure, as described below.

By assuming liberties to touch women, particularly black women, men who harass cement the idea that "African American women are sexually promiscuous, potential prostitutes" who can be sexually consumed on the street through touch or other sexualized gestures.[40] Reducing black women to animalistic and sexualized objects through the act of (non-consensual) touch or attempts to pet them, constructs women as objects or property, and pets, not humans. The controlling image of the Jezebel continually enables harassers to consume black women's bodies visually and verbally, as a result of interlocking oppressions.

Given that most women respondents reported same-race harassment, the mistreatment of black women stemmed primarily from black men. Once men who harass develop an awareness that the construction of black women's sexuality hinges on or intersects with the construction of black men's sexuality as similarly animalistic (though not necessarily subordinate to black women's sexuality), they can experience a shift in consciousness necessary to effect social change.[41]

This shift in social consciousness and away from controlling images had not yet happened for the man who harassed Katie, another heterosexual black woman in my sample. While Katie faced a lot of street harassment here in the United States, she also shared her experience of being harassed in her home country:

> I was younger then, 18 or something. I was wearing a t-shirt and some pants or something and walking down the street and it was a guy who was working in a shop but he was kind of standing in the doorway and I think his job was to kind of get people to come in off the street. . . . Yeah, and the t-shirt I had on had "Hakuna Matata" on the front of it and that means, "No problems," right. And he made a comment which sounds funnier in the language. He said, "Hakuna Matata Hakuna Matiti," which means, "No problem, but you got big breasts." So, basically, I think I was really, really embarrassed. It was just very blatant, very graphic, so I just ducked into a store again.

The respondent's use of "again" marks the repetitive nature of this strategy, in response to her repeated encounters with men who harass. Her observation about her embarrassment conveys the extent to which she found the man's comments undesirable. That he uses what she deems "graphic" language to comment on her body illustrates how powerfully stereotypical images control the collective imagination and shape social interactions.

Black women are always already public, in terms of their bodies, made spectacular under the disciplinary and fetishizing lens of controlling images.[42] Black women respondents provided countless examples of their efforts to counter controlling images, and harassers' assumptions of their presumed availability. The dilemma here is contained in the act of challenging these images, in getting out of the kind of trap that controlling images establishes for women targets of street harassment.

This trap operates as one mechanism of social control of women during street harassment, as it establishes a double bind or Catch-22 for women who respond (or not, as the case may be). In other words, what discursive practices (speech or silence) most effectively challenges or undoes these images? Are women targets of harassment responsible, especially if they are fearful for their lives, of challenging and confronting men who harass?

Some respondents wanted to challenge street harassment, but did not want to endorse controlling images. For example, Katie also commented on her desire to refute other controlling images of her, as she wanted to reject being "that kind of woman" (who invites questionable attention, and thus brings her reputation into question). Katie explained that she rejects men's attempts to interpellate or hail her:

> For me, it's well, I think that what they are doing is demeaning and I'm not going to lower myself to that level, you know. If somebody was upset at me, and I knew that they were upset with me, and they were cursing, I probably would say as little as possible because I don't want to go there with you; I don't want to go down that level and curse back at you.

In other words, Katie perceived street harassment as an unflattering kind of behavior, on a level that she cared not to deign to, as it would taint her reputation, or others' public perception of her.

It is interesting that she views her non-response, her refusal to respond, as a way to preserve this image of respectability, decorum, and decency. She acknowledges her refusal in this way:

> This may sound something "-ist," not "classist," but I don't know what. For me, I feel as though somebody whose walking down the street and saying something out loud to a woman he does not know would probably say it to just about any-body and so I take no—I'm not particularly impressed with myself for having attracted that kind of attention. . . . People just approach me differently. If they are interested in dating me or whatever, or flirting with me, they would approach me differently than just calling something out.

Some scholars trace the controlling images of the hypersexual and promiscu-ous black woman back to slavery: Researchers speculated that Black women are reluctant to label their experiences sexual harassment because, ". . . in their struggle against the image of sexual promiscuity, Black women may not want to draw attention to themselves as targets of sexual attention."[43] The conundrum in identifying oneself as the target of sexual attention is in the suggestion that one might affirm the controlling image of "deserving" such attention due to myths of hypersexuality and hot-bloodedness. Katie and others wrestle with this in their interviews about and experiences with street harassment.

In Katie's estimation, women who get harassed are inviting that attention, but as she notes, men who harass are likely to harass other women as well. This is important to note, because the interpretation shifts attention away from her to the harasser, who should ultimately feel responsible for his actions. Katie implies feeling a bit of shame around being the spectacle of street harassment. As more and more women face street harassment, and see the increasingly common way women are under assault, they can also see the shame-blame connection[44] in a new way, one that sees men as responsible and holds them accountable for harassment.

Katie also shared the horrifying experience of being called the "n word" while she was quite young and still in college. Racism gets expressed in offensive public speech, and becomes a "dangerous way of speaking," as I explore in chapter 5. The experiences that she and other respondents shared during the interview reveal how pervasive and persistent, and how damaging, these dangerous ways of speaking remain.

Controlling images, then and now, inform(ed) the multiple ways that black women are (mis)represented in the media, how they are (mis)perceived, seen, and/or located with society, and how people interact with them in any number of settings, including urban public spaces. The compulsory heterosexuality that accompanies these controlling images helps frame the way black women's sexuality gets scripted. This imagery links to the historical residue of slavery, and the particular gendered, racialized, and sexual oppression and abuse black women experienced at the hands of white men.[45]

Researchers find that sexism and racism converged uniquely to create gendered racism. Specific to my study, many respondents reported experiences of this, in terms of racialized sexual harassment. Men expressed this harassment in varying degrees of hostility and incivility; expressions of harassment ranged from covert, subtly overt, and overt forms.[46]

> Sexual and racial harassment may be combined in unique ways for African American women. Specifically, the cultural and historical contexts of slavery and sexualized stereotypes of African American women result in sexual harassment that is perceived as racially motivated.[47] Moreover, the harassment is likely to take different forms in the lives of Black women than in the lives of White

women. For example, although a coworker may refer to a White woman as a whore or a slut, an African American woman may be called a *Black* whore, which creates an experience that combines aspects of both race and gender oppression.[48]

This painful history produced a legacy of stereotypical and grossly offensive images of black women, images that continue to get reproduced, reinvented, and ultimately consumed for capitalist gains and cultural commodification and gratification. Examining the lingering impact of this power asymmetrical history and society helps illustrate how images of black women, among other less structurally powerful groups, maintained a disciplinary and regulatory effect on people.

For African American women, sexual harassment is inextricably linked with racism and posit, "victims often perceive multiple forms of harassment to be more severe."[49] Other researchers echo the point that sexual and racial harassment are amplified for black women.[50] Scholars see the urgency of more research that examines the following: 1) "whether women of color are differentially exposed to and affected by sexual harassment"; 2) "whether sexual and racial harassment are inextricably linked for Black victims"; and 3) "whether the range and severity of outcomes for women of color are different from that of Caucasian women."[51]

The unique experiences and stereotypes of women of various social positions necessitate a discussion of the ways that intersections form different experiences. Applying intersectionality theory throughout allows for the exploration of the unique and different experiences women have, while still providing the space for women's experiences to converge. However, while these convergences do exist, highlighting and explicating the divergences and particularities in women's experiences resulting from their unique social locations, subjectivities, and personal histories allows for a richer and more complicated understanding of women's lives.

Controlling images of white women exist alongside that of black women, and prove as problematic and contradictory in comparison. Most controlling images of white women exist as "positive stereotypes," since whiteness is synonymous with ideal femininity and/or womanhood. The construction of ideal femininity marks thin, young, blonde-haired, blue-eyed bodies as more valuable than other women's bodies; ideal femininity also always gets attached to or associated with women's bodies, not that of men.

The construction of black women as hypersexualized and white women as virginal and pure has been contested and challenged. Researchers have illustrated how Filipina women construct "'American' culture as deviant" and white women as sexually promiscuous; they argue that women of color have been systematically devalued, yet can produce counternarratives to challenge their devaluation in society.[52] They do so to craft morally superior narratives about themselves, with stand in contrast to morality of white women which they call into question.

The construction of white women as promiscuous challenges hegemonic femininity and the dominant images of white women as ideal (having moral integrity), and the "sexualized racialization" of black women as promiscuous themselves.[53] Both sets of controlling images compete with and contradict one another, as feminist scholars have attempted to expose.

Creating these contradictory images proves beneficial in producing a gap where "real" women can exist. As mentioned earlier, the false dichotomy of good girl/bad girl, along with other prevailing controlling images of white and black women, attempts to discipline women and distract women from the structures (patriarchy) and people in power (men) creating these images in the first place.

Because women are expected to be good girls who are passive and "forced to submit to someone else's desires," we are punished when we behave in ways that assert our agency, and center our own desires. While many women may fantasize about "being admired and ogled at from afar because they look sexy,"[54] women may not fantasize about this attention turning into street harassment. Lamb's work pushes readers to consider whether street harassment plays on this fantasy, by encouraging boys' (or men's) sense of entitlement, and girls' (or women's) victimization.

Does street harassment feel like a game that makes it difficult to distinguish between its objectification and its pleasure? In an attempt to answer this, I draw from Lamb's discussion of the (dangerous?) games girls play: "It was a game. In this game, she became the pursued and they the pursuers, which is a lot like the games little girls are taught about anyway, concerning sexual response: The boy pursues, the girl resists but really wants it. It's a dangerous game, I might add, as it will confuse boys about how to read girls' desires."[55]

If this ambivalence and confusion exists between women and men, then it makes sense that street harassment is so slippery to identify. How does one know when such attention is desired, or not? To my earlier point, the blurred lines between hello and harassment must be clarified, in order for women to feel safe in social interactions and urban public spaces, and in order for men to discern the difference between social interactions and street harassment.

The controlling images made myopic the individual and collective vision of women. Throughout history, women have been viewed narrowly, and through a distorted lens, or "the slanted room,"[56] that race creates, tilting the perspectives to skew reality. These distortions have enabled some men to perpetuate sexualized violence on both white and black women, for different reasons and in different ways, with different consequences.

This violence continues to this day in the form of street harassment, and works to limit women's bodily autonomy and freedom. Women are largely unable to walk "with dignity and pride,"[57] when the potential and actual dangers of sexualized violence persist, in public and in private. Women have learned, throughout history as well, that recognizing, naming, and challenging this violence offers rewards while producing serious risks.

The contradictions that exist, as documented in the literature, show that women can talk back[58] to men harassers, as well as to these controlling images, to dispute their claims, and disrupt their disciplinary potential or power, just as women can talk back to men during street harassment. Women who challenge/d controlling images (and men) by talking back could risk their personal safety, assuming that they felt they had their personal safety to risk. While I explore the act of talking back and introduce and elaborate upon the concept of "dangerous ways of speaking" elsewhere, here, I briefly consider the implications of challenging controlling images during street harassment here.

Challenging Controlling Images and Hegemonic Femininity

The controlling images that circulate about white and black women's bodies reflect the danger in discourses produced about and by people. Since women are generally no longer legally men's property, they must be controlled discursively. Images produced to create representations of women remain controlling, when women are typically not the ones creating these images. The words that reflect (or build upon) these controlling images operate in similarly disciplining ways.

Thus, it is equally important to acknowledge the constructions and contradictions surrounding women's bodies, so as to also expose the power structures that encourage the association or connection between women's bodies and vulnerability, and men's bodies with dominance. The discourses discipline bodies to be understood as vulnerable and/or powerful, in relation to intersections of race, class, and gender, or as Rosemarie Tong posits, "when racism, sexism, and classism combine, a qualitatively different type of sexual harassment is the result."[59] Paying attention to the different social constructions of bodies in our society helps us understand how people see one another.

In the case of my study, both black and white women have to contend with existing controlling images. This illustrates that white women must also contend with controlling images and the impossibility of ideal femininity:

Mothers teach daughters that if a girl presents the right kind of femininity, she will attract romantic interest and respect from boys and men. In the fifties and sixties, being taken care of in life was an important future goal. But in the seventies, eighties, and nineties, being a good girl was protection against being abused and raped. So mothers thought.[60]

Mothers seldom warned their daughters about the consequences of fitting into the feminine ideal; few conversations about these consequences as negative, and violent, take place:

> In aspiring to (ideal) femininity girls are encouraged to seek power through their appearance and their manners. The ideal of femininity is pretty, nice, desirable, and popular. Truth be told, there really is power in this ideal, but it is a borrowed power, a granted power—granted by men who benefit most from girls' niceness. When girls are encouraged to seek power through their actions and accomplishments, something that the girl-power movement aims for, there usually follows an outcry that boys are being displaced.[61]

Many of the respondents in this research spoke about their uneasy relationship to power, given the power asymmetries in society and in social interactions.

It is interesting to think about women's relation to power, in terms of their embodiment and performance of femininity. Some interesting narratives emerged from respondents who centered physical activity, perhaps in pursuit of the beauty ideal, but found themselves being street harassed while being physically active outdoors. Next, I discuss how some of these women managed to find some balance between being fit, and being harassed (and trying to find the right responses to men who harass).

Several of the white women respondents in my sample identified as fitness walkers or runners. Julie, an avid runner, expressed how harassment heightened her sense of vulnerability in certain moments:

> Well, I do feel like a target when I'm jogging, like I feel very vulnerable and exposed but . . . I don't know that it's any different if I'm walking down the street in my jeans and t-shirt. . . . I think I feel vulnerable because of the stories in the media of women joggers who get kidnapped or raped. . . . And sometimes, basically just being physically exhausted when I'm jogging and I just think—consciously saying, like, "I'm gonna kick somebody's ass if they mess with me." Like I try, even though I feel vulnerable; I try not to have this victim mentality where I like, I don't think I can defend myself because I think it's important for women to consciously re-enact [imagine] in their minds what they would do if they were attacked, because we have not been socialized to fight, you know, so we have to learn how to fight, and then we visualize it. So, I'm constantly going, "I'll kick their ass. I feel sorry for someone who tries to mess with me." And sometimes I think, "I'm really tired; I'm *really* tired. How could I kick somebody's ass? I've just run five miles, uphill both ways, and . . . what would I do now?"

My interview conversation with Julie allowed us both to acknowledge the unfair burden of having to devise contingencies, possible escape routes, or exit strategies for those situations that escalate in danger, and otherwise make women feel increasingly vulnerable, especially while engaging in exhaustive activities like distance running. When men harass, they enact a performance of masculinity that imposes on women, in multiple ways, including forcing women to figure out how to more/most safely maneuver around street harassment.

Pamela, another white woman respondent, had ample experiences with street harassment, past and present. The previous experiences informed the present ones. Pamela also shared her concerns about her safety while fitness running in public:

> Well, I ran down a road, and yeah, it was obvious [that they had circled around], and the car was on the street perpendicular to me and it was a brand-new SUV, so you notice it; you notice the person in it. He had plenty of time to turn and didn't—and I didn't really think anything of it at first, and I kept running. Well then, two or three blocks later, he was at, or perpendicular to the intersections again, and okay, that's a little strange; so, then I turned down the street that I live and he was at the complex next to mine . . . and so at that point I thought, "Okay, I'm definitely being followed and I am definitely going to keep running."

Pamela describes the experience as an "unnecessary fear," which stems from not knowing what to anticipate by way of men's street harassing or stalking behavior. She alludes to the web of violence here, verbally gesturing toward the possibility of escalated violence (such as being abducted or kidnapped, assaulted, sex trafficked, and/or murdered).[62]

As a roadrunner, Pamela faced a number of evaluative remarks from men strangers, including the following: "Hey, you're looking great." "You look really nice." "Well, you look very nice today." "You need to keep up the running." Pamela reported that she found neither flattering nor complimentary the comments that men strangers made to her about her body. Instead, she found them disingenuous at best and offensive at worst (given them coming from strangers, as opposed to people she knew more and from whom she might appreciate compliments).

Furthermore, she lamented, and arguably resented, being put in a position to respond to harassers accordingly, while feeling frustrated (rather than pleased) by their undesired and unsolicited attention. The kinds of comments that Pamela received might be considered "sexist compliments," given the way they speak to her aesthetic appearance and attendant value, and in their insistence on her keeping up said appearance. That Pamela is a relatively thin and fit white woman who is told by a man stranger what she "needs" to do reflects the imperative imposition of the beauty ideal[63] as it matches the imposition of individual and societal views onto her.

White women and girls are generally located closer to this ideal femininity; as a result, they face different social expectations regarding this real or imagined proximity to the ideal. When white women are viewed as departing far from the ideal (or further than strangers would prefer), they often encounter increased hostility or are regarded as invisible.

In this sense, ideal femininity operates as a controlling image, intended to encourage—some might say mandate—women's conformity and constant aspiration, if not embodiment of, physical perfection. Women who do not conform can encounter harassment as men harassers attempt control of them. Consider Tammy's experiences, which involve men attempting to touch her during their street harassment of her:

> My most recent one (time I was harassed), the one that annoyed me the most, and I don't know why, was some boy outside. I mean, he was a man; he was at least probably 18. He was kind of like hanging there in a very stereotypical way, kinda like talking to everyone who passed, and when I walked by, he like grabbed my tattoo, and was like, "Hey! Hey, nice tattoo, nice art. Lemme see that!" And then I was like, I mean I was like, I reacted badly, I don't like to grab. And I was like, "Get your hand off me!" And I mean, it was kind of a weird reaction. Then he kept following me and trying to touch my tattoo, but at that point it was no longer about the tattoo. He was controlling me, like he, he was mad that I . . . [had a reaction]. Yeah, I mean, I wasn't supposed to *do* that. I was supposed to run away or not say anything. I was supposed to shrug him off but I was mad. It just pissed me off and I was having a crappy day.

During our interview conversation, Tammy described herself as a fat woman whose heavily tattooed body is often viewed as a transgressive one. Her account above suggests that her failure—or refusal—to perform hegemonic femininity may offer partial explanation for men's harassment of her. She recalled her experience with street harassment, including being called names:

> Both times I've been called a "fat bitch," it's been by a white guy and it's been at a grocery store, in the parking lot, and I was walking and it was different reasons, like one was mad because I cut him off apparently, and one guy, I don't even know why he was yelling but that, those were my two experiences, and they, I don't know, they were kinda mortifying because it's like, to me, the worst thing. Not because I'm not fat and not because I'm not necessarily a bitch, but those words are the ones that there's no response to . . . to me.

Tammy continued, explaining how her impulse to respond aligns with a "female masculinity"[64] rather than respectable femininity:

I feel like this is where my masculine side comes out. I never feel like I'm able to respond the way I wanna respond. I always wanna respond in a more physical or demonstrative way than I allow myself. Like, I really don't wanna get called "fat bitch," especially when you're [the harasser is] just commenting on my physical appearance or clothes. . . . It's not for you [the harasser] to touch. "Go away." 'Cuz people always want to touch my hair or my lip ring; like, it makes it more tangible. People touch my lip ring, as if they aren't touching my mouth. So, I back off, and then they realize, "No touches." I'm always doing things sub-tly . . . I always wanna be physical and in-your-face and I'm not. I don't wanna be called "fat bitch," because there's no response. . . . If I were skinny, I could say, "Not as fat as your mother." No one has ever called me a "smart pretty girl."

Existing outside of the "skinny is pretty" beauty ideal[65] may exclude some women from some forms of harassment, while potentially intensifying spe-cific fat-phobic-fueled comments. To the former point, any exclusion may yield the positive results of minimizing harassment for women. To the lat-ter one, women who are viewed as fat may feel further marginalized, as the comments they hear during harassment speak to their distance from ideal-ized beauty.

Fat-phobic harassment serves as a reminder of fat women's putative "unde-sirability" in society. So much of this logic and language is predicated on compulsory heterosexuality and presumes that women who are perceived as desirable by men actually appreciate such a designation or perception and/or also desire men. Fat-phobic harassment underscores the beauty ideal and hegemonic femininity; it targets women who are viewed as falling outside of the beauty norm and, thus, failing to measure up. Typically, this sort of atten-tion is verbally assaultive and judgmental.

Having a body that falls outside of the parameters of hegemonic or empha-sized femininity means that Tammy gets policed as a result of this perceived transgression. The controlling images of idealized beauty set up expecta-tions for women's appearance. That white women are expected to be always already pretty, and skinny is often equated with pretty in this society, leaves Tammy lamenting never being "called a smart pretty girl." Yet, a dilemma in that exists. To be called a "smart pretty girl" within the context of harass-ment could be understood as both an affirmation and an invalidation. It may be liberating for some women to be recognized as such, but for otherwise, it may operate as a box, a limitation around who they are and what is (perceived as) possible for them.

The underlying themes embedded in what Tammy says include the fol-lowing: a resentment of being fat and feeling socially vulnerable, devalued, or marginal, and in some sense powerless (as a result of existing outside of the beauty norm), censured, and silenced by a society that overvalues skinny women. She reportedly feels like her body, full of tattoos and adorned in other ways, is "Othered," which intensifies others' surveillance and scrutiny of her.

Tammy expresses a frustration at facing these injurious, evaluative comments and not having (or giving) a response. This multiplies her silence in two ways: 1) not feeling comfortable or entitled enough to respond to men harassers, and 2) being at a loss for words (when confronted by harassers' critical evaluation of her). This intensified silence (connected to experiences of shame) cements the "good girl" image that supports the idea that women should not be sassy or talk back.

Ironically, Tammy is typically anything but quiet. However, during moments of street harassment, she displays a hegemonic femininity that masks her otherwise loud or bold personality). While she may try to resist or refute traditional gender role expectations in terms of behavior in social situations, Tammy also risks reproducing these ideas: that performing masculinity relates physicality and performing femininity relates docility. For this respondent, then, being feminine equates being docile, silenced, policed, and accommodating to others, particularly men.

In moments where Tammy is not being forced to think of a response or passively react to street harassment, she subversively reports *initiating* "street harassment," as her way of humorously highlighting how that attention works or what it feels like. Her action aligns with other women's efforts to mirror the behavior back to men who harass.[66]

CONCLUSIONS

This is the way in which street harassment operates as a mechanism of social control. Men who harass may be relying on controlling images of the women targets, and enact harassment as a result of women fitting into or falling out of the scope of those stereotypes and controlling images. Ironically, controlling images not only work to discipline and regulate women (to encourage the pursuit of perfection and the embodiment of the beauty ideal, for example) but also men. Future research should investigate and explore this further.

NOTES

1. Melissa Harris-Perry. *Sister Citizen: Shame, Stereotypes, and Black Women in America.* New Haven, CT: Yale University Press, 2011.

2. Darlene C. DeFour. "The Interface of Racism and Sexism on College Campuses" in Michele Paludi's *Sexual Harassment on College Campuses: Abusing the Ivory Power.* Pp. 49–55. Albany, NY: State University of New York Press, 1996: 54.

3. Donna Haraway. "The Persistence of Vision" in *Writing on the Body: Female Embodiment and Feminist Theory.* Edited by Katie Conboy, Nadia Medina, and Sarah Stanbury. Pp. 283–295. New York: Columbia University Press, 1997: 283.

4. Patricia Hill Collins. *Black Feminist Thought: Knowledge, Consciousness, and the Politics of Empowerment.* New York: Routledge, 2008.

5. Patricia Hill Collins. 2008; Patricia Hill Collins. *Black Sexual Politics: African Americans, Gender, and the New Racism.* New York: Routledge, 2005.

6. Donna Haraway. 1997: 288.

7. Reflecting on Haraway's work provokes many questions: How is it that we know what we see? How does our situated knowledge stem from our abilities to see and not see? How does this relate to my earlier argument that street harassment is hard to see, because it hides in plain sight, because the blurred lines between hello and harassment make it look like a conversation, not interactional vandalism? What situated knowledge can we gain from our respective standpoints, in order to share our vision of a world free of violence?

8. This carves out space for women's voices to be heard, rather than minimized, questioned, or dismissed. Typically, ways of knowing and ways of seeing have been largely defined by the power elite (white, male privileged modes of being in the world). In exploring these notions of ways of knowing, and in this chapter, ways of seeing, people can begin to appreciate the variety and complexity of vision (and knowledge).

9. Patricia Hill Collins. "Toward a New Vision." *Privilege: A Reader.* Edited by Michael S. Kimmel and Abby L. Ferber. Pp. 331–348. Cambridge, MA: Westview, 2003.

10. Donna Haraway. 1997: 285.

11. Donna Haraway. 1997: 286.

12. See Betsy Lucal. "What It Means to Be Gendered Me: Life on the Boundaries of a Dichotomous Gender System." *Gender and Society 13(6)*: 781–797, 1999.

13. Angela Davis. *Women, Race, and Class.* New York: Random House, 1981.

14. Evelyn Brooks Higginbotham. "African-American Women's History and the Metalanguage of Race." *Signs 17(2):* 251–274, Winter 1992.

15. Sharon Lamb. *The Secret Lives of Girls: What Good Girls Really Do—Sex Play, Aggression, and Their Guilt.* New York: Free Press, 2002.

16. Timothy Beneke. *Proving Manhood: Reflections on Men and Sexism.* Berkeley, CA: University of California Press, 1997: 108–9.

17. Laura Mulvey. "Visual Pleasure and Narrative Cinema." *Screen* 16: 6–18, 1975.

18. Margaret Hunter and Kathleen Soto (2009). "Women of Color in Hip Hop: The Pornographic Gaze." *Race, Gender, and Class.* Volume 12 (1 and 2), 2009: 170–191.

19. Timothy Beneke. 1997: 86.

20. Sharon Lamb. *The Secret Lives of Girls: What Good Girls Really Do—Sex Play, Aggression, and Their Guilt.* New York: Free Press, 2002: 43.

21. See Deborah L. Tolman. *Dilemmas of Desire: Teenage Girls Talk about Sexuality.* Cambridge, MA: Harvard University Press, 2002.

22. Nikki Jones. *Between Good and Ghetto: African American Girls and Inner-City Violence.* Piscataway, NJ: Rutgers University Press, 2008: 7.

23. Evelyn Brooks Higginbotham. "African-American Women's History and the Metalanguage of Race." *Signs 17(2)*: 251–274, Winter 1992.

24. Adia Harvey Wingfield. *Doing Business with Beauty: Black Women, Hair Salons, and the Racial Enclave Economy.* New York: Rowman & Littlefield, 2008.

25. Nikki Jones. *Between Good and Ghetto: African American Girls and Inner-City Violence*. Piscataway, NJ: Rutgers University Press, 2008.

26. Nikki Jones. 2008: 7.

27. Patricia Hill Collins. *Black Feminist Thought: Knowledge, Consciousness, and the Politics of Empowerment.* New York: Routledge, 2008: 67–68.

28. Patricia Hill Collins. 2008: 67–68.

29. Dionne P. Stephens and Layli D. Phillips 2004. "Freaks, Gold Diggers, Divas, and Dykes: The Sociohistorical Development of Adolescent African American Women's Sexual Scripts." *Sexuality and Culture* 7, 3–49 (2003). https://doi.org/10.1007/BF03159848.

30. See Adia Harvey Wingfield. "The Modern Mammy and the Angry Black Man: African American Professionals' Experiences with Gendered Racism in the Workplace." *Race, Gender & Class* 14(1/2): 196–212; Patricia Hill Collins. *Black Feminist Thought: Knowledge, Consciousness, and the Politics of Empowerment.* New York: Routledge, 2008.

31. See Phillip Brian Harper. 2000.

32. Laura Nielsen. *License to Harass: Law, Hierarchy, and Offensive Public Speech*. Princeton, NJ: Princeton University Press, 2006.

33. Kimberly Springer. "Divas, Evil Black Bitches, and Bitter Black Women: African American Women in Postfeminist and Post-Civil-Rights Popular Culture" in *Interrogating Postfeminism: Gender and the Politics of Popular Culture*. Edited by Yvonne Tasker and Diane Negra. Durham, NC; Duke University Press, 2007.

34. See Mitch Duneier. *Sidewalk.* New York: Farrar, Straus and Giroux, 1999.

35. See Moya Bailey. *Misogynoir Transformed: Black Women's Digital Resistance.* New York: New York University Press, 2021.

36. Notably, Olivia identifies as black but acknowledges a multiracial heritage. This similarity suggests something about the experiences of multiracial women and social expectations about racial identity and loyalty. Failure to respond in kind to black men can result in reflected rejection, a way of black men recuperating their pride and perhaps perpetuating any sting of rejection, as they see it. Black men who harass must understand that women targets are under no obligation to respond, and choosing not to respond should be no indication of anything more than agency. It is not necessarily a sign of racial loyalty. In fact, the harassing actions of these men says more about their sense of solidarity and community than the subject positions and racial locations of the women they target during street harassment.

37. Peggy McIntosh. "White Privilege and Male Privilege: A Personal Account of Coming to See Correspondences through Work in Women's Studies." Working Paper 189. Wellesley College Center for Research on Women, Wellesley, MA, 1998.

38. Patricia Hill Collins. *Black Sexual Politics: African Americans, Gender, and the New Racism*. New York: Routledge, 2005; Karla Holloway. 2011.

39. Mitch Duneier. *Sidewalk.* New York: Farrar, Straus and Giroux, 1999.

40. Patricia Hill Collins. *Black Feminist Thought: Knowledge, Consciousness, and the Politics of Empowerment.* New York: Routledge, 2008: 174.

41. Patricia Hill Collins. 2008.

42. Karla Holloway. 2011.

43. L. Kalof, Eby, K. K., Matheson, J. L., & Kroska, R. J. (2001). "The Influence of Race and Gender on Student Self-Reports of Sexual Harassment by College Professors. *Gender & Society, 15,* 282–302, 2001: 297–298.

44. See Brené Brown, *Daring Greatly: How the Courage to Be Vulnerable Transforms the Way We Live, Love, Parent, and Lead.* New York: Avery, 2015.

45. Patricia Hill Collins. *Black Sexual Politics: African Americans, Gender, and the New Racism.* New York: Routledge, 2005.

46. NiCole T. Buchanan and Alayne J. Ormerod. "Racialized Sexual Harassment in the Lives of African American Women" in *Women and Therapy* 25(3/4): 105–121, December 31, 2002.

47. Patricia Hill Collins. *Black Feminist Thought: Knowledge, Consciousness, and the Politics of Empowerment.* New York: Routledge, 2008.

48. NiCole T. Buchanan and Alayne J. Ormerod. December 31, 2002: 108–109.

49. NiCole T. Buchanan and Alayne J. Ormerod. December 31, 2002: 109.

50. See Tara E. Kent. "The Confluence of Race and Gender in Women's Sexual Harassment Experiences" in *Gender Violence: Interdisciplinary Perspectives (2nd Ed.).* Edited by Laura O'Toole, Jessica Schiffman, and Margie Kiter Edwards. New York: NYU Press, 2007.

51. NiCole T. Buchanan and Alayne J. Ormerod. December 31, 2002: 109.

52. Yen Le Espiritu. "'We Don't Sleep Around Like White Girls Go': Family, Culture, and Gender in Filipina American Lives." *Signs 26(2)*: 415–440, Winter 2001.

53. Yen Le Espiritu. Winter 2001; Patricia Hill Collins. 2005.

54. Sharon Lamb. *The Secret Lives of Girls: What Good Girls Really Do—Sex Play, Aggression, and Their Guilt.* New York: Free Press, 2002: 71.

55. Sharon Lamb. 2002: 72.

56. Melissa Harris-Perry. *Sister Citizen: Shame, Stereotypes, and Black Women in America.* New Haven, CT: Yale University Press, 2011.

57. Danielle McGuire. *At the Dark End of the Street: Black Women, Rape, and Resistance.* New York: Vintage, 2011: 95.

58. See bell hooks. *Talking Back: Thinking Feminist, Thinking* Black. 2nd Ed. New York: Routledge.

59. Rosemarie Tong. *Feminist Thought.* New York: Routledge, 2017: 165.

60. Sharon Lamb. 2002: 43.

61. Sharon Lamb. 2002: 43.

62. Meda Chesney-Lind and Nikki Jones (Eds.). *Fighting for Girls: New Perspectives on Gender and Violence.* Albany, NY: SUNY, 2010; Barbara Sutton. *Bodies in Crisis: Culture, Violence, and Women's Resistance in Neoliberal Argentina.* Piscataway, NJ: Rutgers University Press, 2010.

63. Sandra Lee Bartky. "Foucault, Femininity, and the Modernization of Patriarchal Power" in *The Politics of Women's Bodies: Sexuality, Appearance, and Behavior* (2nd Ed). Edited by Rose Weitz. Pp. 25–45. New York: Oxford University Press, 2003;

Susan Bordo. "Feminism, Foucault, and the Politics of the Body" in *Feminist Theory and the Body: A Reader.* Edited by Janet Price and Margrit Shildrick. Pp. 246–257. New York: Routledge, 1999.

64. See Jack Halberstam. *Female Masculinity*. Durham, NC: Duke University Press, 2018.

65. Sandra Lee Bartky. "Foucault, Femininity, and the Modernization of Patriarchal Power" in *The Politics of Women's Bodies: Sexuality, Appearance, and Behavior* (2nd Ed). Edited by Rose Weitz. Pp. 25–45. New York: Oxford University Press, 2003; Susan Bordo. "Feminism, Foucault, and the Politics of the Body" in *Feminist Theory and the Body: A Reader.* Edited by Janet Price and Margrit Shildrick. Pp. 246–257. New York: Routledge, 1999.

66. Her strategy also echoes or mimics what Maggie Hadleigh-West documents in her film, *War Zone*.

Chapter 4

Discourses of Danger and Dangerous Discourses

I center the first of two chapters focused on "dangerous ways of speaking" around the matter of street harassment as "discourses of danger" or "dangerous discourses." To explore this topic, I connect the concept of controlling images of people to that of places, linking both back to the web of violence that reflects "geographies of violence." I attempt to illustrate how people construct, rely on, yet seldom challenge "discourses of danger" in an effort to organize and make sense of their own safety and/or vulnerability within the web of violence.

By constructing some geographical spaces as "safe" (the home, for instance), and others as "threatening" (the public sphere, for instance), people perpetuate notions about safety and danger, about vulnerability and violence where they may or may not exist. These constructions ignore the extent to which "for women, the home is a high-risk situation."[1]

Furthermore, these constructions obscure how geographies of violence map onto bodies across time and space, making the web of violence possible and extensive. Seeing spaces (and people) as safe or nonthreatening overlooks the extent to which "the silence of violence" masks its presence or creates the false appearance of safety in the face of violence.

Secondly, I consider "dangerous discourses" to be people's perpetuation of "discourses of danger." Drawing from examples provided by some of my respondents, as well as work on violence against women, I show how easily and extensively we internalize rape culture and patriarchal ideologies, to support sexist notions of safety and danger. That is, I draw from the interviews to show how some women targets of harassment understand their experiences as "the exception rather than the rule," and inadvertently invest in narratives that victims blame other targets of harassment.

These discursive maneuvers construct legitimate victims who are pitted against women who "deserve" to be harassed. Street harassment has been historically normalized through narratives that construct targets as "deserving of" or "asking for" such harassment.[2] I interpret these discursive maneuvers as "dangerous discourses," given the frequency and extent to which women report being harassed.

Generating discourses that set up hierarchies or distinctions between women who deserve to be protected versus those who putatively do not, exposes a double standard regarding respectability. It becomes a danger, in terms of potentially exacerbating women's vulnerability to violence (as an action or behavior, and through discourses that exact harm, or operate as a form of violence).

The web of violence connects to the concept, "geographies of violence," and further encourages exploration of the disparate ways we have collectively attended to or ignored the concerns of violence in this country. I consider the discourses of danger that explain some of those inconsistencies in how groups of people are constructed as violent and/or vulnerable, or dangerous and/or in danger/endangered.

"DISCOURSES OF DANGER" AND "DANGEROUS DISCOURSES"

Street harassment persists as a problem because, as a society, we do not discuss it as such. In this way, society's refusal or inability to recognize street harassment as a social problem reflects a bigger issue, composed of different, but related parts: "discourses of danger" and "dangerous discourses." These terms operate as cousin concepts that contrast with "the silence of violence."

In the next section, I explain and then illustrate each concept, as well as their connection and relation to one another; in addition, I include how they apply to street harassment. To this end, I examine the extent to which violence represents "danger" yet dominant discourses can reframe who is actually or potentially dangerous. That is, at the intersections of power and perception, those with more institutional power can construct victims as "dangerous," while ignoring this characteristic in perpetrators of violent crimes and behavior. Often, powerful people produce discourses that actually endanger the lives of people likely to be targeted by violence, to be victims of violence.

I argue that a number of "dangerous discourses" exist that relate to the people, places, and spaces depicted or misread as "dangerous" that we must minimize contact with, if not avoid altogether. Similarly, "discourses of danger" circulate to warn people about these "dangerous" people, places, and spaces, even if that danger is experienced as an imposition, an association attached from outsiders who falsely view difference as danger.

Discourses of Danger

Ideas about safety and danger constitute what I call "discourses of danger," and, I argue here, operate as "dangerous discourses." Discourses of danger distract attention from statistics like these: "Men are 150 percent more likely to be the victims of violent crimes than women are. Men are more likely to be assaulted, injured, or killed when alcohol is involved. Men are more likely to be victimized by someone they know (62 percent of violent victimizations). Women are more likely to be victimized in their home or in the home of someone they know, whereas men are more likely to be victimized in public.[3]

Discourses of danger intersect with gendered discourses that encourage women to equip themselves with (a non-exhaustive list) of tools to "protect themselves from public stranger assaults"[4]

> [G]o out with a friend, don't drink too much, don't walk home alone, take a self-defense class. Well-meaning as they may be, such suggestions send the false message that women can prevent rape. Certainly, on an individual basis, self-defense and other trainings do help women to protect themselves. But while these trainings are invaluable for the women they assist, they place all of the responsibility on the individual women who use them—in other words, they are not the answer to dismantling rape culture.[5]

Discourses of danger become "dangerous discourses" when women are viewed as neglecting, or "failing" to follow directions about how to protect themselves. Discourses of danger that become dangerous discourses can be disrupted by drawing attention to their limits.

The *danger* of discourses (that operate as directives insisting upon women's self-protection from harm) stems from the potential to doubly victimize women or create a double impact whereby women are first victimized and then held accountable for their victimization. It is a dangerous practice, one with potentially damaging effects on victims (and vicariously, on those in contact with them). Some might argue that these discourses are dangerous because they can feel *more injurious* than the initial actual moments of violence; they can become a secondary kind of violence.

Discourses of danger appear to provide sufficient caution to warn women of potential danger. However, these discourses are dangerous because they do little to address the actual danger that women face in public spaces. That is, they attend more to what women should do when confronted by violence than addressing the actions that support and strengthen the web of violence. These sorts of discourse prove dangerous partially because they protect the perpetrators, and fail to name the perpetrators, or the violence they enact, as the problem. This is how dangerous discourses operate, by and large.

Consider, for example, how girls raised in neighborhoods considered "dangerous" are "socialized into survival."[6] That is, they likely have relatives who help prepare the girls for, and to be able to handle themselves in, violent encounters. Through this socialization, girls learn to be "fighters," where they assertively display that they are "streetwise," or experientially knowledgeable about the "code of the street."[7] Notably, being streetwise proves helpful but cannot entirely prevent encounters with violence; rather, it offers some protection while navigating various spaces.

As this work centers on the various ways women negotiate street harassment, I do not suggest that the failure to employ any strategy successfully should be understood as a failure of the women victims or targets to protect themselves. Instead, I problematize the idea that being "streetwise" ensures that women will not be harassed.[8] Certainly, how people maneuver streets gets informed by their perceptions of safety and danger and hinges on their ability to navigate streetscapes with ease, comfort, and cool. However, no empirical evidence exists to suggest that being streetwise is an always already effective defense against street harassment.

For young girls and women, being streetwise and ready to fight can compromise their respectable femininity. However, not all women and girls are socialized to be streetwise, nor are they prepared to specifically deal with street harassment. So how do young girls and women learn how to respond to verbal harassment in urban public spaces?

Answers to these questions surfaced during my interview conversations with women who had experienced street harassment. Their narratives reminded me of the importance of drawing connections between what happens on the streets, in our neighborhoods, in our families, at our places of employment, in prisons, in schools, and more helps us see the problem of street harassment as directly and indirectly connected to other social problems.

Some research on urban spaces indicates that many young girls and women may "work the code," in attempts to safely inhabit these landscapes.[9] More broadly speaking, girls everywhere, not just neighborhoods deemed "dangerous," are arguably socialized to protect themselves, even as they are taught to see men as their protectors, too. Many of my respondents talked about their concerns regarding the way certain spaces compromised their "physical, emotional, and social safety," (as Olivia put it). So often, too, these spaces are assumed to be public, when dangers to young girls and women can exist and emerge across various sites. Next, I explore how spaces are constructed as safe and dangerous in *discursively* dangerous ways. How might these discourses of *potential* dangers bring into sharp relief (or further bury and veil) the *actual* dangers that threaten women's lives?

The Gap between Potential and Actual Dangers

In examining the embodied experiences of women who navigate street harassment in urban public spaces, I noticed an interesting pattern emerge in the data: many of the respondents offered narratives that suggested they had been socialized to avoid talking to men strangers in public; they also expressed fear of, or were encouraged to avoid "certain" people and places.

Paradoxically, just as some women confronted controlling images of them in their interactions with men harassers, so, too, did some of these women view through the looking glass, stereotypically. In other words, "We are subject to the power of our own mental categories, and to the power of communication to evoke those categories, and avoiding these effects is extraordinarily difficult, if not impossible."[10] To this point, women targets can encounter dangerous discourses that constitute street harassment, while also producing their own, depending on how they describe the people and places in relation to their experiences with street harassment.

Throughout this chapter, I focus on how the women respondents learned to follow or reject the "discourses of danger" in their lives. These discourses of danger narrate where danger and safety exist. Much like controlling images, discourses of danger operate as a form of social control, steering people in the right direction, and ostensibly out of harm's way. The trouble with discourses of danger stems from its mythical qualities, as well as its seductive perpetuation. That is, discourses of danger circulate widely, just as controlling images do, and therefore are easy to internalize, though arguably less easy to recognize.

As a result, people who rely on these discourses of danger begin to produce their own discourses of danger. The combination of existing and new discourses of danger result in the creation of "dangerous discourses." Dangerous discourses are the result of an overreliance on myths about people and places, as I illustrate throughout this chapter. Discourses of danger operate as a double-edged sword, since they can incriminate "innocent" people by constructing narratives about their "dangerous" presence or wrongdoing in society.

Alternately, discourses of danger become "dangerous discourses" in their absence. As I mentioned in chapter 2, the web of violence that exists often gets surrounded by silence. This silence that surrounds violence speaks to the way, for example, that street harassment is seldom talked about or recognized as a social problem or a national public health issue regarding safety. The silence that surrounds violence reflects how little we speak of street harassment as a problem, as something dangerous to its targets. This is a curious, and dangerous, discourse, given how many women report street harassment.[11]

The blurred lines between social interaction and street harassment do little to facilitate public conversations on what, ironically, get misinterpreted as public conversations between strangers. The absence of these discussions and attention to the problem of street harassment is itself a dangerous discourse, as is all of the verbally assaultive and offensive public speech that is street harassment.

To women who experience everyday violence, inquiries that challenge or express doubt about the integrity or accuracy of their accounts become dangerous discourses, as victim-blaming discourses are dangerous. They deflect attention away from street harassment, on small(er) and large(r) scales. Attending to street harassment as a form of everyday violence may seem a peculiar, perhaps even futile endeavor, given its ubiquity.

Street harassment is so commonplace that studies about it may seem mundane.[12] However, it is in the very focus on this everyday violence that people gain a greater understanding of how dangerous discourses emerge within harassment, and around it—through the previously discussed "silence of violence." The silence keeps the violence invisible or illegible, through its discursive erasure of both perpetrators and targets alike.

Clearly, there is a danger in the problem of street harassment itself, but an attendant injury emerges that extends beyond the incivility and aggressive, assaultive behavior and/or offensive speech that targets encounter. Ignoring or minimizing street harassment works to minimize the impact of this form of everyday violence.

Trivializing street harassment facilitates normalizing it, eviscerating a problem that arguably does not exist, because it remains illegible to many. In this way, street harassment could have, at one point, been considered a different "problem that has no name."[13]

This work is important in centering the voices of women who challenge and confront these discourses of danger and dangerous discourses; women who experiences these discourses are not immune from participating in and potentially perpetuating them themselves (a topic I address later in the chapter). Many people do not discuss street harassment because they view it as a part of social interactions and social life. This view skews attention away from harassment as the problem, thereby making silence something that compounds the problem.

Why do we collectively fail to see street harassment as a social problem? Why do we seldom discuss it in public discourse, or recognize it as forms of individual and structural violence? What will draw attention to the problem of street harassment, and the problem of not talking about it as such, as this reflects the silence of violence?

In addition to the silence that surrounds violence is the silence that exists within or emerges from violence. When targets of violence impose or choose silence, they silence their stories and experiences, but also evidence of the problem. This work grapples with the dilemma, or danger, of talking about street harassment, especially for women targets who habitually face this offensive public speech.

When targets of street harassment silence themselves, they risk minimizing the problem. My research aimed to explore, as well as counter, some of these silences, as a way to reveal, not conceal, the everyday violence that is street harassment. During the interview conversations with respondents, and in the consequent analysis of that data, I closely examined the ways in which women contributed to (or disrupted) the silences in regard to street harassment. What were the silences that exist within the space of the interview? Do they replicate any silences women experience during street harassment?

Unveiling the silences also helps to link them together, to make them more visible and legible within the web of violence. In this way, recognition of the problem precedes the solution. This recognition undoes any silences that perpetrators rely on to deny their own complicity in violence, as if to suggest street harassment never occurred if no one ever mentions anything. Within the aforementioned context of a rape culture, such silences speak volumes about the (mis)recognition of the problems of street harassment and violence against women, more generally. Understanding the relationships between these forms of violence provide greater insight into the pervasiveness of rape culture, as I theoretically considered in chapter 2.

Exploring the silence of violence remains important because this silence reflects a "dangerous discourse" in its inability or refusal to articulate an obvious problem: violence against women. The silence of violence is dangerous to victims of violence who feel silenced or keep quiet about their victimization to (ironically) "keep the peace." This silence is also dangerous in supporting people's refusal to recognize and name a problem that affects millions of people. Finally, this silence is dangerous because it is potentially deadly.

As victims of violence suffer in silence, they may experience adverse effects from any initial impact of violence, as well as the assortment of attendant traumas stemming from the silence of violence (not wanting to disclose victimization, feeling silenced during and after that victimization, facing retaliation or intensified violence after disclosure of victimization, and more). The silence of violence slowly suffocates victims of violence, in their search for justice.

Curved Spaces: Where the Public and Private, and Danger and Safety Meet?

Within the web of violence, danger lurks everywhere,[14] with almost everyone implicated. Pervasive, ubiquitous violence in this society exposes the rough

terrain (socially, physically, mentally, and more) of the geographies and car-
tographies of violence and danger.[15] Conceptually, the term, "curved space,"
knits together the public and private. The "curved space" between the public
and private helps to illuminate other "blurred lines."[16] Those lines pertain to
where real and imagined danger exists. Several scholars contest this notion
that the public and private are separate spheres; muddying the distinction
helps draw out the connections within this curved space. It also allows people
to see how street harassment becomes a public expression of violence that
likely gets expressed privately as well.

To link these expressions of violence is to disrupt the idea that women are
safe in private spaces and vulnerable or in danger in public spaces. Exploring
the connections or overlap between the public and private helps solidify the
connections between the various forms of violence and their problematic
expressions through curved space (or various spatial locations).[17]

Within the web of violence, everyone is exposed, vulnerable, and potentially endangered. However, recognizing "discourses of danger" as "dangerous discourses" helps expose the ways that discourses of danger attempt to
discipline women and operate as a form of social control of them. In *Fighting
for Girls*, the authors demonstrate how "discourses of danger" seldom speak
to the increasing violence among or expressed by girls, as they fight for their
own survival.[18] They also urge us to consider discourses that see violence
as the same, rather than differentiating violence as a reactive, self-defensive
strategy, versus an initiated or retaliatory kind of violence.

The discourses of danger that might dissuade women from entering public
space alone, or at night, or in certain neighborhoods operate as a form of
social control. If these discourses of danger fail to dissuade women from
being in public, they often succeed at fueling women's fears.[19] The social
control of women's bodies becomes a currency for young men who lack the
traditional access to economic resources. As Anderson explains in *The Code
of the Street*,

> [M]any young black men form strong attachments to peer groups that emphasize
> sexual prowess as proof of manhood, with babies as evidence. These groups
> congregate on street corners, boasting about their sexual exploits and derid-
> ing conventional family life. They encourage this orientation by rewarding
> members who are able to get over the sexual defenses of women. For many the
> object is to hit and run while maintaining personal freedom and independence
> from conjugal ties; when they exist, the ties should be on the young man's terms.
> Concerned with immediate gratification, some boys want babies to demonstrate
> their ability to control a girl's mind and body.[20]

As the above suggests, some women can easily become part of the sexual game that men play to satisfy their desires and secure street credibility among their peers. This game makes women vulnerable as men's prey in their pursuit of pleasure, and in men's loyalty to their peers.[21] In the sexual game, the "winner" gets the most women, so we could see street harassment through this frame. Talking to girls and women in the frame of this sexual game illustrates Anderson's points, that "[t]he peer group places a high value on sex, especially what middle-class people call casual sex."[22] In Anderson's observation, young men are motivated to do the following:

> [F]ind as many willing females as possible. . . . The lore of the street says there is a contest going on between the boy and the girl even before they meet. To the young man the woman becomes, in the most profound sense, a sexual object. Her body and mind are the object of a sexual game, to be won for his personal aggrandizement. Status goes to the winner, and sex is prized as a testament not of love but of control over another human being. The goal of the sexual conquests is to make a fool of the young woman.[23]

The sentiment embedded in and expressed in Anderson's ethnographic work exposes the paradoxical pursuit of and simultaneous devaluation of young girls and women in this particular urban landscape. The theme of conquest and control link the public and the private, in that curved space mentioned earlier, and reflect the web of violence framing the lives in the youth Anderson studied and described here.

Despite the time that has passed since the inception of his ethnographic study, it seems little has shifted the geographies of violence. In fact, one could argue that the violence described in the devaluation of women during interactions or relationships persists, if not has intensified in the interim. Anderson's discussion of the code of the street reminds us to see how urban spaces are in fact dangerous to men and women, and that this danger gets reflected in the home as well (as evidenced in his discussion of the mistreatment of the young women in relationships with the men players).

The legitimate "discourses of danger" about spaces that prove to perpetuate violence stand in contrast to the less substantiated discourses of danger. An example of the latter includes discourses of danger about public spaces that might actually be safer for women to occupy than the private spaces they call home. Young girls and women experience a significant level of victimization in the home: "Thus, when we speak of *girls' violence* it is important to look through a wide lens, and to include violence enacted against girls, particularly violence within the context of primary caregiver relationships."[24]

Discourses of danger seldom seek to exert the same control over men, their bodies, behavior, and mobility to the degree that they socially control women. (Or do they??) Yet this social control does little to keep women safe. Why? Because violence against women is a global epidemic, not an isolated incident that only occurs occasionally in public. While discourses of danger may dissuade some women from the public, or increase women's fears, these discourses do little to address the *everyday violence* that women face or encounter.

Women who ignore the social conventions or fail to internalize these discourses of danger ostensibly put themselves at risk (socially, morally, and even physically and/or sexually). The discourses of danger that attempt to regulate women's mobility in this fashion align with discourses of danger about particular spaces and places. Discourses of danger then work to shape the perceptions of people, and the spaces and places people are willing (or not) to inhabit.

Discourses of danger casually inform people about the places to avoid, at night, maybe even altogether. Embedded in these discourses of danger about particular places and spaces are the social values attached to them. As bodies populate spaces, they arguably absorb the social values of these spaces. Bodies in space then seem to share social value, in ways that can improve or worsen the social value of both. In fact, when particular groups of people inhabit spaces, those spaces can be contaminated by bodies that do not matter (socially speaking). As other groups enter that space, they may find that they enjoy increased social status for transgressing such boundaries, or that their social status diminishes, as they assume the properties of the space. Thus, women in public becomes "public women."

Women are kept "in their place" through dangerous discourses, and discourses of danger. Dangerous discourses are ones that tend to demonize women for being "out of place," thereby compromising their respectable femininity, and risk embodying 1) controlling images or stereotypes of femininity (a variation of "blaming the victim"), or risk embodying 2) dangerous spaces that do not suit them or have their best interest in mind.

By investigating both the dangerous discourses (including who is viewed as dangerous and/or endangered), I also investigate how some urban *spaces* can be inhabited and informed or shaped by dangerous discourses. That is, a) that these spaces are dangerous, present the threat of danger, or should be (are?) perceived as dangerous; and b) "dangerous discourses" also reflect or involve the kinds of interactions characteristic of street harassment, but that people regard as evidence to support perceptions—whether that be that such interactions put women in danger, illustrate how "dangerous" street harassers really are, or how "dangerous" certain spaces are (where street harassment occurs). I contend that these discourses perpetuate power asymmetries that are raced, classed, and gendered. They also maintain the illusion of domesticity as safer for women than the statistical reality suggests/supports.[25]

While the "silence of violence" conceals violence under a veil of silence (which suggests that the violence does not exist or ever did; in other words, it ignores the web of violence I discussed earlier, discourses of danger and dangerous discourse disrupt the silence of violence, but in potentially harmful ways. This adverse impact registers as "dangerous discourses," in that it perpetuates myths about where violence, danger, and crime exist, and who the true victims and perpetrators of violence are.

Discourses of danger point to a plethora of people or places "known" as dangerous or violent, whether empirical evidence exists to support such claims. In the next section, I will elaborate on the concept of "discourses of danger" to more fully flesh out its implications in regards to street harassment. Instead, discourses of danger typically include (over)generalized advice about people and places to avoid publicly. For example, women who are in urban public spaces are often advised to avoid talking to strangers,[26] or to ensure their safety by never walking alone at night or after dark.

Women may be encouraged to avoid being in public at certain times of the night, or to avoid urban public spaces altogether. These discourses negatively sanction women for being in public. They draw little attention to the conditions or factors that compromise women's safety, or the explanations that contextualize the ways in which women are "in danger."[27] Instead, they create or encourage "disappearing acts" of women such that women stay home or sometimes are forcefully removed from public spaces.[28]

In many ways, telling women to avoid danger by not going out alone and/ or after dark parallels a similarly dangerous discourse that urges women to "not get raped" instead of urging rapists to "not rape." The parallel discourses that develop and exist around rape and street harassment show the troublesome trend of imposing responsibility for violence against women onto the women themselves. This work urges a clearer understanding of the problem of street harassment and a reframing of the way we collectively identify, address, and remedy such social problems.

It invites a closer inspection of the discourses that frame our social lives, and that reinforce myths about where dangers exist. It encourages a re-examination of our own construction of and participation in these discourses of danger. This work wants to challenge and dismantle the rape culture that supports street harassment, as well as these "dangerous discourses."

Discourses of danger rely on problematic imagery or mythologies of gender and race to perpetuate and endorse the culture of fear in our society.[29] Discourses of danger code urban public spaces as "dangerous" because of prevailing mythologies about who inhabits these spaces. (The language around—or used to describe—urban spaces usually accommodates references to "that kind of people" or "those people.")

Various historically contingent racial projects offer partial explanation for the coding of urban spaces ("chocolate cities")[30] to be associated with danger, and suburbia (whiteness) with safety. My earlier discussion of domesticity and publicity should counter some of those problematic associations of safety and danger (being attached to spaces that prove otherwise).

Social etiquette and socialization partially explain people's reluctance to explicitly define spaces as dangerous because of the public presence of "certain" groups. Instead, these discourses of danger become a kind of "race talk" that enables people to refer to spaces, not (just) particular people, as dangerous (or danger as associated with spaces that are stereotypically associated with specific social groups). This explains why discourses of danger tend to take on a generalized quality, such as that encourages individuals to "be careful" of "others" without the need to clarify of what or whom one is being careful.

Race talk enables people to cloak or conceal disparaging thoughts with "smiling racism."[31] They reframe their otherwise offensive language with more palatable and seemingly nicer words. Upon closer inspection, the mask of benevolence reveals the uglier truths of statements sugarcoated for public consumption.

These discourses construct urban public spaces as dangerous, perhaps due to the size, density, diversity, or heterogeneity characteristic of urban areas.[32] Talking about people and spaces as dangerous, in the abstract, obscures attention away from the specific dangers that people face on local and global levels, and which women face partially due to global patriarchy. That is, discourses of danger become dangerous discourses in their ability to deflect attention away from *actually* dangerous people and places that exist.

Anticipating and Perpetuating Discourses of Danger and Dangerous Discourses

In a rape culture, women have generalized fears of violence. These fears are partially informed by rape myths that promote "stranger danger." This relates to street harassment to the extent that women fear men's verbally, physically, and/or sexually assaultive speech and behavior. Some women learn to manage this fear through anticipatory socialization, expecting to be, yet never knowing exactly when they may be, victimized. Facing harassment from strangers complicates the realities of women's lives, as they are seldom free from danger anywhere.

The legitimate fears that women have with regards to prior or anticipated victimization challenges discussions about preparatory socialization. A "dangerous discourse" in itself, narratives that aim to protect women from harm form a dangerous discourse about victims' ability to arm or protect themselves from harm, such as that experienced during street harassment.

That many women regularly experience street harassment offers partial explanation for why people commonly confuse it with consensual casual conversation. A blurred line between "harassing" and "conversing" exists in and across curved space. The slipperiness of this distinction likely means that, for many women, they anticipate street harassment will occur.[33] Preparing to experience street harassment conveys how commonly its targets encounter it. Anticipating its occurrence may make some women feel better equipped to handle whatever might unfold during or following it.

Despite how commonplace women's experiences with street harassment have become, few women in my sample reported being taught to expect it, nor did they feel equipped to handle it. In other words, they were not specifically socialized to navigate street harassment. This may seem curious, the absence of any "anticipatory socialization," given the statistics on street harassment.

While women report a variety of strategies for responding to threats embedded in or expressed as street harassment, few women reported learning any management styles from particular sources, such as parents, respected community leaders, friends or school peers. This type of anticipatory socialization would entail talking to girls and women about the web of violence, while being taught a general set of skills or equipped with the tools to navigate street harassment. Such socialization coexists with education that informs the public about civility in conversation; this approach would more broadly communicate the problems and pitfalls of harassment.

The absence of anticipatory socialization runs the risk of burdening targets of street harassment, but so, too, does its presence. In the latter case, women are expected to learn how to navigate street harassment, when the emphasis should be on teaching those who harass not to do so. To the former point, not knowing to anticipate and/or not knowing how to handle harassment can leave women feeling unprepared to navigate the kinds of street remarks and verbal assaults they may encounter throughout the life course.

What makes anticipatory socialization a "dangerous discourse" rests in the potential misreading of it as holding victims accountable for their own protection. Conversely, the aim of anticipatory socialization involves preparing girls with responses to street harassment, so that they can navigate it (and ideally, avoid any further harm or escalation of violence). This socialization may help them feel better equipped and less alone or alienated when confronting violence in their everyday lives.

While not much has been written about anticipatory socialization, more has been discussed in terms of what I call "anticipatory victimization." The latter refers to the extent to which women fear what they perceive, and are socialized to see as, the likelihood of violence impacting them, and the specific inevitability of rape. Author Jana Leo speaks to this point in her memoir:

> My friend L told me that when she was raped, the thought "here it is" came to her, as if rape is something every woman fears and expects to happen. The probability is that a woman has to assume that if she hasn't already been raped, she very possibly will be in the future. And if she has, she may be raped again. The ghost of rape is attached to being a woman.[34]

For women socialized in this way, the web of violence remains a haunting possibility or presence in their lives, looming over or shadowing them. The process socializes in this society toward what I see as "embodied vulnerability." This contrasts with embodied empowerment and strength. Different discourses (and controlling images) about women's (real or imagined) "strength" complicate this vulnerability in important ways. Given the statistics about and frequency with which women are victims or targets of sexual violence and street harassment, this "anticipatory victimization" in some ways accurately (if not unfortunately) reflects the extent of women's "embodied vulnerability."

The statistical reality of violence against women underscores my point about the web of violence. The geographies of violence map onto everyone's lives in problematic and persistent ways. The ghosts that haunt women reveal the harsh reality of how unregulated violence remains a part of our everyday lives. A part of that haunting and a part of that harm stems not only from the lack of regulation of street harassment (among other forms of violence against women), but also the silence of violence that stings as well.

What connects to women's fear of rape is a whole variety of ways women can experience violence. Global misogyny and patriarchy largely explain patterns of violence against women.[35] Street harassment is simply one manifestation of this devaluation of women; it is a practice that alienates and objectifies women in ways that encourage their disappearance from social life and public spaces.

The disappearance of women, in literal and figurative terms, reflects how "undesirable" they are considered. Women disappear from public life in many ways, and for numerous reasons. Women's efforts to achieve equity and parity in society elicit strong responses, their desire to participate "in political society, the state, and the public sphere" provoke violent reactions.[36]

Evidence of how women are intentionally and systematically disappeared from public spaces and public discourse highlights the role that "discourses of danger" play in the process. "Anticipatory socialization" that prepares women to anticipate (being victims of) violence, in its various forms (gendered, sexualized, racialized, and otherwise) can combine with discourses of danger to serve as part of the socialization process.

Women are often warned about people and places to avoid, in order to stay safe/r or minimize risk. These discourses may do little to actually protect women from the violence visited upon them. So often, these discourses quickly become "dangerous discourses" in the circulation of ideas that suggest people can fully control their safety and/or protect themselves from harm. Discourses of danger include false notions of such illusive safety, and ignore that danger can (and does) emerge in the "safest" of places amongst people deemed "safe."

Disappeared Women

As scholars who study the "disappearing acts" of women argue, street harassment reflects and connects to violence against women. Street harassment exists in the curved space between the public and private, and thus exposes and builds upon the tensions that link together in the web of violence. Perhaps one could argue that street harassment erodes the false distinction between the public and the private precisely because of how commonly violence gets expressed within and across these spaces.

Street harassment also links the public and private through discourses: Just as public elements of discourse enter the private sphere, so, too, does the private enter the public sphere. Arguably, street harassment provides a clear example of this, given the ways that many women are (mis)treated in society. In other words, the ubiquity of violence against women, the normalization of feminicide,[37] the policing and surveillance of women, and the disappearance of women provides evidence that what happens "behind closed doors" does not always stay that way.

Violence enters public space in the form of street harassment, and otherwise, as an extension or reflection of the violence that so often occurs in private. Some women in public have been policed into the private sphere, where they are similarly policed (but in the *presumed* privacy of the home).[38] Recent concerns about technologies of surveillance suggest that publicity and privacy, much like the public and private spheres, have eroded to the point of dissolution. These "blurred lines" suggest troubling questions, then, about the lack of intervention in an age of such surveillance. If people's behaviors are being scrutinized or are under surveillance, why does the "silence of violence" persist? How do women get "disappeared" from the societies in which they live?

The "demonstrated disappearance of women from the city streets and workplaces"[39] can be evidenced in the recent recovery of three women, kidnapped when they were teenagers, and then held captive in Cleveland, Ohio, and, then in the privacy of the stranger/perpetrator's home, tortured sexually, socially, and physically, for ten years. How is it possible that these young girls were "disappeared" in this country? Wright explains:

> By female disappearance, I mean the removal of women and girls from some place where they once were. The efforts to make women disappear can be legal—making female presence illegal in some place—or can operate beyond the law, through such practices as kidnapping and harassment. . . . While these different types of disappearances are not equivalent—to be denied access to public space is not the same as to be kidnapped and murdered—they are knit together through a discourse deployed by the city's political and corporate elites that equates any form of women's vanishing from public space with urban development and industrial progress, as evidence of how the city has progressed from its renowned "traditional" past of prostitution and labor-intensive manufacturing to a more modern place organized around high-tech facilities and middle-class sensibilities.[40]

The normalization of violence against women results in women getting blamed for the harm visited upon them (as opposed to holding to account the perpetrators of these disappearing acts). Through "the valorization of female degradation" and "the discourse of negation," women, in life and death, get discredited; popular and largely uncontested (misogynistic) perceptions of women being always already of questionable character fuels their disappearance.[41] Among multiply marginalized groups of women, the risk of disappearance is heightened, as efforts to eliminate "alleged transgressive sexual behavior" prevail.[42] When patriarchal societies find women "out of place," they take measures to ensure the erasure of women in public.

Research on disappeared women and their erasure crafts broader connections between various forms of violence across time and space. Disappeared women are made invisible symbolically, socially, politically, culturally, and physically. "The invisible is not what is hidden but what is denied, that which we are not allowed to see."[43]

In the United States, this erasure takes many forms. In part, it arguably takes place through harassment.[44] Street harassment often erases women from public spaces if we fear for safety (and avoid being) in the spaces we encounter such harassment. The erasure of women links to an erasure of the problem of street harassment itself: both provoke a problematic kind of "nothing to see here" energy. Consequently, street harassment is often denied as a problem because people are not allowed—or refuse—to see it as such.

People typically view street harassment as the social interaction that takes place in public between strangers. Based on il/logic, if women are harassed, they "deserved" it; consequently, some women prefer not to want to be in public afterward. The denial supports the disappearance, but does little to undo the problem of patriarchy, of street harassment.

Through the denial of this phenomenon of street harassment and its depiction as an individual problem rather than a larger social issue, the government can locate blame on flawed women "asking for it," who somehow provoke such attention and justifiably warrant a reaction, rather than assume responsibility for flaws embedded in the patriarchy. Fregoso explains:

> The patriarchal state's initial preoccupation with women's morality and decency is a form of institutional violence that makes women primarily responsible for the violence directed against them. Thus, those women who do not conform to the mother/wife model of womanhood (lesbians, working women, women who express sexual desire, and so forth) are suitably punished. In effect women are transformed into subjects of surveillance; their decency and morality become the object of social control. What's more, shifting the blame towards the victims' moral character in effect naturalizes violence against women.[45]

Fregoso describes the negation of violence against women as an "obscene, interpretive strategy."[46] The consequent disaggregation, or breaking apart, of the problem of violence moves beyond denial. Instead, it presents the problem as an individual or personal one, as opposed to a social and national one. Scholars' attention to the economic, social, and political factors in globalization guide people toward an understanding of the exploitation, eradication, and/or extermination of women's bodies, locally and globally.

The disappearance of women again should not be understood in only literal, but rather figurative, terms. The state should seriously consider the aggregate consequences of such treatment of women by men, but instead negation and disaggregation of violence result: "Feminicide . . . makes evident the reality of overlapping power relations on gendered and racialized bodies as much as it clarifies the degree to which violence against women has been naturalized as a method of social control."[47] One might argue that the United States relies on the aforementioned strategies (of negation and disaggregation) in its response to street harassment. Handling street harassment in this way (read: not at all) makes it, too, disappear.

Through the denial of this phenomenon and depiction of it as an individual problem rather than a larger social issue, the government can locate blame on flawed women "asking for it," who somehow provoke such attention and justifiably warrant a reaction, rather than assume responsibility for flaws embedded in the patriarchy.

As Fregoso posits, "It (the Mexican government) has justified its failure through a rhetorical strategy of deflection that has taken two narrative forms: negation and disaggregation."[48] We can steadily draw parallels between the state-sanctioned violence in Mexican cities like Juarez and numerous American cities.

Where women face a variation of this violence, in the form of assaultive, offensive speech on the street, they are often seen as nonnormative or transgressive in some way. Any presumptions of women's immorality and promiscuity enables the social regulation of women, rather than the perpetrators of violence. These views and judgments of women can get cast as legitimating the violence visited upon them.

Women who habitually endure street harassment engage in what I find to be akin to the "politics of gender extermination."[49] This occurs in cases where the social encounters intensify, escalate, insult, or repeatedly and consistently berate, degrade, or otherwise wear women down with words. And while women might choose to use their words as weapons, they may also tire of the seemingly exhaustive verbal assault from strangers on the street.

While this may not directly lead to a literal extermination of women, the cumulative effects of habitual harassment must carry some costs to its women targets. Surely the perpetual yet inevitable conversational vandalism and verbal entanglements[50] from men who harass negatively impact women in some ways. And what are the costs to societies where women's lives are at stake, if not socially, then physically?

"And while silence, as a strategy of resistance *for women*, needs to be historicized, especially in this scenario of forced 'confessions,' it has generally been a sign of women's public and political invisibility." Research draws attention to the double-edged sword of simultaneously silencing women and "while ostensibly giving her a voice."[51] Much of this work draws attention to global efforts to erase, disappear, and silence women.

Throughout history, the harassment of marginalized groups extended far beyond street remarks and include murder, lynchings, and shootings. Specifically, these acts symbolically and socially controlled blacks, denying them their human rights for freedom,[52] or "freedom with violence."[53] In particular, black women face various forms of violence, including public harassment (in the form of pejorative and offensive name-calling) and sexual assaults.[54]

Black women who faced sexual violence felt particularly compelled to stay close to home. They did so as one way to manage or minimize the sexual violence that racist white people committed against them. "The sexual violence enacted and enforced rules of racial and economic hierarchy,"[55] such that everyone learned their "place" in the social order at the time. This hierarchy has changed little since the 1940s. Instead, the hierarchy has arguably crystallized the persistent position of white men as powerful actors. Keeping black people fearful of their lives kept them largely out of the public, a different kind of disappearance related to that previously discussed.[56]

One could understand social hierarchies as a form of structural violence, complicated or enhanced by agitating action that calls into question these structures. In the fight for freedom, "respect, and bodily integrity,"[57] black women, who practiced "walking in pride and dignity,"[58] they "demanded that they be treated like human beings worthy of protection and respect"; challenging social hierarchies has meant that women have faced violence.

CONCLUSION

Feminist scholarship demonstrates much of the failures of patriarchy. The literature speaks to how some men not only fail to protect women from violence, but are often the very sources of such violence. Scholars also show how the fight for freedom, the fight for civil rights, makes women's rights human rights issues.[59] In recognizing their shared suffering of "humiliation and mistreatment,"[60] black women have collectively banded together in the struggle for their basic human rights and respect in historical and contemporary society.

Women who face sexualized and racialized violence offer important lessons. They speak to the empowering acts of talking back and fighting for freedom. These acts of resistance have often met with retaliation, across time and space. In many ways, women who attempt to defend themselves face not only the dangers of violence, as well as any amplified, retaliatory violence that follows.

In discussing street harassment, then, one can also look to other forms of violence that prove dangerous to women. Various attempts at some sort of annihilation of women exist. Feminicide, the disappearance of women, and other acts reflect misogyny and speak to how the hatred of women links to these various forms of violence.

In the next chapter, I explore the ways that women who are harassed respond to street harassment. I consider how these responses demonstrate the tensions between speech and silence; how the women produce a variety of discourses, even participating in the production of dangerous discourses themselves on occasion.

NOTES

1. Jana Leo. *Rape New York.* New York: The Feminist Press of CUNY, 2010: 87–88; 90.

2. See Danielle McGuire. *At the Dark End of the Street: Black Women, Rape, and Resistance.* New York: Vintage, 2011.

3. Jill Filipovic. "Offensive Feminism: The Conservative Gender Norms That Perpetuate Rape Culture, and How Feminists Can Fight Back." In *Yes Means Yes!: Visions of Female Sexual Power and a World Without Rape.* Edited by Jaclyn Friedman, 2008: 23.

4. Jill Filipovic. 2008: 23.

5. Jill Filipovic. 2008: 23.

6. Nikki Jones. "'It's About Being a Survivor . . .': African American Girls, Gender, and the Context of Inner-City Violence" in *Fighting for Girls: New Perspectives on Gender and Violence.* Edited by Meda Chesney-Lind and Nikki Jones. Pp. 203–218. Albany, NY: SUNY, 2010: 17.

7. Elijah Anderson. *Code of the Street: Decency, Violence, and the Moral Life of the Inner City.* New York: W.W. Norton, 1999

8. See Elijah Anderson. *Streetwise: Race, Class, and Change in an Urban Community.* Chicago: University of Chicago Press, 1992.

9. Elijah Anderson. 1992; Nikki Jones. 2010.

10. Nicholas Winter. *Dangerous Frames: How Ideas about Race and Gender Shape Public Opinion.* Chicago: University of Chicago Press, 2008.

11. Holly Kearl. *50 Stories of Stopping Street Harassers.* New York: Praeger, 2013; Holly Kearl. *Stop Street Harassment: Making Public Places Safe and Welcoming for Women.* New York: Praeger, 2010a; Holly Kearl. "Street Harassment: A Real Problem that Requires Legal Regulation," *Huffington Post,* March 12, 2010b; Maria Ochoa and Barbara K. Ige. *Shout Out: Women of Color Respond to Violence.* New York: Seal Press, 2008.

12. Melody Berger. *We Don't Need Another Wave: Dispatches from the Next Generation of Feminists.* New York: Seal Press, 2006.

13. A nod here to Betty Friedan and her book, *The Feminine Mystique.* New York: Penguin Books, 2010.

14. Aaronette White. *Ain't I a Feminist?: African American Men Speak Out on Fatherhood, Friendship, Forgiveness, and Freedom.* Albany, NY: SUNY 2008.

15. Nikki Jones. "'It's About Being a Survivor . . .': African American Girls, Gender, and the Context of Inner-City Violence" in *Fighting for Girls: New Perspectives on Gender and Violence.* Edited by Meda Chesney-Lind and Nikki Jones. Pp. 203–218. Albany, NY: SUNY, 2010.

16. This is a nod to the song of the same title, that proved both provocative and a source of musical plagiarism for singer, Robin Thicke.

17. See Susan Gal. "A Semiotics of the Public/Private Distinction." *Differences: A Journal of Feminist Cultural Studies.* 13:1, 2002.

18. Meda Chesney-Lind and Nikki Jones (Eds.). *Fighting for Girls: New Perspectives on Gender and Violence.* Albany, NY: SUNY, 2010.

19. Jill Filipovic. "Offensive Feminism: The Conservative Gender Norms That Perpetuate Rape Culture, and How Feminists Can Fight Back." In *Yes Means Yes!: Visions of Female Sexual Power and a World Without Rape.* Edited by Jaclyn Friedman, 2008.

20. Elijah Anderson. *Code of the Street: Decency, Violence, and the Moral Life of the Inner City.* New York: W.W. Norton, 1999.

21. Elijah Anderson. 1999: 150.

22. Elijah Anderson. 1999: 150.

23. Elijah Anderson. 1999: 150.

24. Judith Ryder. "'I Don't Know If You Consider That as Violence . . .': Using Attachment Theory to Understand Girls' Perspectives on Violence" in *Fighting for Girls: New Perspectives on Gender and Violence.* Edited by Meda Chesney-Lind and Nikki Jones. Pp. 129–148. Albany, NY: SUNY, 2010: 143.

25. See Emilie Buchwald, Pamela R. Fletcher, and Martha Roth (Eds.). *Transforming a Rape Culture.* Minneapolis, MN: Milkweed Editions, 2005.

26. In her documentary, *War Zone*, Maggie Hadleigh-West observes that what people really mean by this saying should be edited to the following: "Don't talk to *men* strangers."

27. See Diana Taylor. *Disappearing Acts: Spectacles of Gender and Nationalism in Argentina's "Dirty War."* Durham, NC: Duke University Press, 1997.

28. Diana Taylor. 1997; Melissa Wright. 2005.

29. Barry Glassner. *The Culture of Fear: Why Americans Are Afraid of the Wrong Things.* New York: Basic Books, 2009.

30. A nod to Marcus Hunter and Zandria Robinson, the authors of *Chocolate Cities: The Black Map of American Life.* Oakland, CA: University of California Press, 2018.

31. Kristen Myers. Racetalk: Racism Hiding in Plain Sight. New York: Rowman & Littlefield Publishers, 2005. Eduardo Bonilla Silva. *Racism without Racists: Color-Blind Racism and the Persistence of Racial Inequality in America.* Lanham, MD: Rowman & Littlefield, 2017.

32. Louis Wirth. *On Cities and Social Life.* Chicago: University of Chicago Press, 1956.

33. The frequency and intensity of the harassment that women experience also explain their view of what constitutes a threat. This threat is not contestable or imaginary.

34. Jana Leo. *Rape New York.* New York: The Feminist Press of CUNY, 2010: 91.

35. Julie Zeilinger. *A Little F'ed Up: Why Feminism Is Not a Dirty Word.* New York: Seal Press, 2012.

36. Chandran Reddy. *Freedom with Violence: Race, Sexuality, and the US State.* Durham, NC: Duke University Press, 2011.

37. Diana Taylor. *Disappearing Acts: Spectacles of Gender and Nationalism in Argentina's "Dirty War."* Durham, NC: Duke University Press, 1997.

38. Melissa Wright. "The Private Parts of Public Value: The Regulation of Women Workers in China's Export-Processing Zones" in *Going Public: Feminism and the Shifting Boundaries of the Private Sphere.* Edited by Joan W. Scott and Debra Keates. Pp. 99–120. Urbana Champaign: University of Illinois Press, 2005.

39. Melissa Wright. 2005: 370.

40. Melissa Wright. 2005: 370.

41. Melissa Wright. 2005: 370.

42. Melissa Wright. 2005: 370.

43. Ana Maria Fernandez. "Violencia y Conyugalidad," La Mujer y la Violencia Invisible. Eds. Eva Giberti and Ana Maria Fernandez. Buenos Aires: Editorial Sudamericana, 1989.

44. Melissa Wright. 2005.

45. Rosa-Linda Fregoso. "Toward a Planetary Civil Society" in *Mexicana Encounters: The Making of Social Identities on the Borderlands*. Edited by Rosa-Linda Fregoso. Pp. 1–29. Berkeley, CA: University of California Press, 2003a: 5.

46. Rosa-Linda Fregoso. 2003a: 5.

47. Rosa-Linda Fregoso. 2003a: 2.

48. Rosa-Linda Fregoso. 2003a: 3.

49. Rosa-Linda Fregoso. 2003a.

50. Mitch Duneier. *Sidewalk.* New York: Farrar, Straus and Giroux, 1999; Mitch Duneier and Harvey Molotch. 1999.

51. Diana Taylor. *Disappearing Acts: Spectacles of Gender and Nationalism in Argentina's "Dirty War."* Durham, NC: Duke University Press, 1997: 7.

52. Danielle McGuire. *At the Dark End of the Street: Black Women, Rape, and Resistance.* New York: Vintage, 2011.

53. Chandran Reddy. *Freedom with Violence: Race, Sexuality, and the US State.* Durham, NC: Duke University Press, 2011.

54. McGuire (2011:58) notes: "For example, Bus drivers . . . disrespected black women by hurling nasty sexualized insults their way. . . . Aside from direct sexual harassment, drivers referred to black women with contemptuous names like 'black ni**ers,' 'black bitches,' 'heifers,' and 'whores.'"

55. Danielle McGuire. 2011: 29.

56. Melissa Wright. 2005.

57. Danielle McGuire. 2011: 43.

58. Danielle McGuire. 2011: 95.

59. See Danielle McGuire. 2011; Melissa Wright. 2005.

60. Danielle McGuire. 2011: 75.

Chapter 5

Between Speech and Silence, or "Dangerous Ways of (Not) Speaking"

BETWEEN VOICE AND SILENCE

Much of the literature on the discursive disappearing acts of girls revolves around their self-selected silence. That is, over time and especially during adolescence, young girls develop a reticence that may persist for years. The scholarship centered around recuperating women's voices draws attention to the ways that young girls learn to question themselves and the importance of their voices; they wonder if anyone is listening to them, and if they are being heard in ways that prove meaningful and important to them.

Given the evidence that exists to suggest that society does not encourage girls to speak up, it is little wonder that women who experience street harassment might feel conflicted and caught between speech or "voice and silence." Little consistent support exists to encourage and accommodate what young girls and women have to say, especially "to speak what otherwise remains unspoken."[1]

While gender socialization persists from birth to death, arguably little attention is directed at preparing young girls and women to handle street harassment (or other types of violence for that matter). Instead, women are encouraged to ignore the problem or the men who create the problem. This "silence of violence" is a dangerous discourse, or a "dangerous way of not speaking" about a commonplace problem that people seldom discuss.

Women's silence, then, intersects with the silence that surrounds violence. As women confront the realities of dangerous discourses during street harassment, they must weigh the promises and pitfalls of speech. This chapter considers these, and the strategies that women employ to navigate street harassment.

In focus groups on girlhood, many girls note the invaluable lessons that could be a part of their gender socialization. They expressed an interest in sharing their experiential knowledge with young girls when they begin "traversing a difficult passage"; some of this knowledge including relating experiences and protecting others from intersectional injustices, including the following:

> . . . injuries of racism and sexism—both the overt acts of discrimination and violence as well as the more subtle dismissals and silencing they might encounter. [They want] . . . to intercept and interrupt the harmful and misleading messages girls risk internalizing including cultural messages that define acceptable standards of beauty and behavior.[2]

Imagine, then, the impact of preparing young women to anticipate and negotiate street harassment. Contrast this with the typical gender socialization that girls and women endure, conversations which eclipse the reality, much less the possibility, that they will likely face street harassment (and other forms of violence against women).

Through gender socialization, girls and women learn about power differences, that their words and voices (and silence) carry different weight (in comparison to other girls' and women's voices, and that of boys and men).[3] They also learn that there is a higher price or penalty to pay for voicing our thoughts, especially when our ideas disrupt gendered norms or do not align with gender expectations. This penalty often applies to all forms of speech acts enacted or expressed by young girls and women, with varying penalties incurred for the uncomfortable truths they tell.

> If girls feel that "no one ever listens," perhaps it is because they are saying what no one wants to hear. Girls' questions raise the possibility of a future that can be different from the past; they urge women—as has Audre Lorde—to "examine their position," to hold up to scrutiny their strategies for survival, their practice of teaching, their daily decisions to speak or remain silent. Girls' questions require women to face pain, to expand their capacity for joy and hope and pleasure. They call upon women to allow themselves to become vulnerable and to risk relationships with girls and with each other across differences and across separations.[4]

Often, girls and women are seen as vulnerable, but are not encouraged to allow themselves to be vulnerable. Being supported in this vulnerability and humanity enables young girls and women to take risks and challenge themselves, to see strength in being vulnerable. As women learn these lessons, they strengthen their ability to express themselves.

The blurred lines that emerge here regarding street harassment stem from the reality that some young girls and women may feel that men harassers are listening to them, engaging them in what might look or feel like other social interactions, instead of street harassment. As a "dangerous way of speaking," it would be dishonest not to acknowledge that some young girls and women might find street harassment a form of attention that affirms that someone is listening to or looking at them. This is a difficult admission, given the ways I argue that street harassment is a form of violence. Perhaps it is that diminishing and devaluing the voices of young girls and women is another form of everyday violence.

As the authors note, and other researchers corroborate, vulnerability is a double-edged sword. For young girls and women who feel invisible and ignored, vulnerability proves possibly risky. Conversely, vulnerability can be a source of power, and should be considered "a relational strength, creating openings for building trust and power in relationship."[5]

This is an interesting point to consider, given that women are frequently associated with or constructed as vulnerable, with men constructed as invulnerable. Rethinking the ways that men harassers may feel a vulnerability that they transfer to or impose on their women targets of harassment opens up new ways of thinking about the power asymmetries that play out in urban public spaces. Perhaps it is that men harass women because the men are in search of respect and recognition, and otherwise feel a certain vulnerability.

Because hegemonic masculinity does not accommodate vulnerability, when misinterpreted as a weakness, men harassers assert their vulnerability in dominant ways. This perpetuates a disconnection, and forecloses the connections that might otherwise be possible among (men and women) strangers in urban public spaces. Because it is human to be vulnerable, but people associate vulnerability with weakness, these moments of potential connections quickly turn into moments where people protect themselves from these human feelings.

Brené Brown echoes this point.[6] She speaks of vulnerability as strength, shifting the connotation away from weakness. If young girls and women learn to equate vulnerability with weakness, not strength, they may similarly see silence as weakness, and speech as strength. They may witness the ways other girls and women respond to or handle being human by being vulnerable,[7] and incorrectly interpret this vulnerability as docility.

Young girls and women can develop self-policing strategies regarding their own speech practices; this facilitates the discursive disciplinary mechanisms of social control. That is, they can see how they silence themselves, or allow others to silence their voices.[8] If young girls internalize the price of speech as a social penalty or liability, why would they use their voices in situations that are much less supportive and much more uncertain and hostile? If the experiences that girls have teach them about "disconnections and violations"[9] in relationships, why would girls *not* normalize this expectation in all of their interactions?

In this way, street harassment takes on the typical quality of "disconnection and violation" and begins to illuminate why women sometimes normalize these interactions. To some degree, this suggests that women are used to discursive aggressive and dismissive interactional styles and settings. Other scholars articulate the dilemma this way:

> In the context of failed or absent or abusive relationships, girls may find that they "don't know who to trust," may be made to feel "like [they are] nothing" or "nobody," may learn that "you really can't trust anybody" and that "people take advantage of you if you care about them too much." They may also be at risk for muting their own voice and their sense of self if they learn too well that it is better to stay "nice and calm" or that it is "always good to be helpful," no matter what they are feeling. If it is girls' experience that "no one ever listens," that "nobody cares" about what they say or do, that they are "never talking to one person," the potential for healthy social, emotional, and intellectual development is severely compromised. What develops instead is an enveloping sense of isolation and powerlessness, a loss of faith that others will come through for them.[10]

As young girls and women continue to crave connection, relationship, and attention, and learn to distrust others, they may misinterpret men's harassment as a form of interaction that fills the void. As discussed above, young girls and women may embrace the ideologies that encourage them to avoid "dangerous ways of speaking." This is a "dangerous discourse," in that it positions young girls and women in ways that promote our voicelessness, or that discipline the way we speak, when we speak. Young girls learn difficult lessons about speaking truth to power, and sharing their realities with others. The gender requisite pleasantness of their speech can silence girls who have messier, uglier, and grittier things to say.

As mentioned earlier, girls learn that silence *can* protect them from other's criticism and censure, even if a palpable pain eventually accompanies or follows that self-silencing. When girls insist on speaking, and then adults silence them (or the girls silence themselves into adulthood), that silencing potentially reverberates in a variety of settings, including urban public spaces and other sites of (street) harassment.

How do girls and women learn to "speak for themselves"? How do they come to intimately know and confidently articulate the challenges of living in or moving through "dangerous" spaces (their own neighborhoods or otherwise)? How do we teach girls and women to challenge the silence of violence, by claiming their voices and exposing the ugly truths about their realities in confronting gendered and racialized violence? What happens when women and girls learn to lift the veil off of violence? What would happen if girls learned to "speak out against injustice"[11] as a form of empowerment, resistance, and social change?

On Voice and Vulnerability during Street Harassment

Many of the women in the sample I drew did not struggle to find their voice when deciding how to respond to street harassment. Instead, they struggled to negotiate the requirements of femininity, the docility and duty expected of them, even—if not especially—with strangers. The layers of silence ensnare the layers of violence, until both conceal one another's ugly truths.

If no one speaks about street harassment, it must not be a problem; this may motivate victims of this everyday violence to minimize or question their own experiences. The perpetrator may feel vindicated or encouraged to continue harassing, because, after all, "what's the big deal?" And if victims do not make a big deal about street harassment or other forms of violence, why would anyone else? Who will intervene on behalf of the victims to validate their experiences with street harassment, or sexual assault, or rape? And why do we expect victims to speak for themselves, when they are trying to survive violence? Perhaps even stunned into silence by the violence they never or always expected to experience.

Speaking up and out can sometimes create the contradictory oppression and liberation attached to discourse. Women targets of street harassment consider a variety of options, in devising strategies responses to men who harass. What impact will our words produce, if spoken at the wrong time, in the wrong place, to the wrong person? How do we assess these dynamics as we traverse public space? What are the right words, at the right time, in the right place, to the right person (the harasser)? Is there such a thing?

I explore this double-edged sword in street harassment, and in thinking about silence and speech among women targets of street harassment. When it comes to various forms of violence, numerous tensions exist between speech and silence. Not all of these tensions are productive ones. Instead, many of the tensions result from the targets of violence feeling silenced or speechless by the violence, and from the contradictory consequences to employing either speech or silence as a questionably effective response to violence. These tensions also exist because of the uneven attention given to violence, especially in its everyday variety.

With street harassment (and other forms of harassment), there is often little discussion of its occurrence, as if talking about the problem is the problem, rather than the problem itself. By extension, targets or victims of a problem are commonly seen as causing the problem, whether when talking about it or experiencing it. This scapegoats or blames the victim, while allowing the perpetrator's behavior and the problem of violence to persist.

The silence of violence exists in ways that create various impacts. For example, the silence that surrounds street harassment makes it a social phenomenon or problem that seems irrelevant, if not unusual or atypical. However, in talking to women about their experiences in urban public spaces (and reading as much as possible about various forms of harassment), I discovered how ubiquitous such harassment remains. That is, a "dangerous way of (not) speaking" about street harassment is precisely that—not speaking about it, or speaking about it as a "women's issue" versus a matter of "street justice."[12]

The silence that surrounds violence works to protect perpetrators of such violence, by suggesting that their harassing or violent behavior is normal. Clearly, there is a danger in ignoring or minimizing everyday forms of violence; there is also a lot of potential danger in the harassment and violence itself. It is one thing to encounter harassment and be impacted by incivility and aggressive, assaultive speech and behavior. It is quite another to have that problem be trivialized, such that it is normalized to the point where it "arguably" does not exist. Many people do not discuss street harassment because they view it as a part of social interactions and social life. This view skews attention away from harassment as the problem, thereby making silence something that compounds the problem.

As evidenced elsewhere,[13] one can see the way people learn how to silence themselves as targets and perpetrators of harassment (as if the harassment never occurred). It is important to understand the ubiquity of the silence that surrounds all forms of violence, and links these occurrences together. Understanding the relationships between these forms of violence provide greater insight into the web of violence I discussed earlier, and speaks to the pervasiveness of rape culture.

In this section, I closely examine the ways women talk about their experiences with street harassment (or do not talk about them—what are the silences that exist in the space of the interview?).[14] I discuss how they deal with and respond to harassment from men strangers in urban public spaces, including relying on speech and silence. I complicate the categories of speech and silence, to consider how both and/or neither can be empowering expressions of agency or disempowering, depending on the situation of street harassment for the women involved.

The Problem that Hides in Plain Sight

Street harassment reflects and becomes another form of violence in a rape culture. It hides in plain sight, and, even under close inspection, often fails to warrant meaningful consideration. While scholars and activists are increasingly attending to street harassment as a serious problem, discussions of street harassment often register a dismissive tone. Disregard of the damaging impact of street harassment minimizes the experiences. It overlooks how traumatic, assaultive dimensions of this dynamic can be.

Why do we collectively fail to see street harassment as a social problem? Why do we seldom discuss it as a public discourse, or recognize street harassment as a form of structural violence? Is not talking about it another form of (or a reflection of) the silence of violence?

In chapter 3, I discussed the ways in which controlling images exist to shape people's perceptions of and interactions with one another. Considering the ways that controlling images impact social interactions involves the "dangerous ways of seeing" ourselves and one another. If we only see people as stereotypes or through a slanted room,[15] then our perceptions rely on and reflect those distortions. I build on the previous discussion by looking next at how people talk about street harassment in relation to danger.

In order to accomplish this goal, I organize the chapter around two central themes: speech and silence. Both speech and silence remain in productive tension with one another. In this chapter I explore the discursive practices that *surround* street harassment, while in the following chapter, I explore ones produced *during* street harassment (and that respondents reflect on after the experience).

The tensions that exist between speech and silence get echoed in discourses about and during street harassment. In this chapter, I will explore how patterns of speech and silence show up in street harassment. I consider the "dangerous ways of (not) speaking" about and during street harassment, to draw attention to the ways women targets of harassment employ discursive speech practices (or not) to navigate urban public spaces. This chapter also draws on the previous chapter, to link the ways women are socialized to their (non) responses to street harassment.

Thinking about the strength of socialization, as well as gender norm expectations, the construction of safety and danger, and spatial locations, helps contextualize women's behavior to street harassment. Understanding the ways such socialization and expectations construct "discourses of danger" specific to women, I consider how women who respond (or not) to harassment produce their own kinds of "dangerous discourses" that might compromise their safety, heighten their vulnerability, or call their femininity into question. First, I consider how speech practices about street harassment.

On Speech

Women may find street harassment subtle, almost a benevolent sexism that sneaks up on them, serving as a gentle reminder that they should occupy the domestic sphere contentedly, and cease infringing on the territory of men. Such benevolent sexism becomes blatant and malicious when men intend to terrorize, antagonize, and verbally brutalize, scrutinize, or scorn women, rather than respectfully regard women, compliment them, or otherwise engage without intended aggravation.

This difference between benevolent and blatant sexism illustrates one possible interpretive scheme for understanding street harassment of women. The multifaceted quality of street harassment necessitates a complex theoretical framework, including an incorporation of Foucaldian theories of docility, discipline, punishment, and discursive practices. Understanding the intersections of docility, gender, and race provides insight into the ways bodies in society are docile, disciplined, controlled, and punished.

Adding gender and race to the analysis extends or complicates Foucault's "docile body" theory by recognizing the differential experiences of docility for diverse groups of people (i.e., white women, black women, white men, etc.). This intersectional approach also recognizes how different discourses produce discourses around different bodies.

The discourses these bodies produce vary in response to these specific social locations. The discursive practices that people produce reflect both hegemonic ideological perpetuations of traditional gendered and racialized, heteronormative scripts, and expectations, and disruptive strategies that resist these scripts.

Examinations of variations such as docility, and discursive practices enable a richer understanding of women's racialized and gendered experiences with street harassment. That a black woman responds to a man harasser's attention reproduces discourses about assertive, emasculating, black femininity (but interpretations of her behavior partially hinge on the race of the harasser).

A black woman who chooses silence may do so not as a disservice to herself, but as a powerful strategy of resistance, resistance to this racialized and gendered expectation that anticipates (and overdetermines) black women's incitement to speak more often than not; conversely, silence can be read as reproducing hegemonic discourses about women as quiet, "better to be seen and not heard."

While speaking up can be read through a traditional gendered lens as being polite and respectably feminine, an against the grain reading of black women's discursive resistance requires some attention to the possibility that these women do recognize these racialized and gendered discourses but find asserting themselves verbally restores and/or affirms their subjectivity.

The risk of reproducing such race and gender stereotypes may pale in comparison to the power accessed through this restoration of subjectivity, to remind male harassers of this subjectivity is to both resist myths of female weakness, subordination, or vulnerability. It also produces new ways of negotiating power publicly, in the case of street harassment. To speak sometimes is to access power often off-limits to women who were punished for speaking. Speech can serve as an act of transforming oneself from an object to a subject of one's own life.

On Silence

There is a peculiar silence that surrounds the everyday injustices and sexualized injuries that women, as targets of street harassment, face. These "mundane" violations hardly register in our collective understandings of violence, yet these occurrences reflect men harassers' attempts to invade women's spaces and control women's lives. Intrusions and invasions on women get normalized in a society that devalues women.

This society accommodates some men's intrusions and everyday violence and violations with a normative silence. To talk about the mendacity of street harassment and its potentially disruptive impact on women targets' lives is to speak of subjects off-limits. Street harassment is one such subject, and the discourses produced to challenge this phenomenon are even more unspeakable. Examples I provide later in the chapter illustrate this point.

Discourses are "principally organized around practices of exclusion. Whilst what it is possible to say seems self-evident and naturalness is the result of what has been excluded, that which is almost unsayable."[16] Sara Mills might argue that street harassment is a set of discourses intended to exclude women from public social life. This is certainly the case scholars who study the "disappearance of women" argue in their work.[17] Because "discourses structure both our sense of reality and our notion of our own identity,"[18] we must contend with them in one way or another.

Discourses about street harassment get entangled with discourses of femininity to further the exclusion of women from public view. As discourses contain disciplinary power, they shape our daily practices. Discourses shape people's thoughts, beliefs, and actions. Additionally, people develop an understanding of the gender expectations society holds for them. "These discursive frameworks demarcate the boundaries within which we can negotiate what it means to be gendered."[19]

Because discourses contain disciplinary power, power that produces knowledge, they can become dangerous. If dominant discourses exist to deny street harassment as a problem, or reject women's critique of men's harassing behavior, this proves dangerous for aforementioned reasons. Producing

counter-hegemonic discourses that tell different truths about street harassment prove just as dangerous.

Exposing the everyday reality of street harassment counters the protective
veil of both private and public patriarchy, in that women—as victims of all
kinds of patriarchal abuses—are expected to be quiet—as "good" female subjects and docile bodies/objects of desire in a patriarchy. Discourses of femininity outline expectations for women to stay silent on the subject of street
harassment (or really, any other abuse visited upon them, including all forms
of patriarchal oppression) as a way of "keeping secrets." Keeping secrets
protects men perpetrators of street harassment, or other forms of aggression
and violence against women.[20]

In this case, women's silence protects men perpetrators of street harassment by not exposing the ugly truths about how intrusive, upsetting, and
disruptive such encounters can be. Women's silence effectively enables men
who street harass to continue what they do. The silence that surrounds street
harassment creates the illusion that street harassment happens all the time, to
anyone, anywhere, or conversely that it does not happen at all. In a sense, the
silence normalizes street harassment.

In her powerful collection of essays and speeches, black lesbian poet,
Audre Lorde writes about the "transformation of silence into language and
action." She grappled with her own mortality, having confronted the reality
of breast cancer and the specter of death. She observed,

> In becoming forcibly and essentially aware of my mortality, and of what I
> wished and wanted for my life, however short it might be, priorities and emis-
> sions became strongly etched in a merciless light, and what I more regretted
> were my silences. Of what had I ever been afraid? To question or to speak as I
> believed could have meant pain, or death. But we all hurt in so many different
> ways, all the time, and pain will either change or end. Death, on the other hand,
> is the final silence. . . . And that might be coming quickly, now, without regard
> for whether I had ever spoken what needed to be said, or had only betrayed
> myself into small silences, while I planned someday to speak, or waited for
> someone else's words. And I began to recognize a source of power within
> myself that comes from the knowledge that while it is most desirable not to be
> afraid, learning to put fear into a perspective gave me great strength . . . I was
> going to die, if not sooner, then later, whether or not I had ever spoken myself.
> My silences had not protected me. Your silence will not protect you.[21]

In this chapter, I reflect on these thoughts, meditating on the contradictions
that emerge for women as they consider speech and/or silence as strategic
responses to men during street harassment.

I rely on the respondents' narratives to grapple with this set of questions
Lorde posed in her work: "What are the words you do not yet have? What do

you need to say? What are the tyrannies you swallow day by day and attempt to make your own, until you will sicken and die of them, still in silence?"[22] I draw inspiration from her inquiries to explore the significance of speech and silence in women's responses to street harassment from men. . . . "For there are so many silences to be broken."[23]

When women remain silent about their experiences of street harassment, they not only fail to protect themselves, they ostensibly fail to protect others from similar behavior. They deny and invalidate their own experiences and truths while inadvertently protecting the man or men who perpetrate the harassment directed at them. Women's silences *about* street harassment are qualitatively different than their silences *during* street harassment. In the following section, I will elaborate on these important distinctions.

On Silence *about* Street Harassment

Women's silences about street harassment partially veil these encounters. Not talking about street harassment disappears the problem, as much as the social phenomenon attempts to disappear women. Street harassment contains a messiness, about and within which silence and speech wrestle. This work explores these productive tensions, and this discussion purposefully troubles and complicates the speech/silence dialectic.

When women remain silent about street harassment, they may have many motivations for doing so. Many women have internalized sexism and willingly participate in a patriarchy by supporting its ideologies. Because street harassment reminds women of "their place," or effectively tries to keep women in their place, women who subscribe to sexist ideology may feel that they, in fact, deserve to be harassed, if they are in public, unaccompanied by a man, dressed [however the women are dressed] and so on.

As discourses of femininity largely dictate appropriate modes of behavior and discipline women who fall out of line accordingly, some women behave in ways that support, rather than challenge, street harassment. In many ways, silence is part of the discourse of femininity, as is the saying: "If you don't have anything nice to say, don't say anything at all." Talking about street harassment would violate the central expectations of femininity as silent and polite.

I would argue, at the risk of appearing victim-blaming, that some women who remain silent about street harassment may not even recognize these interactions as problematic. They are silent in the arbitrary (or neutral) sense of not speaking out about street harassment as a social issue. Their silence is simply the alternative to seeing street harassment as problematic and speaking out about it; their silence indicates that street harassment is a nonissue. This is precisely illustrative of my point about the "silence of violence."

When victims of street harassment deny or normalize it, failing to see street harassment as a problem, they normalize the violence.

Conversely, some women may remain silent when asked about street harassment because they have experienced it as problematic and may not want to relive the traumas of those experiences in their telling and re-telling.[24] Others make this point:

> To reveal personal history may also entail revealing one's survival strategies, however, and this requires enormous trust. As one of the black women remarked, once revealed, survival strategies are no longer effective. Consequently, in the retreats, the desire to break silences and connect across difference continued to vie with the pull to remain cautious, to draw back, to defend against the repetition of past hurts.[25]

This quote illustrates how the recollection of dangerous memories or past experiences, can create a re-traumatizing effect for the person making the disclosure. The quote also illustrates the way that discrediting or questioning the "truth" disrupts the healing potentiality of truth-telling or "telling to live."[26]

If sexual, social, and street injustice always already exists as an "unlikely" violence or "impossibility," survivors of such violence are going to feel silenced by that distorted perception of the reality of violence. This makes the unspeakable truths about violence in particular settings or communities more difficult to acknowledge, and makes the individual survivors of such violence question the benefits of disclosure or other confessional discursive practices.

In this entanglement, we see the complexities and contradictions of speech and silence, or the ways in which words can wound, and words can heal. As a result, some people respond to trauma through silence, protective of their privacy (and intimate relationships with others). Sometimes, silence suggests that traumas "would, somehow . . . just get better."[27] Sometimes, speech enables survivors of violence to feel connected to others, to feel less isolated or alienated from their experiences.

Importantly, neither speech nor silence has consistently proven to be the more effective mode for managing trauma, surviving violence, or negotiating street harassment. Each person must find their own way to navigate this violent world, until the "silence of violence" is loud enough to signal the significance of these problems, and demand more serious efforts to secure social justice.

In American society, discourse and speaking are privileged forms of communication. However, speech acts, throughout history, carry the weight of memory. Speech acts signal the many strategies people employ to survive social life. While everyone is generally encouraged to speak up and be heard, not everyone's voice is heard. This reality shapes the way women choose to respond (or not) to men who harass them in urban public spaces.

Black women often strategically employed "silence and secrecy" to challenge disreputable (mis)representations of them, and keep their "inner lives . . . hidden from white people."[28] Different historical moments made "testimony and openness" possible, while at other times, silence, and what Darlene Clark Hine calls a "self-imposed reticence," proved just as useful a strategy for survival.

For many women, silence threads through experiences with everyday violence. It proves a central theme for so many survivors of sexual violence. Silence exists in many forms and dimensions: the silence that surrounds sexual violence as it occurs; the silence often required (demanded) of those being victimized and violated during their violations, and then the silence stigmatized (in the moment and afterward); the silence of the known violent offenders who perpetuate sexual violence crimes; the silence expected of survivors at times, as the silence supposedly might conceal the shame and stigma that so often accompanies sexual violence; the silence of supporters or allies who are at a loss for words (or are afraid to say the wrong thing so they say nothing).

In the wake of violence, some women "never share with another the fact of their trauma. They do not speak words of acknowledgment that begin to unlock the silent pain."[29] Such silences can mask the painful reality, obscuring (to others) that violence occurred. However, for some survivors, speaking out about street harassment and/or other forms of violence might not be decidedly liberating, though some may experience it as such. Speech and silence can feel liberating and/or oppressive.

What remains an important consideration is understanding the ways women choose to (not) speak about and during street harassment. Pierce-Baker notes,

> I am now able to articulate without fear, guilt, or shame that I am a black woman who has survived rape. I have survived my own silences. . . . Each day brings new revelations. . . . The way out is to tell: speak the acts perpetrated upon us, speak the atrocities, speak the injustices, speak the personal violations of the soul. Someone will listen, someone will believe our stories, someone will join us. And until there are more who will bear witness to our truths as black women, we will do it for one another. . . . For now, that is enough.[30]

This admission attempts to detach shame and stigma from the experience of sexual violence. People often feel shame when they (falsely) believe that they are something versus that they did something.[31]

Author Laura Gray-Rosendale provides a related example of this in her work.[32] When she calls her mother, she reports her experience in this way:

"I am raped." Connecting the dots here means recognizing the powerful linguistic impact of "being" versus "doing" or having something done to you. This linguistic move is critical in lifting the veil off of violence, or of disrupting the silence of violence. That is, in saying that one "is" raped, instead of "has been" raped, one removes the responsibility of the actor, the perpetrator of the crime of rape. While it may help victims of violence to disclose their experiences as a means of minimizing the shame, I argue that it is equally, if not more important, to encourage men harassers and perpetrators of such violence, to acknowledge and speak through their shame, to assume responsibility for their actions, in an effort to move toward a more just society.

In a recent talk delivered at a small liberal arts college, the author, Gray-Rosendale, highlighted the importance of "telling our stories."[33] When legitimate legal or criminal justice eludes or escapes the victims of sexual violence, sometimes the way to seek justice is through remembering and retelling, speaking about the atrocities, and disclosing the details, so as to not let them prove self-destructive. "'Speak, keep on talking, don't keep quiet, no matter what, because silence frightens; I'm afraid, it seems to me that a long hand in the shadows is going to grab us by the neck and strangle us!'"[34]

Dorothy Alison echoed these thoughts when she noted that stories ensure our survival. She argues, "To go on living [we] have to tell stories . . . stories are the one sure way [we] know to touch the heart and change the world . . . 'Re-memory' would make itself a felt process of daily living. Wholeness, I would learn, is a forever journey."[35] That is, reassembling the pieces of our lives may be an easier process when accompanying by a remembering and retelling. Again, this illustrates how speech can prove empowering for some, while silence can feel protective to others, or can both be experienced in myriad ways, depending on the situation.

In ways that echo Alison, Sharon Lamb sees speech as a form of survival, and women's storytelling and sharing as a form of liberation:

> Both women and girls told me sexual stories—truths, partial truths, memories, but stories nonetheless. . . . In the 1960s, after centuries of silence, women began to tell their stories of coercion and rape, in books, consciousness-raising groups, and 'Take Back the Night' rallies. These individual stories created one large historical narrative about the lives of women. It served to bring women and girls together, together in their victimization. . . .[36]

Following the idea that "storytelling is community building," Lamb posits:

> Storytelling can also be subversive. It can change the way we view the past and it can overthrow what we think is normal to create new norms. The public form of storytelling takes individuals' acts of rebellion and unruliness, brings

them together as a body of stories, and by virtue of making them "women's stories" . . . gives them a power all their own.[37]

To underscore an earlier point about the ways in which society recognizes and registers women's voices, I will say that it is important to consider the value of speaking, when people may or may not be listening. This begs the questions, "What is the point of talking, if/when no one is listening?" "Is silence self-protective and a mode of preservation when you are being seen but unheard?" I consider silence next, as women targets of street harassment report relying on silence as a strategy for navigating urban public spaces.

On Silence *during* Street Harassment

Many women in my sample reported choosing not to respond to men during street harassment, a decision contingent on a variety of factors, including the time of day, if they were alone in public with the harasser, and so on. As I described in an earlier chapter, the social pressures on women to maintain respectable femininity offers partial explanation for women's non-response to men who harass. This differs considerably from not responding out of fear of verbal or physical retaliation. That is, choosing silence qualitatively and experientially differs from feeling silenced as a constraint.

Women's non-response to men harassers relates to the social penalties women targets would possibly incur, were they to respond to men harassers. Ignoring the interpellations of men harassers, women who refuse to respond often do so in order to perform respectable femininity. They do not want to compromise or make questionable their social status by engaging men harassers. If women respond to or are interpellated by men harassers, the women may feel responsible for any ramifications to their response.

While some see women's non-response or silence as a failure "to make life together,"[38] others see this response as a way to make life together. Sometimes, women's silence during street harassment is their way of expressing civility, not docility, during such exchanges. This is not to say that talking back to men harassers constitutes incivility, but rather that women's silence is not always already oppressive. Sometimes, women choose silence as a purposeful, intentional strategy for dealing with street harassment.

Some women rely on silence as a cautionary measure to avoid further accusation of being "the type of woman" to talk to strangers (or talk back to men, by extension). This depiction of the woman would cast her in unfavorable terms, compromising the respectable femininity she may actively be working to preserve. In such cases, then, women who get verbally entangled by men in urban public spaces may possess a generalized fear and anxiety, not of the men themselves or any attendant hypothetical danger or threat they may pose, but rather of her image.

Some women remain silent as a way of also attempting to remain respectable, or good repute, and decent looking simply. Speaking back to men strangers makes women appear subversive, which is not an appearance that all women care to make. Thus, silence can be deployed as a way to reject being a certain kind of woman. In this way, "dangerous ways of (not) speaking" link to "dangerous ways of seeing" in the sense that silence among some women can challenge controlling images of them.

For example, silence can prove subversive for black women who wanted to disrupt problematic public perceptions, such as being seen as sassy, emasculating loud mouths. Not talking back disrupts that notion and forces people, who misrecognize black women and see them only in these limited ways, to expand their understandings of this group of women. Silence then not only challenges these misperceptions but the behavior that relies on these misrecognitions. That is, when women choose to be silent during street harassment, they expose (sometimes successfully, sometimes not) the interactional vandalism that they face. Being silent in the face of such aggressive assaultive speech magnifies all that is going awry during such interactions. As it challenges "dangerous ways of seeing," it can facilitate the "dangerous ways of speaking" that men harassers perpetuate against women targets.

When someone is silent during a conversation, s/he is breaking, or at least challenging, the rules of social interaction. Being silent may make the women target seem rude or awkward, upon first blush, but really, it is the men who street harass who are breaking the social interactional rules. They are not, however, violating the code of the street,[39] or any codes of gender,[40] specifically related to masculinity.

In contrast to the silence that magnifies the harasser's speech, the men's speech continues beyond the scope of the public space in which they harass. As they tend to share stories and accounts of their harassing behavior with men peers, as a means of 1) proving manhood, 2) establishing or strengthening homosocial bonds and getting/gaining respect, and 3) confirming or displaying their heterosexuality.

So to keep quiet *about* street harassment for men is almost a break with the male contract, which is why being silent about street harassment for women protects men who harass and enables their harassment to continue largely unchallenged. Women choosing silence *during* street harassment exposes the extent to which men violate conversational expectations or rules. This selective and strategic silence encourages a revisiting of Audre Lorde's idea, "Your silence will not protect you."

Given this violation in interactional rules, I would argue that *sometimes* strategically choosing silence over speech can, at least temporarily, protect a potential target or victim of street harassment. Certainly, the spirit of Lorde's words resonates with targets of street harassment who want to *not* be afraid, who want to say what they need to say, except when the fear of survival and death or violent harm outweighs fears of being misrecognized or misheard.

Given the regular occurrence of violence against women in the United States and the rates of abuse reported (not to mention the extent to which violence against women goes unreported), women's silence indeed does not protect them against the everyday injustices they face in the context of the curved space connecting public and private patriarchies.[41] Though women are theoretically protected by the ideological discourse of patriarchy, women who have experienced violence and harm directly and indirectly (witnessing it) know the failures of patriarchal discourse intimately and sometimes tragically.

In light of this frequency of various kinds of assaultive behaviors directed at women, it is no wonder that some women, when confronted by men harassers in public spaces, they might opt for silence as a protective mechanism. This opting for silence reflects more of a constrained choice, as discussed earlier by Susie (see chapter 1).

Her observation reminds me of the concept of "freedom with violence," and she astutely notes whose freedom and right to speech is recognized, accommodated and encouraged. Her silence complicates current understandings of how people use themselves and their bodies (including, but not limited to their voices) to negotiate being un/seen and un/heard. On the one hand, we can interpret her silence as a docile or deferential kind of silence, and on another, as a strategic deployment of silence to avoid violence.

Different groups of people have voices that are heard or registered in meaningful but varied ways; marginalized voices encounter difficulty entering public discourse, in political terms,[42] and often get marginalized and silenced in society. Drawing connections to the various sites and strategies that silence women provide important parallels to understanding street harassment. Women's speech and silence remain a complex part of the process of addressing street harassment individually and on a broader sociopolitical level.

> Attempting to use the public sphere as a way to address, understand, and transform gendered social and sexual violence perpetrated not only by white men but by all men of color made it seem that black men were corroborating the outlandish discourse of black depravity that was used to justify white mob violence, Jim Crow race riots, and lynchings. . . . Under these conditions, black women most likely experienced various forms of gendered violence as well as forms of racialized violence, as most of the women were racialized urban women workers and domestics who could not be engaged through the larger international or transatlantic public sphere.[43]

The social structure of society makes (black) women's "efforts to gain autonomy the false promise of modernity."[44] That is, the prevailing gender, racial, and class hierarchies mask the ways in which women's lives are often circumscribed by systems of oppression, or interlocking oppressions. Women in general, and black women in particular, resisted this oppression through their writing. Others have echoed this idea of "women writing resistance"[45] as a way to do the following:

> [E]ngage the violence and norms that could not be spoken of easily in the public sphere. . . . That is, black women encountered the public sphere, so crucial to the progressives' vision of democratically run societies, as the source of an aporia: without participation in the public sphere, they would have no chance to mobilize the state against historical forms of antiblack violence; yet in lending their speech to the public sphere, they supported the norms that give speech its authority, norms that made particular forms of violence become inconsequential or meaningless to private, public, and political life.[46]

Given the complexities in strategically opting for speech or silence, women who experience street harassment further update our understandings of how their participation in social life is compromised by the practice of gender inequities and spatial injustices. The curious thing about silence in particular is the way that it makes women appear docile and obedient, but it can also be an expression of quiet resistance and strength.

Remaining silent, or choosing to be silent, allowed these women to "fake docility" or appear to be docile bodies in a public special landscape. At the same time, these women were also able to use their silence to follow the script of respectable femininity—by appearing to not "talk back" or "mouth off" to men. Rather than engage public strangers in unwieldy and unpredictable conversations, the women who chose silence felt they could "manage" these interactions by basically not interacting with men.

In the sample I drew, many respondents spoke of this strategy as a means of avoiding "intensified street harassment," or trying to de-escalate men's verbally assaultive speech. Indeed, women's silence did not protect them from being harassed in the first place, but to some of them it seemed to temper and diffuse some of the street harassment they faced. Some women made apparent the power of gender and family socialization in their informal education about dealing with street harassment.

One respondent, Red, noted, "Well, I think also seeing my mother . . . people make remarks to her and she doesn't pay them any attention. I guess I went along with her, also you know like, it doesn't bother her; it *really* doesn't bother me. You know, it's just someone voicing their opinion about you."

In our interview conversation, I gently invited this respondent to reflect on her consent to willingly participate in my study, knowing it focused on street harassment, and yet she minimized the impact of harassment on her life. This moment revealed the extent to which women are socialized or taught to do this, to disregard or diminish their experiences, perhaps especially with everyday violence.

When I asked her what had drawn her to participation in my study, she admitted or revealed more of her feelings about being harassed: "Well, yeah, it does bother me to the point where every day I have to go walk through the park, I have to worry about so many—it's uncomfortable kind of, just because you never know how far this person may take it, even though I've never experienced anything like that, you still have to be cautious."

Red's comments convey the extent to which she experiences street harassment as an everyday violence, which she reported facing five to six times a day, every day. Her concerns about her safety surface in her reluctance to discuss street harassment within the relative safety of the interview. This reluctance extends to public spaces, where she chooses or prefers to remain silent, in an attempt to remain safe/r, in the presence of potential risks. We can understand the various "dangerous ways of speaking" as dimensionalized in talking *during* and *about* street harassment. Red's reluctance to reveal her feelings of fear and frustration regarding street harassment suggests that the perception of danger extends beyond the site(s) in which she faces street harassment. In this way, we see the importance of recognizing the web of violence that exists individually for respondents, and more broadly in society. We can also gain an appreciation of the reasons guiding women's decisions to remain silent, rather than employing potentially "dangerous ways of speaking," by talking back to men who harass (and intensifying or accelerating their harassment).

So even though women's silence can endorse proscriptions about being "better seen and not heard," women opting for silence can also allow them to feel a sense of agency as they navigate public spaces and interactions with strangers. For example, some respondents spoke of the ways that men offered them compliments, which, even if they found flattering, they typically opted not to respond in kind. Some appreciated the flattery, but did not want to be interpellated as the kind of woman who publicly displays said appreciation. To some, that might suggest a woman did not mind being harassed by men, if she found their comments "complimentary."

Women reported negotiating silence and speech in a number of ways. For example, Amy, a white middle-class respondent, noted that she never felt men responded with hostility to her non-response when they harassed her. Instead, she felt this way: "But on the street, I'm just this generic female and there's this sexual energy directed at me and it's fleeting. I've never had, that I can recall, any negative response because I didn't respond. They're just giving a shout out to the girl." Amy's example illustrates that she does not think much of the street harassment, and therefore chooses not to respond to it in turn. However, by not responding, by being silent, does she appear to be actively silent to the men who harass her, or is she just a "generic female" who they silenced (if this is a more intentional part of their harassment)?

How do women such as Amy convey that they are acting choosing to be silent, without having to articulate that action with words to clarify their decision? In other words, some women may gain an appreciation for their decisions not to respond to men harassers during our interview conversations, rather than during social interactions that turn into street harassment. Women may see the value and agency in their silence, in reflecting on these experiences, not actually within these experiences when they are making important decisions about if, how, and/or when to respond.

Other respondents commented on the dynamics of street harassment, as they sometimes seemed to have more to do with men speaking than attempts to silence women. For example, Red recalls, "I don't really think they care what you look like; you're just a woman." This suggests that women are interchangeable to men harassers, and that men harass women because the men think that they are supposed to interact with women in this manner.

Red's comments present the reminder: do not read too much into what seems like behavior centered on women that in some ways has very little to do with women; the interaction, she suggests, remains quite generic. "Well, it seems, it's flattering when I'm not dressed my best and they're like, 'Hey, beautiful,' or 'You look pretty today' or just something, because you know, anybody can give you a compliment and that would boost you way up." I jokingly replied, "So when you're feeling a little frumpy, it's nice to hear." Thus, these women believe that harassment should not be internalized, or taken personally.

Other respondents commented on the way street harassment seemed to have very little to do with women, and in fact, much more to do with men, particularly when men harass in groups. Jenny also made comments that alluded to the homoerotic nature of harassment; Snow, another white woman respondent, noted that harassment seems to her a ritual between men. Scholars discuss this form of male bonding that implicates women but argue that it has more to do with men forming a social and/or sexual connection amongst themselves.[47]

When women respondents felt they were the center of men's unwanted attention, some of them used silence as a way of normalizing men's attention, to present the appearance of being familiar with being fawned over, rather than being annoyed by the harasser's words and behavior. For example, during our interview, Tammy revealed this:

Well, I was walking to the (club) to see a concert and I was in my go-go boots, and a mini-skirt and I was feeling sassy and . . . some man stopped his truck and for the first time in my life I got acknowledged by a man on the street in the way that a sexy little blond minx does. And he was like, "Hey, gimme some of that. Woo!" You know? And just hollered at me, and then everyone turned around and looked and I was just like, I didn't make any face, I just walked on like it happened every day. You know? I pretended that I was a cute sexy blond minx, like, "I'm so used to this." You know, I didn't smile. I didn't frown but inside I thought, "Hmm, I got acknowledged. Hot Stuff!" Yeah.

Tammy provided another illustration of how she negotiates men's interpellation of her:

I mean, there are plenty of times when I feel like I shouldn't respond and I get used to being a spectacle, and I honestly, because I've always been "the freak," I don't know how much of it is sexualized and how much of it is "You're looking freaky," and how much of it I'm . . . I have to admit I've never felt safe to acknowledge any comments, like "Hey, nice tattoo" or "Hey, check the hair," unless it's a group of people that I'm familiar with, I've never felt like I could look you in the eye and acknowledge it. I'm always doing this "Latino chin nod," that "I hear you" gesture.

This discussion illustrates the ways in which Tammy experiences some ambivalence about how to handle harassment, an ambivalence compounded by feelings of self-defined deviance and a spirit of doing things differently (as materialized by body modification in the forms of piercings, tattoos, "extreme" hair coloring such as purple, and so forth; doing gender imperfectly; and likewise).

By offering some acknowledgment of people's comments with a small social and physical gesture, Tammy can appear civil while controlling or containing the interaction, by discouraging others from engaging her more, or otherwise expecting more from her.

To gain a sense of the policing that Tammy experiences, I offer this anecdote from our interview:

When I walk into a store, when my tattoos and lip ring's out, I always get security guarded like I'm a black man. They see a tattoo on a young person and they immediately follow me and I'm always followed in stores, not that this is harassment, but anyways. . . . I was just buying my boyfriend $300 worth of shirts and ties the other day, and I was just matching the ties up to the shirts and the security guard was just following me . . . for like 8 minutes. I mean, it was significant . . . and he followed me from section to section. So, I knew it, and finally he came up and asked, "Can I help you?" and I said, "No thanks, I'm just buying ties and shirts." And I was like, "Also, just because I have tattoos doesn't mean I'm going to steal stuff, so I'd really appreciate if you're gonna surveill me to do it a little more so that you're more than 5 feet away from me." . . . And large women always spend money; we're older usually, and have better jobs; and we spend more, we drop a lot of money on clothes; at least that's the stereotype and I think that it's true. And then I walk in with this tattoo and it supersedes my fatness and turns into like something bad. . . . And the funny thing is that I snapped and it was really funny that the security guard did this thing where he waited one more minute on principle and then walked away. I was so mad.

The above statement shows how the respondent drew parallels between her experience in quasi-public spaces such as shopping malls and that of black men who she argues gets policed in a publicly acknowledged yet obviously/admittedly problematic manner.

While not equivocating the two social positions (i.e., being a white woman v. being a black man), the respondent clearly points out how her body appears as a walking contradiction, such that having tattoos and being female and decent remains an oxymoron or an anomaly, and how these tattoos work to justify and intensify others' surveillance of her given and despite their unfounded suspicions of her decency, legitimacy, and right to be respected.

Dangerous Ways of Speaking: Un/Doing Gender and Performing Femininity Im/perfectly or In/appropriately

For many women, the risks attached to responding to street harassment remain comparable to that attached to choosing silence. One of the black women respondents, Susie, noted that, once when she was harassed, the harasser implied that she failed to respond in the way he anticipated or expected. He informed her, "'You just ain't acting right.'" Because Susie failed to reciprocate the man's interest in her, and instead feel silent in surprise at what she felt were sexually charged and inappropriate remarks, she found herself facing evaluation from this male stranger.

The gender imbalance that exists in this society serves as a reminder that some women feel neither entitled nor empowered to impose their opinion of men onto them. Most of the women in my sample did not feel particularly emboldened to confront men with the same sorts of evaluative comments as the men shared so openly and boldly with the women. This partially suggests that men enjoy a freedom with discursive speech practices that eludes many women, especially in potentially and actually threatening moments such as street harassment.

One of the white women respondents, Tammy, shared how hostile harassment has been in her experience:

I didn't feel, the first time I didn't feel threatened but the second time, I felt like he was going get outta his truck, like he was slowing down. And he was pissed because I stopped in front of him, I mean, and you know, he was *mad*, and I was like, "F—k you!" and I wasn't (giving) him s—t but I felt though like, because I had responded back to him, like "F—k you, I'm from [the Midwest]; I'm from a trailer park. I'm not taking this." I felt though, because I took him on, I really did feel like he was gonna get out, and then I was all like, "S—t. I'm glad I'm walking into the store." You know, like the shop keeper will protect me (laughter). . . . I was scared; I felt like he was following me. And I don't know why . . . but I don't know what I thought he was gonna do, but all I felt is this I need to protect myself by walking quickly into the store and you know, just kind of being aware. I remember that sense of, I wanted to yell back and be like, "F—k you more!" but also felt the overriding need to protect myself.

Tammy's example here foreshadows the discussion in the next section, which explores how talking back can be empowering and a "dangerous way of speaking" for exactly the reasons Tammy illustrates in her own example. Whether women are silent or not, we still may be vulnerable to the threats contained within and expressed during street harassment.

As Tammy noted, sometimes the street harasser says something to which there is no response, or there are no words. Sometimes, the "right" words are angry, volatile words that women use to express their sense of outrage at the spatial and social injustice of street harassment. The same words that might feel empowering may simultaneously intensify a woman's feelings of vulnerability and also the very harassment she faces from men. Paying attention to protecting herself reflects how much street harassment presents dangers to women.

That Tammy and other women reported seeking further protection from service workers in public arenas also reveals the level of vulnerability women feel in the face of street harassment. That they actively resist street harassment and disrupt traditional gender role expectations by enacting or mimicking harassment, mostly in a parodying way, with men, shows that they have some agency, amidst their feelings of vulnerability.

In some ways, Tammy's responses to street harassment convey her attempts to be both comical, and disruptive of the expected gender norms. That is, she performs femininity badly, to the degree that she deploys humor as a way to subversively critique street harassment. In their "harass and get harassed back" moments, these women show men that the tables can easily be turned socially, even if balancing out power differentials prove a more arduous task. Julie offers another example:

Well, I think of times when somebody has said something to me that's so ridiculous that I laugh and then he laughs, and then I move on. This happens a lot and this always makes me laugh. Sometimes when I'm jogging some guy, when I'm passing will say, "Hey, honey. Can I run with you?" and then I say, "You couldn't keep up," and then I keep running, and we both laugh. That happens a lot actually."

Here, Julie shares how she negotiates men's intrusions or attempts to entangle her with humor; being clever and witty enables Julie to engage in banter (camaraderie) with men, without feeling controlled by them. This levels the exchange.

Julie also described moments when responding to street harassment proved impractical or heightened her awareness of her vulnerability. For example, being insistently asked to smile by male harassers worked to discipline her display of femininity, to regulate her expression of accommodation. Because of her feminist consciousness, she rejected this interpellation by male strangers, and instead disrupted men harassers' "good girl" notion that the men may hold of her by saying, "F—k off!" She offers the disclaimer that she says this on "really bad days." Later on in the interview, Julie adds,

> The experience [drive-by versus street harassment] is different. I wouldn't say that my reaction or level of anger differs, but there is a certain amount of frustration when somebody's in a car, and I can't flick them off, or tell them to f—k off. And, so, it's like this drive-by catcall, and eeerr—I just wanna like throw a brick in their window when they're gone. And when they're walking down the street and they harass me, um, if I can say, or flip them off or tell them to f—k off, there's a little bit of satisfaction in that.

Julie distinguishes between the curt comments that originate from men driving by in cars, and that which stems from men who confront women in face-to-face social situations on the street.

While both circumstances can seem assaultive, the former seem more daunting to deal with simply because they inhibit a woman's ability to respond given the quickness with which the harassment happens. In contrast, street encounters can unfold over a period of time, and unfortunately escalate into discursive debates and heated contestations between strangers.

Notably, in the space and relative comfort of the interview, Julie can describe what she might like to say to men harassers, but in reality, as she describes, talking back to some of them may prove to her (and other women targets) to be "dangerous ways of speaking." Furthermore, the articulated desire to seek retribution, albeit imagined, speaks to the dangers of violence. As women continue to experience street harassment, they may grow increasingly impatient with, and reactively violent to, this everyday problem of violence.[48]

In discussing civility and authenticity in social interactions, Gardner mentions ways she observed lapses in civility, such as when a group of African American men harasses white passersby, but ignore African American women passersby.[49] As a point of comparison, Amy's experience relates; she observes that most of the men who harass her are black. Here we can link the examples as illustrations of street harassment as gendered and racialized.

That Amy self-identifies as a white woman and is aware that most of her harassers are black men draws our attention to the social landscape of the harassment and the social dynamic between her, as a white woman, and her harassers, mostly black men. Amy describes Southern City as the site of most of the harassment she experiences.

At the intersections of race and gender, as well as target and harasser, some—mainly speculative—explanations can be offered about Amy's experiences with harassment. Her comments arguably raise more questions than answers. Is Amy a target of black men's harassment because of her whiteness, her womanhood, her femininity (or some combination thereof), or their blackness, their black masculinity, their potential experience as a marginalized (versus hegemonic) masculinity, or their perception of her as deserving of—perhaps even desiring—their attention?

For those answers, we would have to turn squarely to the very source of harassment and discomfort—the men harassers themselves. As a researcher, I had to manage my own levels of discomfort while negotiating harassment directed at me. Securing answers to, or exploring, the above questions and more would require more emotional labor than I felt equipped with at the time of this research endeavor. I recognize that acknowledging this discomfort troubles and potentially upholds stereotypes about categories of men. However, I also recognize that the hazards to women targets of harassment are very real, and that engaging men about this topic might intensify such hazards to women's health.

For example, what if the men perceived as harassers *were* in fact simply trying to say hello? What if their need for respect and recognition interrupted their ability to communicate and engage women with civility? Are men misunderstood or misrecognized in unfair ways? Ways that condemn them for behavior that they do not realize they are guilty of enacting? What if street harassment marks the reflection of the socialization of men and boys to be oriented to women, and to be assertive and aggressive with women in ways that they understand as an appropriate performance of masculinity, and not evidence or an intentional expression of harassment (even as that is the impact)?

As Amy explains, men who harass cross "the line." She spoke of the privilege that men assert with women in public spaces, and their aggression in expressing their entitlement through animosity and hostility (when the women do not respond to the men's attention in what the men deem appropriate):

> I've also noticed that in terms of masculine privilege, and you're in a bar, and a man approaches you and you aren't interested, "Well, you don't have to be a bitch." And then I'm thinking, "Well you're pushing me into this conversation without asking my permission, whether I want to engage in this conversation, and you're calling me 'the bitch'?"

This type of antagonistic and accusatory behavior from men operates as a disincentive for women to further engage the men. It clearly demonstrates to most women the amount of male privilege afforded men in public spaces, speech practices, and social interactions with others, if not in general.

This also is a dangerous discourse, for a man to call a woman a "bitch," in that it denigrates women, discursively associating them with animals. This is "dangerous" if only because it again opens up the space for women to be mistreated and disrespected, stemming from the initial dehumanization that starts when equivocated with animals.[50]

Notably, Amy subverts the meaning of "bitch," a derogatory word typically associated with women. By posing the question in such a way, she dislocates the term from women, and attaches it to men who complain about and argue with women, and then effectively whine when they fail to get their way with women. While Amy may have had this thought at the moment of harassment, she makes clear that she did not speak her thought about him being a "bitch." In this moment of harassment, she may have felt silenced, or chose to stay silent, refusing to speak her mind.

However, in the space of the interview, she could recuperate and reclaim her thoughts, breathing life back into them during the interview. This point underscores the importance of the interview as a space to accommodate and encourage women to speak their truths. Who knows what price Amy would have paid were she to insinuate that the man harasser was "the bitch"?

Amy described an experience where she acted back (versus talked back) to a man harasser. As she ponders the penalties of doing so, she wonders about the threat to her, and her threat to femininity:

> It's mostly, I don't know if it's so much, "Don't talk to strangers," as [it is] the notion that it's going to go back and forth. Don't respond, because they'll respond back. And you'll get into this pointless exchange or in some cases, like downtown, you could, I don't know. . . . Is this person going to get angry? If I, when I actually, that's the way I think about it, but when I actually made the gesture [flicking some guys off], I felt I had violated a gender role, like I wasn't being feminine. I didn't recognize that at the time, but I must have felt that.

Amy's comments illustrate how dangerous her violation of a gender role proves, threatening her own safety, as well as the construction of appropriate or emphasized femininity.

Amy proudly suggests that she violates a gender role, which the reference "bitch" works to confirm. Otherwise, the man harasser might be more generous and benevolent in his street remarks (offering a compliment, or infantilizing her even, versus insulting her arguably more harshly with the term, "bitch"). Amy's action might be a dangerous discursive practice, but she finds it to be empowering. Her anger reflects an expression of embodied resistance. Paradoxically, it is dangerous, yet emboldening, for women to express. How often can women feel empowered in their attempts to access survival strategies in the face of street and social injustice?

The cost of challenging hegemonic femininity relates to the social control mechanisms of street harassment. Amy's comments underscore the price that women pay for being in public. Gendered discourses also prescribe the "proper" places for women to be present, so that they might preserve respectable femininity.

This, in part, explains the extent of the harassment Amy experiences. She shared that she gets harassed a lot in public places (such as bars) versus spaces (streets, parks, plazas, etc.):

> I never, the only time I get [called a] "bitch" is in not the street, but a bar setting, because that's when the person is coming toward me. On the street, I'm just this generic female and there's this sexual energy directed at me and it's fleeting. I've never had, that I can recall, any negative response because I didn't respond. They're just giving a "shout out" to the girl.

Several other respondents noted the generalized quality of street harassment. That is, they understood their experiences as a reflection of being harassed because of their gender and racial group memberships, not necessarily as a function of details particular to them as individuals.

This is an inversion of the position about gaining an appreciation for the general in the specifics. That many women report feeling that they were being harassed because of their gender is instructive of the pervasion of violence against women. Maybe this is more about the interchangeability of women and the degree to which men who harass see women as categorically subordinate to men.

In addition, men who harass may feel threatened by more assertive and confident women than submissive or docile ones. Women who fail to adhere to the tenets of respectable femininity will likely threaten men who harass, as these women appear more like "masculine women."[51]

Turning Discourses of Danger into Dangerous Discourses?
Or, When Victims Blame the Victim by Internalizing Rape Culture

Perhaps discourses of danger become more problematic when internalized or endorsed by victims of violence, such as street harassment (or women who face street harassment). Take Felicia's narrative as a useful example. Felicia identified herself as an educated, middle-class white woman. As she began to describe her most intense and upsetting incident of street harassment, Felicia said, "I went out walking and it was like sundown, and um, you know, we were wearing like yoga pants and a t-shirt and tennis shoes, and we went for a walk, and this guy walks by."

Here, she sets the stage for the events that follow: she is sure to carefully construct herself and her friend as quite uninviting or enticing to others, and thus by extension to show how undeserving they are of any attention that might mark them as indecent, provocative women (i.e., bad girls who arguably deserve whatever adverse attention they receive). Discourses of danger are also divisive, in drawing false distinctions between people who "should" be protected from violence, and those who "should not" (the "sympathetic" victim or the pitiable one, in contrast to the arguably "deserving" one).[52]

She explains, "It wasn't like baggy shirts but like, you know, what you go walking in. It wasn't like we were wearing skirts and high heels; I mean we would come home from work and put our hair in a ponytail to go out for a walk. . . . We definitely were not looking like, 'Hey, check me out.'" Discourses of danger infer that well-dressed (respectable) women do not get harassed, while women who dress questionably may call similar kinds of attention to themselves.

Felicia's comments draw the line between women who ostensibly "ask" to be harassed (as evidenced by poor choices in appearance or behavior), versus those who do not. Notably, this discourse picks up the victim-blaming tone so central to rape discourse (she "asked for it"). We see that women victims of violence can discursively protect themselves from further victimization by constructing themselves as virtuous, while discursively re-victimizing victims they view as promiscuous or provocative.

This dangerous discourse reveals the extent to which anyone, including women (victims) can internalize sexist patriarchy to blame the victim and produce dangerous discourses. Perhaps this technique allowed them to feel better about their own encounter with violence, to make its likelihood comprehensible. This should not take much, since most women *will* experience street harassment, as I indicated earlier. Felicia continued,

> So, we were walking, we walked down this street and this guy came up towards
> us in a bike, and [my friend] and I both smile, nod, make eye contact, and then

he went right in between us, and we were going to both go to one side of him, or the other, and he rode right between us, and as he was riding up, both of us, afterwards, talked about the fact that we could tell he was looking at us, like he was checking us out, and all of a sudden we had made eye contact with him just to be neighborly cause you're walking past them in your neighborhood. You know? So looking back we were like, well, maybe we shouldn't have made eye contact, maybe we invited, oh I don't know. So, he rode his bike right in between us and we both thought, "Well, that was weird," and then we just kept walking. You know, and the sun went down, and we were walking down, we did all of the things that you probably shouldn't do, because we were walking in a not-well-lit area, but we were walking in the street as opposed to the sidewalk, because it was darker on the sidewalk, and, because we were together, we didn't feel like, I guess you're just not as conscious, like I would not have gone out that late at night if I were by myself.

The other series of "dangerous discourses" embedded in Felicia's comments are the (stranger danger) rape myths that she refers to and the checklist that she runs through—no eye contact with strangers; walk in street, not sidewalk, walk in pairs, not alone. This reflects the anticipatory socialization and/or victimization embedded in the discourses of danger with which girls and women are so often socialized.

In their attempts to minimize or avert the male gaze, Felicia and her friend found out that dressing down does not prevent dangerous encounters with others. What she described next involved her anxious conversation with her friend as they decide what to do as this suspicious stranger lurks behind them on his bike.

The streets are very wide and there are street lights, so we were walking on the side of the street, instead of the sidewalk, and we could tell that he was behind us, like we could hear him back there, and we kind of glanced back and he was just kind of keeping his distance from us, he was keeping that distance at a steady pace, like he was staying a certain distance away from us, and so we both noticed it but we didn't say anything. Because anything we said he could have overheard, which not that it would have mattered but . . .

The two friends wondered,

Like, what are we going to do? This guy's following us on his bike. So, we both could tell; we kind of gave each other these looks like what the hell is this guy doing back here? And then before we had a chance to say anything, he comes riding up on his bike and he goes, "Excuse me." And we kept walking, we didn't turn around, just because of the incident that we had had before [the man riding his bike between the two women], . . . and then he yelled—So we were like, we're just going to ignore him. And he kept saying, "Excuse me, excuse me."

And then finally, he had said it so loud, that I turned around and he had unzipped his pants. . . . It just gives me the creeps [thinking about this]. . . . And he had his penis out and he was like riding towards me on this bike . . . showing me, you know. And so, I turned around, and my first instinct, I didn't know what to do. I was like, not expecting that at all, and there were some people out in their yard, and I just started heading to their yard, and like, "C'mon, girl" to my friend, and she turned around, because he said, "Excuse me" again. And I guess she didn't realize [what was going on]; it happened so fast that she didn't know what was going on, and so she turned around, and actually she never saw that he had his pants unzipped, with, you know, everything hanging out. She looked him in the face, like, "What do you want?! Why are you messing with us?!" She's the more upfront; our personalities are [different]; she's more confrontational.

This respondent believed, prior to this incident, that avoiding "stranger danger" entailed avoiding eye contact and blending in, in terms of choice of clothing and behavior. She also suggested that she might expect to be street harassed in the downtown urban public spaces, not in a neighboring part of the city.

She noted, "He rode towards us, so he rode up and both of us looked up and nodded or you know, just made casual eye contact which you wouldn't probably do on the streets of Southern City, but when you're in somebody's neighborhood, it's different." Felicia assumed a qualitative difference in the character of social spaces. Although she was in a metropolitan area, she believed that she could expect people to "act better" (less harassing or violent) in a quasi-suburban part of the city versus that in/of the downtown area (a more decidedly urban setting). As mentioned earlier, this fallacious idea stems from popular belief that urban areas attract or house undesirable people and that one can encounter nicer, more polite people the further from a city center one goes.

Put more succinctly, her comments solidify this equation: downtown = dangerous; suburb = safe. This equation (assumption) reveals the faulty assumptions guided by it. It also neglects to consider people's individual mobility and travel through various urban areas (or the geographical mobility and travel within and across areas).

Even in this Southern city that is densely populated, people curiously maintain a level of familiarity amidst one another (read: millions of residents); people constantly move in and out of spaces, so there is no fixed quality to the urban landscape (i.e., the same guy on a bike could be found downtown or in the surrounding area, especially if his travel is facilitated by public or personal modes of transportation.

Once Felicia and her friend reported her harassing incident of indecent exposure to the police, they felt dissatisfied with the insincere and dismissive way the officers handled the reporting of the incident. The officer assuaged the women's fear with a disingenuous and conciliatory, "'We'll keep a look out. . . . If we see him, we'll pull him over.'" Felicia noted:

> [The office] wrote our information down on his little note pad, but not on a police report because we didn't want him to keep that so I think that we didn't think the police officer took it as seriously and when we went to the gift shop, the minute we said something about it, she immediately said, "I'm calling the police" but the other [man] owner, he thought it was a little funnier [entertaining].

Her comments reveal the extent to which others trivialized and failed to take seriously the event she experienced and details she described. Dismissive and disingenuous responses to street harassment are themselves dangerous discourses that support the "silence of violence." That is, disregard for the everyday violence of street harassment enables it to (is what precisely) hides in plain sight.

Ironically, discourses of danger and gendered discourses again meet (or get entangled) as the two women find validation from the women versus the men. This example reveals some of the complexity of these dangerous discourses. She continued,

> I mean he knew it wasn't right but he didn't take it as seriously as the wife. I mean, immediately she called the police, and said, "Forget it, you're not going home; stay here, we're calling the police." I guess we ended up being there an hour. It took up our whole evening. And afterwards we were so disturbed by the whole thing. We had to go home and process it. And she said, "I'm not sleeping in my house. What if he saw us come home?" I'm sure it was a random thing. We didn't feel like the police took it seriously. He, the police officer, wasn't like, "Um, we're going to get him."

Felicia felt as if she and her friend did not receive the response, the protection, they expected. When I asked her whether she believes she would have been more respected or gotten a better response from a female police officer, she replied:

> It's hard to say. Based on the response, it's funny, she [Felicia's friend] and I have talked to our friends about it and several of our friends live in that neighborhood (You'll never guess what happened this weekend!). So she wanted to let them know, don't be so carefree when you're out walking your dog because it's not as safe as you want to think that it is. And she said that she saw a difference, because we talked about the difference between reactions between men and women, like my boyfriend, when I told him, he was like, "Oh, that's terrible," but it wasn't like the reactions that I got from my girlfriends who were like, "Oh my God. What did you do? I bet that was so scary." Because men just don't have that imposed, like I don't think they ever have to worry about

someone doing that to them. It's not something in their consciousness. But for women, they teach you, "Oh, you need to learn self-defense" from like the 5th grade on and you know it's sort of ingrained.

Felicia's comments gesture toward the way men may not feel the same vulnerability in public. However, racializing any gendered double standard complicates the story. Accounting for race and gender simultaneously, one arrives at various intersections and negotiations of safety and danger. Who feels more or less vulnerable and/or protected in public? Felicia's comments reveal the extent to which gendered discourses shape our experience with street harassment and our reactions to street harassment.[53]

Felicia concluded,

But you know men just don't have to think about that. I think and even my boyfriend was like, "What's the big deal? He didn't hurt you." I'm like. . . . my friend said, she said, "Well, who's to say he wouldn't have hurt us? Who's to say he didn't have a gun in his backpack? Or who's to say he wasn't planning on doing something?" . . . My friend was like, "*That* thing (his penis) could have hurt us. Who knows what he wanted to do with *that*!" And men just don't have that fear of someone, of someone of another gender that could scare them or hurt them.

These comments reveal the extent to which street harassment is potentially and actually dangerous. As Felicia noted, men who harass can use their bodies against women, not just their voices. This highlights how harassment operates as an everyday violence for women, when men weaponize themselves in the process.

Despite reporting only occasional (versus routine) experiences with street harassment, Felicia illustrated how intrusive and evaluative men's comments could be. Felicia's experience powerfully demonstrates the extent to which men (both familiar and strangers) trivialize and diminish her experience as insignificant. Her narrative shows how imperative it is to address street harassment with more efficacy and immediacy. Without adequate interventions, street harassment could unfold or escalate into other forms of violence.

Is Talking Back to Men Who Harass a "Dangerous Way of Speaking" or an Empowered, Emboldened Speech Act?

In her article detailing how she felt about street harassment and male harassers in particular, author Michelle Roberson describes a feeling of daring: to go out alone, to talk back to harassers, to refuse or reject offers, and to continue walking away "as he hurled insults at me from behind."[54] She also described a perpetual desire to do the following:

Like I want to hide, disappear, or pray that I don't get sniped by another insult from another man today. But I can't give into fear. The group of women at that discussion group taught me that not only am I not alone, but that I can stand up to harassers on the street. That I can tell a harasser to "Stop Harassing Women! I don't like it, no one likes it" and that he may actually stop harassing me for that moment. And, if enough women tell him this enough times, he may actually stop harassing for good. You see, when a man harasses a man it boosts his ego, but if he doesn't get that satisfaction, if he's met with resistance, he will stop.

If a woman confronts him calmly and loudly and in a matter-of-fact way, he loses the reward of making a woman cower. And if another man overhears his harassment and also confronts him, he loses male approval of his behavior. And, if every time he harasses, he meets loud confrontation, the stakes become too high, the visibility too much of a risk, the humiliation too great. . . . I can't say this approach will subdue every harasser. There may always be the man who will retaliate with insults no matter what you say to him. But afterwards, it feels better to have said something constructive than to have said nothing at all.[55]

Or does it? Is the liberation that Roberson experiences in her direct confrontations with harassers equally freeing to all women who engage in such disruptive discursive speech practices? Does every woman feel similarly empowered and inspired with confidence in the act of talking back to men, particularly in cases like Roberson, where they have insults such as "dumb bitch," "piece of s—t," and likewise hurled at them? Would they take Roberson's advice, and try "not to listen," because like her, they are "too busy feeling broken down"?[56]

In several situations, speaking to men who harass may seem like the least likely (least effective) and most unsafe strategy. How do women assess the "dangerous discourses" produced by men who harass; do women ever participate in their own "dangerous discourses" in their responses to them (such that they escalate the very danger they are attempting to escape in moments of harassment)? Do women targets of street harassment produce their own "dangerous discourses" when they report their experiences, such that they rely on problematic narratives to explain these encounters (of why they, instead of someone else, faced harassment)? Here, I consider how women make determinations about how, when, and to whom they respond to men's street harassment.

Shifting the burden of managing street harassment to women targets of harassment absolves men who harass from that responsibility. The reality of street harassment is that victims are seen as the problem, and expected to solve the problem that is them (themselves). Given that, women must bear this burden by maneuvering around street harassment, in discursive and physical terms.

As women targets of street harassment illustrate, they are precariously positioned in relationship to street harassment. Many women report not knowing how to respond, or worrying about how a male harasser might respond to their own responses. Women also wonder about the impact of their responses. Will talking back provoke a harasser even more, or encourage him to be reflective about and reconsider his harassment? Will keeping quiet incense a harasser or similarly subdue or silence him? Does verbally disrupting harassment begin to diminish its occurrence, or does the next woman harassed pay a higher price for previous targets talking back?

When women have the chance to speak, to voice their stories, and embrace their subjectivities, it creates space for disrupting discourses. Women who talk back to men who harass them may articulate subjectivities that are hegemonically, conventionally or commonly, read as bad, inappropriate, unacceptable, or otherwise not respectable subjectivities or femininities.

Additionally, women who talk back may be read as rebellious, resistant, or otherwise. They may be viewed as asking for trouble. They are frequently held accountable for possibly initiating or further provoking undesirable attention or prompting unpredictable responses from men, ones (men) who escalate or elevate the level of sexual violence, antagonism, or animosity toward these women.

In this way, the woman who talks back to her harasser may be (mis)understood as troublesome, as deviant, as someone who departs from normative expectations regarding public interaction and civility. Perhaps she is naïve or clueless to any number of possible consequences of *her* (re)actions.

The pregnant possibilities of this potential (read: "inevitable" moment) is intended or designed to haunt the woman who talks back, is meant to contain her incitement to speak, is meant to silence her into submission. But does her speech liberate her from the subordination or sexual objectification she feels on the street, in the moments of, or leading up to and/or following encounters of street harassment (particularly if one sees street harassment as a mere expression or extension of the plethora of ways women experience patriarchal and/or racial domination, as well as sexual intimidation, violence, or harassment in other arenas or facets of their life?

At what point or in what instances are women's words, their speech acts or verbal practices, disruptive of the hegemonic discourses that so keenly shape their behavior and that of others? The disruptive potential of women's speech practices appears to stem from an (their) effort to engage and humanize the harasser. Doing so can be seen as an attempt to restore the subjectivities of both the harasser and the woman experiencing the harasser.

Understanding how women engage in discursive strategies requires recognition of the potentially recuperative and/or repressive potential of speaking up or staying silent in social encounters of street harassment. Following feminist scholarship,[57] I recognize the possibility that women choose talking back as a subversive strategy, one that may empower them on the streets and equip them with the tools to negotiate complicated or tenuous situations. This is a point made below, as discussed in an interview between Michelle from the Street Harassment Project and intern Elizabeth Brookbank of *Off Our Backs*:

> In a one-on-one situation though, if you feel like you can confront the harasser, that's great, because every time a woman tells a guy who harasses her that what he's doing is not appropriate behavior that is one step towards him not harassing women anymore. One reason why street harassment is so prevalent is because, for the most part, the men who do this get away with it. And it's not that women are letting it happen, but there is such an intimidation factor that goes along with it that most women feel that all they can do is just walk away or ignore it. But that gives the impression to the sexist mind of the street harasser than he can get away with that behavior.[58]

Brookbank's view is an optimistic, but myopic one, to the degree that street harassment has not appeared to have diminished but rather intensified within rape culture.

Given the persistent *collective* efforts to address interlocking oppressions in this unjust society, the efficacy of individual efforts that challenge harassment can be called into question. Perhaps some combination of both individual and collective efforts will eventually remedy the problem of street harassment, by calling attention to individual harassers, as well as the structures (including rape culture) that support street harassment and street injustice.

Without more empirical evidence about street harassment, it is difficult to determine if the impact of a woman target's confrontation of her harasser produces the immediate effect of stopping (or curbing) his harassment. In fact, it may be the case that a woman target who tells a harasser that his behavior is inappropriate may face amplified or intensified harassment; alternately, the harasser may redirect that verbally assaultive behavior toward other women.

By evaluating the disciplinary mechanisms that operate to control women, including their speech, I examine the emergent trends and patterns in which women engage in verbal strategies of resistance and which do not.[59] Exploring racialized and gendered narratives about who employs such speech practices will complicate notions of speech and silence, and will uncover how both can prove empowering and disempowering in various situations of street harassment.[60]

This work aims to disrupt the notion of women as relatively silent or passive passersby on the street, and suggests instead that women possess the power to resist patriarchy and the oppressive and disciplinary elements of street harassment from men. This goal remains important to me, since much of the literature on street harassment effectively erases the women's subjectivity, which parallels the objectification of street harassment itself.

Highlighting women's agency in their negotiation of street harassment recognizes their subjectivity. Future research could offer nuance to current understandings of women's experiences, in part by attending as much to the playfulness and respectful reciprocity that unfolds in urban spaces, alongside the problematic aspects of power differentials that shape social interactions between strangers.

Such research would carve out space to see the possibility of camaraderie in social interactions on the street between strangers.[61] How might women participate in such interactions as a form of sexual banter or play rather than merely a response to harassment? This shift attends to women's agency, remains sex-positive in approach, and appreciates people's abilities to engage others as a form of self-expression that is not always already limited, curtailed, or inhibited by street harassment.

This creates the space for women who appreciate and enjoy men's sexualized social attention. Women might engage this interaction while inadvertently escalating the attention. Such escalation thereby facilitates or potentially fuels the harassing, sexually objectifying aspects of the social encounter. Thus, it remains important to simultaneously recognize how the same behavior (this attention)—when unwanted and unappreciated—can be considered harassing. It can be seen as an infringement on the rights of the women experiencing this sexualized attention/interaction.

If the hazards of harassment outweigh the pleasures of such attention, the behavior seems more problematic than playful. Clarifying boundaries or establishing the difference can be complicated but a worthwhile endeavor. How women accomplish this amidst their interactions with strangers in urban public spaces remains to be seen.

The comments that women make when talking back to men harassers can seem like "dangerous discourses," because men are so often angered and annoyed by women's resistance. Suggesting that women should *not* talk back to men who harass may prove to be a similarly "dangerous discourse" that denies women their agency and right to spatial justice, including not being harassed. Some women noted that they negotiated street harassment by talking *to* versus talking *back* to men who harass them.

Many women, such as Olivia, recognized some "discourses of danger" as "dangerous discourses" or "dangerous ways of seeing men." She was among several black women respondents who worked to challenge the controlling images embedded in and perpetuated by these narratives. They recognized that these discourses reflect a generalized culture of fear predicated on misinformation. They remained dubious of myths that questionably regarded some groups of people as "threatening."[62] They refused to invest in the "discourses of danger" associated with urban public spaces. Rather, they understood street harassment as specific to men who harass (as opposed to spaces, on the whole, proving "dangerous.")

For Olivia, talking back to street harassment did not prove a dangerous endeavor. However, she did use these encounters as opportunities to engage men with civility, which worked to humanize everyone involved. Doing this also disrupts the controlling image of black women as emasculating, angry, and likewise:

> To me, that's all they're saying. Or one time I gave a dollar to some homeless guy and I walked off and this guy who saw me do that said, "I don't want a dollar; I just want a phone number." [I said], "Hmm, no." And he was like, "Oh well. It don't hurt to try." You know? So, or if someone says something, like, "Speak," or they ask you if you are interested, then I tell them, I tend to say, "No. I'm not interested right now," or I will tell them it's bad timing for me; they tend to take that and respect it. Or I'll tell them—I know that maybe I shouldn't have to do all of that or I'll say that, "I recently got divorced" and "I'm dating somebody." A lot of times I do the, "I'm not emotionally ready for anything" so it's not one guy. . . . and the ones that don't take that for an answer are the ones I take the time out to give them a piece of advice, because then I'll say, "You know, any woman would probably be flattered by that but not right now. You should take the hint. Take the hint!" You know?

Olivia expressed compassion and respect for men who tried to engage women but also recognized that they should respect women's boundaries in such interactions. She and some other black women respondents in particular noted the courage required by men to approach women, even if their approach was misguided (i.e., harassing).

Maintaining a reciprocity and sense of community in public interactions remained more important for some of the black women respondents than the white women in the sample. For example, Mickie, a black middle-class heterosexual woman, reportedly ignored her mother's advice that warned her "not to talk to strangers." She opted instead to offer a simple greeting as a means of being polite.

When men did not come across as "sleazy" to Mickie, then she would usually reciprocate their attention by saying hello, if they initiated such a greeting. She explained, "I at least respond to the hello. . . . If I respond, it depends on my mood. If I'm in a flirtatious mood, I don't care who chats me up, it's only going to go so far. I may not give you my name either."

Mickie's experience exemplifies the kind of agency that women who are harassed may employ in any number of moments. She heeds the maternal warning which cautions her against "stranger danger," yet decides for herself who she responds to in urban public spaces. She also decides how friendly, enthusiastic, or indifferent she may be during the interaction. By attempting to set some parameters for these conversations or interactions, Mickie believes that she exercises some control over the situation, rather than feeling silenced or limited by the interactions.

Another respondent shared her experiences negotiating speech during street harassment. As Olivia explained, she does not want men harassers to feel rejected, so she responds to their advances tactfully. Interestingly, she confirmed that she is simultaneously shutting them out when seemingly engaging them. She accomplished this by not stopping to walk when she engages men who harass her:

> [B]ecause I didn't know that these people could try and grab me or what they would do when you originally tell them, "No." That's giving you—You're giving them a response they don't want, so you don't ever know. So, I just keep going. . . . I think I'm trying to still be nice but I'm also trying to not let them know that they are becoming more of my world in that small, small exchange.

Olivia conveys both her clear awareness of the potential threat that harassers pose, but she also makes sure that she displays respectable femininity, by recognizing the humanity of the men (and women) who harass her.

Though she does not get overly involved in the interactions (as a self-protective mechanism), she made efforts to recognize the men who harassed her as desiring attention, and often being misguided, or hopeful even, in their verbal entanglements. While she did not condone this behavior, she did not condemn it. She felt this strategy actually minimized the potential dangers of engagement, because she remained respectful and courteous (another posture that disrupts controlling images of black women) of her harassers.

By politely engaging men who harass, Olivia endorses and embodies gender expectations regarding niceness and care of others; (the racial kinship that seems to exist with black men who harass allows her to respond to them civilly, but not fully engaged). The street etiquette that Olivia expresses stems from childhood lessons about kindness and consideration of others' feelings, arguably a gendered (feminine) lesson.

Transferring that kindness from one space and time to another allows Olivia, by her accounts, to navigate urban public spaces in ways that minimize danger. She is arguably able to see men who harass her as people "in search of respect"[63] but also as potentially dangerous given their harassment (not on the basis of color or perceived race, for example). She does not construct particular men or places as dangerous, but rather understands situations as potentially dangerous in that the interactions could escalate to create harm for her.

By refusing to see men harassers through the lens of controlling images, she complicates the narratives about men who harass. On the one hand, these men harass, yet they receive her respectful attention. On the other hand, she is careful not to share (or care) too much, though she strategically shares just enough to be self-protective, in her estimation.

We could interpret Olivia's kindness and caring as emotional labor that protects a "good girl" image. Conversely, her talking back to men harassers could convey a "bad girl" one. These are not mutually exclusive options. Further, they nuance collective understandings about black girls and women, who tend to be stereotypically viewed as loud, angry, boisterous, and so forth. Scholars contend that "loudness is associated with badness, but for African-American girls who are loud, it means presence. The paradox for African-American girls is that the louder they are, the more visible, yet the more they risk being seen as bad, wild, unruly, or simply unacceptable."[64] For many black girls and women, "loudness is a way of taking up space and garnering attention." It is a form of resistance, a way of countering invisibility and managing hypervisibility. Being loud proves self-protective, as it is equivocated with men, "being pushy," "taking up space, and making oneself known."[65]

Black girls and women have to contend with how to perform femininity in ways that limit *and* liberate them.[66] While "[c]ursing and loudness are associated with being lower class,"[67] speech and silence differ for black women than women of other racial groups:

> [Loudness is] associated with telling the truth. It also speaks of a lack of division between private and public life. On the one hand, it has been true historically that people who have less power have less privacy from those who do have the power. On the other hand, loudness and telling it like it is are seen by those who cultivate a more private life as a lack of class or restraint. What people forget is that those who have the luxury of cultivating a private life can do so without fearing that their beliefs, their visions, their opinions will go unheard, because these opinions already are preserved in the dominant society. For other girls, being good means suppressing disagreements; the louder one disagrees with what's going on, the harder it is to be viewed as good.[68]

When girls speak their mind, they "disrupt the boundaries between private and public lives, private and public speech."[69] Truth-telling, without much "regard for the consequences"[70] illustrates a way women talk back and challenge institutional impulses to silence them.

Yet, *how* women use their voice and/or silence can resist or reproduce gendered and raced stereotypes or controlling images of them. I discuss in more depth, in the following chapter, the dilemmas of deciding between speech and silence for women targets of street harassment. These choices are fraught with broader frameworks of voice, visibility, and vulnerability.

According to researchers, some black girls learn to be loud (versus "naturally" are) in order to be seen, to announce, "'I am here and I will not be made invisible.'"[71] This demand for visibility and recognition, on their own terms, contests the ways that black women are (not) seen. As previously discussed, the media perpetuates problematic controlling images of black women; so, too, do they sometimes participate in the problematic ways of seeing black women.

The impact of racist, sexist images and the perceptions that people generally form (from these images) of black women may arguably "increase their vulnerability to harassment."[72] Much like black women, other groups of women of color have been constructed in the media as "desiring" such attention. For example, "Hispanic women have been described as hot-blooded, ill-tempered, religious, overweight, lazy, always pregnant, loudmouthed, and deferential to men. Native American women are perceived as poor, sad, uneducated, isolated, and devoted to male elders. Asian women have been described as small, docile, and submissive. However, they are also viewed by some as exotic sexpots who will cater to the whims of any man."[73]

Black women have been perceived as domineering, having low morals, highly sexed, heads of households, and "loose." "Sexual harassers tend to take advantage of those whom they perceive as most vulnerable, and whether we care to face it or not, black women enflesh the vulnerability of their people's slave past."[74] While this may be true to some extent, I also want to acknowledge the way that some black women can transform vulnerability (or being seen as vulnerable and then potentially victimized) into strength. This is not to solidify the stereotype of "strong" black women but to recognize the ways that women made to feel vulnerable, historically and contemporarily, have agency.

Arguably, all women and their bodies are generally constructed as vulnerable and victimizable. Women are always already victims in a rape culture, given the construction of women's bodies as weak, docile, or dominated in this patriarchy. Beyond this recognition of all women's bodies as vulnerable then, we must consider the contradictions of this vulnerability by asking what contributes to or complicates this vulnerability.

Certainly, while black women embody vulnerability in relation to slavery and sexual exploitation (among other forms), they have also resisted and endured many forms of exploitation. White women have had to confront society's sexualization and objectification as well, but with the advantage of white privilege attached to their bodies.

Thus, we can understand the negotiations that women make during street harassment as one where they can contest this construction of vulnerability. Street harassment then serves as an illustration of the ways power operates, such that the harasser attempts to assert control over both individual and collective bodies (as representative of a group, in the latter case). Patriarchal ideology guides much of the desire men harassers have to control women's bodies, where discourses discipline (indirectly, instead or as an extension of the men).

Much like "fighting back is a matter of survival,"[75] so, too, is talking back. For Olivia, talking back is not so much about "loudness," as it is a strategy to talk to harassers, to equalize the engage, and diffuse any tensions from palpable power differentials. If loudness ensures one's visibility, then verbally engaging harassers might draw attention to social interactions (so there is an audience or witnesses); in situations that might otherwise put Olivia in some danger, she might boost her safety by talking back.

However, evidence exists to suggest that people do not always intervene when they observe others in dangerous or threatening situations. Thus, Olivia's decisions to respond to harassers may align with the view that women who talk back are "bad" (and thus, "deserved" to be harassed in the first place. Such a view must be challenged in order for the criticism to land in the appropriate place, where men who harass (not their targets) are held accountable for street harassment.

One can interpret her responses to men who harass her as interventions. However, one can also recognize the great potential they hold in agitating harassers who may be angered or worse, enraged, by her pointed and critical remarks. Olivia noted that if men harassers use offensive public speech with her, then she draws the line, refusing to "entertain anything they have to say."

Despite the boundaries that she attempts to maintain with them, Olivia noted how men violate or intrude upon women's personal space, gesturing an impending touch, or feigning it altogether, then denying these efforts, as a way of getting women's attention:

> But they won't touch you, but, and then they'll tell you, "Oh, I wasn't trying to touch you, I was just trying to get your attention." "Hmmm, don't reach out for me, because that's scary." Um, and I don't entertain anything they have to say. If the first thing they say is, "Where's your n— at? I really, I really don't . . . and depending on my mood, I may very well say, "I have no idea because I don't date n—s." And then I tend to go into that whole political spell that they really don't want to hear, and then they tend to walk off.

Olivia noted retracting or coiling in from this offensive public speech, and purposefully changing the course of her path in public afterward. Sometimes, the men harassers apologize, saying, "'I wasn't trying to touch you. I'm sorry, I didn't mean to scare you.'"

Upon realizing that the women have interpreted their attempt to touch horrifying, the men offer disingenuous apologies to the women, possibly to appear considerate of the women's feelings, even after provoking the women in a negative way in the first place. The men often mistakenly assert their male privilege and find that many women have different triggers that provoke certain rejecting reactions and adverse consequences for the men who have intentionally crossed that line of comfortable social distance between themselves and the women they attempt to entangle.

This moment of transgression highlights some productive tensions that could prove dangerous, if the harasser took it poorly. The productive tensions make space for Olivia to assert her respectability, but also to challenge pejorative language of black people (men, in this case). This moment is quite instructive, for if the harasser wants to see himself as someone Olivia will consider, he certainly cannot be the "n-word." He may realize she will not entertain his advances, since he has collapsed all black men under that umbrella.

That she confronts his use of arguably offensive language is dangerous but delightful. She has created a consciousness-raising moment that invites him to do the following: 1) contemplate his approach to her, 2) (re)consider his perception of himself and other black men (and the men he presumes her to date), and 3) his presumption of her favorable response (which was *not* inevitable).

This example shows that women who encounter street harassment might engage *with* dangerous discourses (the use of the n-word to refer to black people), and *produce* potentially dangerous discourses (by not only talking back, but also challenging language use *and* rejecting his advances). Her engagement with strangers who harass her could perpetuate the idea of black women as promiscuous or easy, since she is responding to strangers (read: women are not *supposed* to do that). Her engagement as *confrontation* could perpetuate the controlling image of black women as emasculating: "The matriarch represents the sexually aggressive woman, one who emasculates Black men because she will not permit them to assume roles as Black patriarchs. She refuses to be passive and thus is stigmatized."[76]

Ironically, the danger in disrupting the notion that one is passive, can be dehumanized or objectified, or seen as for others' pleasure, is that it challenges patriarchy and hegemonic masculinity, even marginalized masculinity (in some cases, where she is harassed by homeless black men, for instance) (not just that she is challenging the actual specific person). Alternately, the benefit of disrupting the notion that one is passive is that women who "talk back" can show that they, too, are in search of respect.

One final example of the ways women who face street harassment struggle with their own responses and strategies for negotiating these interactions comes from Red. During our interview-conversation, I asked her, "Is there an effective way to respond without being nasty?" She cleverly confessed, "Um, I'm pretty sure there is; I just haven't found it."

With that, we laughed, almost in mutual agreement that confronting street remarks and harassment marks a constant negotiation. It is one that we must maneuver delicately and strategically. Since the outcome of these encounters are hard to anticipate (i.e., whether a man's attention will escalate into some unwieldy expression of anger, animosity, or likewise), it is similarly difficult to anticipate responses that are "best practices."

CONCLUSIONS

While talking back has often been described as having liberatory potential and proves resistant to patriarchal domination and silencing effects,[77] talking back also remains quite risky, given the extent to which street harassment is still not recognized as a social problem, and no formal legal protections exist for targets of street harassment.

The women's effort to engage and talk to versus talk back to men seem admirable, in the context of this lacking legal and social protection. The various strategies and interpretations that targets of street harassment share help illuminate how much of a problem street harassment potentially and actually is, and reminds us of the "dangerous ways of speaking" that both target and perpetrator of street harassment produce. In the final substantive chapter, I consider "dangerous ways of looking" during street harassment.

NOTES

1. Jill McLean Taylor, Carol Gilligan, and Amy M. Sullivan. *Between Voice and Silence: Women and Girls, Race and Relationship.* Cambridge, MA: Harvard, 1995: 131.

2. Jill McLean Taylor, Carol Gilligan, and Amy M. Sullivan. 1995: 132.

3. Jill McLean Taylor, Carol Gilligan, and Amy M. Sullivan. 1995: 162.

4. Jill McLean, Carol Gilligan, and Amy M. Sullivan. 1995: 172.

5. Jill McLean Taylor, Carol Gilligan, and Amy M. Sullivan. 1995: 172.

6. See Brené Brown, *Daring Greatly: How the Courage to Be Vulnerable Transforms the Way We Live, Love, Parent, and Lead.* New York: Avery, 2015

7. See Judith Butler. *Precarious Life: The Powers of Mourning and Violence.* New York: Verso, 2006.

8. Jill McLean Taylor, Carol Gilligan, and Amy M. Sullivan. 1995.

9. Jean Baker Miller. *Toward a New Psychology of Women (2nd Ed.).* Boston: Beacon Press, 2012.

10. Jill McLean Talyor, Carol Gilligan, and Amy M. Sullivan. 1995: 154.

11. Joanne Smith, Meghan Huppuch, and Mandy Van Deven. *Hey Shorty! A Guide to Combating Sexual Harassment and Violence in Schools and on the Street.* New York: The Feminist Press at CUNY, 2011.

12. Nikki Jones. *Between Good and Ghetto: African American Girls and Inner-City Violence.* Piscataway, NJ: Rutgers University Press, 2008.

13. See Joanne Smith, Meghan Huppuch, and Mandy Van Deven. 2011.

14. GGE discuss the frequency of sexual harassment, and I find this question limited in its sensitivity and insight. Sometimes, a person can have infrequent yet traumatizing experiences with street harassment, or have milder but more common experiences with street harassment. Rather than be tempted to rank oppressions, I find it more powerful to demonstrate the wide range of experiences with, and responses to, street harassment. . . . In *Between Voice and Silence*, Taylor, Gilligan, and Sullivan (1995: 128) observe, "The interview process also demonstrated one of the most important benefits of speaking with and listening to girls in this way: it can help girls to develop, to hold on to, or to recover knowledge about themselves, their feelings, and their desires. Taking girls seriously encourages them to take their own thoughts, feelings, and experience seriously, to maintain this knowledge, and even to uncover knowledge that has become lost to them."

15. See Melissa Harris-Perry. *Sister Citizen: Shame, Stereotypes, and Black Women in America.* New Haven, CT: Yale University Press, 2011.

16. Sara Mills. *Discourse.* New York: Routledge, 1997.

17. Melissa Wright. "The Private Parts of Public Value: The Regulation of Women Workers in China's Export-Processing Zones" in *Going Public: Feminism and the Shifting Boundaries of the Private Sphere.* Edited by Joan W. Scott and Debra Keates. Pp. 99–120. Urbana Champaign: University of Illinois Press, 2005; Rosa-Linda Fregoso. "Toward a Planetary Civil Society" in *Mexicana Encounters: The Making of Social Identities on the Borderlands.* Edited by Rosa-Linda Fregoso. Pp. 1–29. Berkeley, CA: University of California Press, 2003a; Diana Taylor. *Disappearing Acts: Spectacles of Gender and Nationalism in Argentina's "Dirty War."* Durham, NC: Duke University Press, 1997.

18. Sara Mills. *Discourse.* New York: Routledge, 1997: 13.

19. Sara Mills. *Discourse.* New York: Routledge, 1997: 17–18.

20. As an aside, the "silence of violence" I discussed in an earlier chapter also reveals the generalized silence or collective refusal to speak about violence in this society. This silence of violence, as a dangerous discourse, connects to gender discourses, to complicate notions of speech and silence as it relates to women and men.

21. Audre Lorde. *The Cancer Journals.* San Francisco: Aunt Lute, 1980: 40–41.

22. Audre Lorde. 1980: 41.

23. Audre Lorde. 1980: 41.

24. Charlotte Pierce-Baker. *Surviving the Silence: Black Women's Stories of Rape.* New York: W.W. Norton and Company, 1998.

25. Jill McLean Taylor, Carol Gilligan, and Amy M. Sullivan. *Between Voice and Silence: Women and Girls, Race and Relationship.* Cambridge, MA: Harvard, 1995: 100.

26. The Latina Feminist Group. *Telling to Live: Latina Feminist Testimonios.* Durham, NC: Duke University Press, 2001.

27. Charlotte Pierce-Baker. 1998: 260.

28. See Danielle McGuire. 2011: 72.

29. Charlotte Pierce-Baker. 1998: 268.

30. Charlotte Pierce-Baker. 1998: 270.

31. Brené Brown. *The Gifts of Imperfection: Letting Go of Who You Think You're Supposed to Be and Embrace Who You Are.* Center City, MN: Hazelden, 2010.

32. Laura Gray-Rosendale. *College Girl.* Albany, NY: SUNY Press, 2013.

33. Laura Gray Rosendale, Invited Talk. March 2014.

34. Rosario Castellanos. "Language as an Instrument of Domination" in *Women Writing Resistance: Essays on Latin America and the Caribbean.* Edited by Jennifer Browdy de Hernandez. Pp. 73–78. Cambridge, MA: South End Press, 2003: 75.

35. Dorothy Allison. *Two or Three Things I Know for Sure.* New York: Plume, 1995: 268.

36. Sharon Lamb. *The Secret Lives of Girls: What Good Girls Really Do—Sex Play, Aggression, and Their Guilt.* New York: Free Press, 2002.

37. Sharon Lamb. 2002.

38. Mitch Duneier and Harvey Molotch. "Talking City Trouble: Explorations" in *Gender, Media, and Public Space.* Cresskill, NJ: Hampton Press, Inc., 1999.

39. Elijah Anderson. *Code of the Street: Decency, Violence, and the Moral Life of the Inner City.* New York: W.W. Norton, 1999.

40. Sut Jhally. *The Codes of Gender: Identity and Performance in Popular Culture.* Videorecording, 2008.

41. Patricia Hill Collins. *Black Sexual Politics: African Americans, Gender, and the New Racism.* New York: Routledge, 2005.

42. Chandran Reddy. *Freedom with Violence: Race, Sexuality, and the US State.* Durham, NC: Duke University Press, 2011.

43. Chandran Reddy. 2011: 110.

44. Chandran Reddy. 2011: 112.

45. Jennifer Browdy de Hernandez. *Women Writing Resistance: Essays on Latin America and the Caribbean.* Cambridge, MA: South End Press, 2003.

46. Chandran Reddy. 2011: 111.

47. Elijah Anderson. *Streetwise: Race, Class, and Change in an Urban Community.* Chicago: University of Chicago Press, 1992.

48. Meda Chesney-Lind and Nikki Jones (Eds.). *Fighting for Girls: New Perspectives on Gender and Violence.* Albany, NY: SUNY, 2010.

49. Carol Brooks Gardner. *Passing By: Gender and Public Harassment.* Berkeley, CA: University of California Press, 1995.

50. Patricia Hill Collins. *Black Sexual Politics: African Americans, Gender, and the New Racism*. New York: Routledge, 2005.

51. Betsy Lucal. "What It Means to Be Gendered Me: Life on the Boundaries of a Dichotomous Gender System." *Gender and Society 13(6)*: 781–797, 1999.

52. Jessica Valenti. "Purely Rape: The Myth of Sexual Purity and How It Reinforces Rape Culture." In *Yes Means Yes!*, 2008: 299–304.

53. Betsy Lucal. "What It Means to Be Gendered Me: Life on the Boundaries of a Dichotomous Gender System." *Gender and Society 13(6)*: 781–797, 1999; Maggie Hadleigh-West. *War Zone*. Video recording. A Film Fatale, Inc./Hank Levine Film. Northampton, MA: GmbH Production, 1998.

54. Amaya Naomi Roberson. "Homeland Insecurity: The Terror of Street Harassment" in *Off Our Backs*. July-August 2003: 66–68, 2003: 66.

55. Amaya Naomi Roberson. 2003: 68.

56. Amaya Naomi Roberson. 2003: 67.

57. See bell hooks. *Talking Back: Thinking Feminist, Thinking Black (2nd Ed.)*. New York: Routledge; Linda Martin Alcoff and Laura Gray. "Survivor Discourse: Transgression or Recuperation" in *Signs: Journal of Women in Culture and Society 18(2)*: 260–290, 1993.

58. Elizabeth Brookbank. "Talking Back: Women in New York City Confront Street Harassment." Interview with Michele from the Street Harassment Project. *Off Our Backs*. September-October 2002: 22.

59. Michel Foucault. *Discipline and Punish: The Birth of the Prison*. Translated from the French by Alan Sheridan. New York: Vintage Books, 1977.

60. Linda Martin Alcoff and Laura Gray. "Survivor Discourse: Transgression or Recuperation" in *Signs: Journal of Women in Culture and Society 18(2)*: 260–290, 1993; Ann Cvetkovich. *An Archive of Feeling: Trauma, Sexuality, and Lesbian Public Cultures*. Durham, NC: Duke University Press, 2003; Michel Foucault. 1977.

61. Kari Lerum. "Sexuality, Power, and Camaraderie in Service Work." *Gender and Society 18(6)*: 756–77, 2004.

62. Angela Davis. *Women, Race, and Class*. New York: Random House, 1981; Mitch Duneier and Harvey Molotch. "Talking City Trouble: Explorations" in *Gender, Media, and Public Space*. Cresskill, NJ: Hampton Press, Inc., 1999.

63. Phillippe Bourgois. *In Search of Respect: Selling Crack in El Barrio*. Cambridge, MA: Cambridge University Press, 1995.

64. Sharon Lamb. *The Secret Lives of Girls: What Good Girls Really Do—Sex Play, Aggression, and Their Guilt*. New York: Free Press, 2002: 206–7.

65. Sharon Lamb. 2002: 206–7.

66. Sharon Lamb. 2002.

67. Sharon Lamb. 2002: 204.

68. Sharon Lamb. 2002: 205.

69. Sharon Lamb. 2002: 205.

70. Sharon Lamb. 2002: 205.

71. Sharon Lamb. 2002: 205.

72. Darlene C. DeFour. "The Interface of Racism and Sexism on College Campuses" in Michele Paludi's *Sexual Harassment on College Campuses: Abusing the Ivory Power.* Pp. 49–55. Albany, NY: State University of New York Press, 1996: 50.

73. See Tara E. Kent. "The Confluence of Race and Gender in Women's Sexual Harassment Experiences" in *Gender Violence: Interdisciplinary Perspectives (2nd Ed.)*. Edited by Laura O'Toole, Jessica Schiffman, and Margie Kiter Edwards. New York: NYU Press, 2007: 177.

74. Rosemarie Tong. *Feminist Thought.* New York: Routledge, 2017: 165.

75. Sharon Lamb. *The Secret Lives of Girls: What Good Girls Really Do—Sex Play, Aggression, and Their Guilt.* New York: Free Press, 2002.

76. Patricia Hill Collins. *Black Feminist Thought: Knowledge, Consciousness, and the Politics of Empowerment.* New York: Routledge, 2008: 79.

77. See bell hooks. *Talking Back: Thinking Feminist, Thinking Black (2nd Ed)*. New York: Routledge.

Chapter 6

"Dangerous Ways of Looking"

THE RIGHT TO LOOK V. THE RIGHT
NOT TO BE LOOKED AT?

Throughout history, people have attempted to regulate and legislate the gaze across time and space. Amidst the power asymmetrical terrain of a hierarchical society, and the pleasure of shared recognition of humanity, people negotiate "right to look."[1] A danger resides in looking, and has resulted in dire consequences, depending on the social location of the observer.

For example, the concept of "reckless eyeballing" speaks to the cultural anxieties that white men had regarding the black male gaze. White men attempted to control white women under the guise of protection. They policed black men who so much as looked at white women, in real and imagined ways.

Take, for example, the case of Carolyn Bryant Donham and the lynching of Emmett Till. Donham's name is less familiar to the public than the 14-year-old black boy whom she alleged "grabbed her and was menacing and sexually crude toward her." In a recent *New York Times* article, Donham admitted, "[T]hat part is not true."[2] As a result of her accusations, Till's young life came to an abrupt, murderous end, while Donham continued to live, in relative obscurity.

The gaze proved so powerful as to potentially result in death. Arguably, the black male gaze is no longer policed to the same degree of harshness; for black men, there is ostensibly more "freedom" to look. This freedom approximates that which white men have enjoyed for centuries. What these men may experience as a form of visual pleasure and liberation could simultaneously be experienced as oppression for the women being looked at. That one person's liberation is another person's oppression remains relevant throughout this work.

This chapter updates the historical penalties assigned to people who engaged in "dangerous ways of looking." The title of the chapter offers a double entendre, to grapple with the "ways of looking" in terms of the gaze (looking/watching/observing), and in terms of appearance (clothing, behavior). I explore the impact of the gaze, to extend the discussion on dangerous ways of (speaking, seeing, and now looking). The power of the gaze lies in looking and being looked at. There is something powerful about inviting the gaze and enjoying it. Alternately, there is something troublesome in not inviting gaze or enjoying being looked at, and not knowing how to deflect attention or avert the gaze.

In this chapter, I consider the blurred lines between the visual pleasure experienced by the harasser and potentially "provoked" by the target of harassment (not as a matter of fault, but as a matter of "fact" that someone might provoke attention, and then receive it, as different from getting attention and getting harassed. To be clear, women do not deserve to be harassed, no matter the way they look. I also continue to discuss dimensions of "danger" in looking: by exploring the discourses that women produce about how men look at them *feels* dangerous; how women look to provoke danger (harassment), and how women look (actively) at, not to, others (a looking back, alongside talking back).

Throughout history, women had to negotiate "dangerous ways of looking," or as one woman reported having men's eyes "all over her"; historian Danielle McGuire refers to the term, "eye rape," noting, "Although the charge of 'eye rape' seemed utterly absurd, it was deadly serious."[3] McGuire's discussion of sexual violence and its curious invisibility throughout history, particularly with regard to black women, suggests that dangerous ways of looking persist to the present.

Terms like "eye rape" illustrate the various ways women could be objectified and viewed through the scrutinizing and sexualizing male gaze. In historical and contemporary society, one can observe how women's "bodies were not their own."[4] For women experiencing street harassment, many of them described similar sentiments.

Women who felt the weight of the male gaze lamented that they could not deflect attention or impede the male gaze. Some women noted the feeling that "reckless eyeballing" created for them. Others expressed frustration at being looked at without profit. They joked (perhaps seriously) about the commodification of their objectification, arguing that they should be paid to be looked at, in the ways that some men harassers visually consumed them. Their comments raised interesting questions about the power differentials and unevenness in street harassment.

They illustrate the many "dangerous ways of looking," in terms of the following: 1) appearing in public and having that appearance generate attention (despite any intention to do so or not), 2) looking at women through the eyes of men harassers, in ways that reproduce the power asymmetries of the male gaze, perpetuate notions of women as sexual objects or objects of visual pleasure for men, and 3) looking at harassers through the lens of controlling images (that solidify stereotypes versus disrupt them to recognize men as people) as a means of acknowledging the limiting and "dangerous ways of looking" at various groups of people, including "victims" and "harassers." I could talk here about the vulnerable, troublesome bodies??

The purpose of exploring "dangerous ways of looking" relates to how people are seen and not seen, how people assert the "right to look" in an historical moment that does not police "reckless eyeballing" in the same way as decades past, and how people are mis/perceived as "inviting the gaze" or "asking for attention" in punitive ways.

This chapter acknowledges the power of looking, but also the pleasure of looking, and attempts to complicate the narrative of the gaze in the context of street harassment. This involves, as stated earlier, an examination of the ways groups of people are constructed and disciplined through controlling images, or in other words, how these images constitute "dangerous ways of looking" or seeing various social groups.

Dealing with Surveillance, Serving as a Spectacle

When women report experiences with street harassment, they often discuss and describe the various ways they become objects that men who harass them view through the male gaze. Under the surveillance of street harassment, where men offer evaluative comments, and unsolicited feedback on women's appearance and attractiveness to the men harasser(s), women frequently face the social pressure of serving as a spectacle.

As men harassers look at women, the women targets feel, to varying degrees, the impact of these "dangerous ways of looking." The male gaze (from men who harass) feels dangerous to many women; many of them already feel a kind of vulnerability in facing men's harassing comments and verbal assaults, much less the scrutiny of surveillance among men who harass.

The male gaze compounds or "complements" the verbal component of harassment, adding insult to injury in these moments of "interactional vandalism." That is, as women may face being evaluated on their appearance and attractiveness, they may also have to endure the "eye rape" that McGuire and others reference in their respective research. What does it mean to be visually consumed while being verbally assaulted during street harassment? How do women feel about this and how do they respond?

The Perils and Pleasures of Looking

At times, street harassment seems to hold both pain and pleasure in the balance. What proves pleasurable for some (harassers) is often painful for those who discontentedly fall under the surveillance of the gaze. The idea of "scopophilia," or visual pleasure, is advanced by Laura Mulvey, as she examines the male gaze in the context of cinema.[5] The concept easily extends beyond the realm of the cinematic to apply to alternate settings, including public spaces. Mulvey posits, "There are circumstances in which looking itself is a source of pleasure, just as, in the reverse formation, there is pleasure in being looked at."[6] Contestations of this point can be found among some of the respondents in my sample, who found little pleasure in the way men harassers looked at them.

Here is an excerpt from my interview conversation with one of my respondents, Samantha (introduced in chapter 1):

> Samantha: "I'm really picky about people looking at me funny, or looking at me, period. If I don't want someone looking at me, then they damn well better not look at me."
> Author: "How do you block that gaze then?"
> Samantha: "Um, I'm not successful at it usually because if I'm out on the street, if I'm talking on [the street], it's kinda hard to hide. I just walk faster . . . I've had two main kinds of street harassment: one is they're hitting on me and two, they see me with a black partner and harass me because of that."

Despite her desire to reject or avoid when "someone is invading my space verbally or visually," Samantha was unsuccessful at countering these men harassers' "dangerous ways of looking." In contemporary society, the consequences to these ways of looking are arguably much less severe, in contrast to the high price black men paid in the past for (allegedly or actually) looking at white women. Historically, black men potentially risked their lives by looking.[7]

Samantha's comments draw attention to the hegemonic, or dominant, performance of masculinity, whereby the "codes of gender" generally require men to take up space. By extension, men learn to invade space. This invasion is evidenced in a bodily way, but also geographically, socially, politically, and visually. Men who harass prove to be "verbally and visually" invasive, taking up space of their own, as well as that of others, especially women. The men who harass may work to create "dangerous ways of looking" themselves—appearing to be tough, menacing, threatening, and hypermasculine.

That Samantha does not desire to have her space invaded visually or verbally by men strangers reveals the dilemma for women who cannot make themselves any less visible to the unwanted attention directed at them by men. Her comments also draw our attention to the ways women are often objectified and commodified, involuntarily serving as a source of visual pleasure for others. This suggests that for women, there may be many "dangerous ways of looking." Women's appearance is frequently viewed as a provocation and an invitation, as opposed to creative expression, or simply, a practical decision to wear clothes. Being seen as provoking attention captures the way that women are held to account for men's reaction to them, rather than the reverse. In this way, "dangerous ways of looking" often prove problematic, pleasurable, or both.

As Samantha falls under the gaze of harassers, she notes different ways that she provokes attention. For some, her presence in public with her black partner proves potentially dangerous. That she describes being harassed because of her interracial relationship provides evidence of the historical residue of racism and sexism that regulated interracial relationships in the past, and continues to do so, albeit differently, in the present.

Samantha's interracial relationship, evidence of "love's revolution,"[8] serves as something of a spectacle, and appears to invite the gaze, in arguably less hostile or violent ways than has historically been the case. What was once a "dangerous way of looking" between black men and white women is now observed, and not necessarily negatively, by others (people outside of the couple).

The men who harass her because of her interracial relationship, or perhaps due to some interest in her, show contrasting reactions: they are engaging in ways of looking that some find socially offensive, but not legally so; they are also simultaneously expressing dis/interest in her, maybe even disgust, as she challenges the legacy of dangerous ways of looking. That is, Samantha stands in pride as a part of an interracial couple. She is aware of the aforementioned history and tensions between white women and black men.

Since street harassment is not regulated, it links to Samantha's frustration at being looked at by men harassers and not being able to do much about it. Notably, the lack of regulation around these "dangerous ways of looking" link to "dangerous ways of speaking," in shoring up the privileges and benefits of doing so disproportionately for men harassers than the women targets. While women targets of harassment employ dangerous ways of doing both (looking and speaking), they arguably risk far more in this process; they have far graver, and more dangerous, penalties or consequences, including intensified harassment, increased or alternate forms of violence, or worse, death.[9]

A more liberated version of reality would encourage mutually respectful, not dangerous, ways of looking and speaking, such that people in urban public spaces could choose to interact with one another in civil and enjoyable ways. Instead, the persistence of social inequities plays out in social interactions and in society in general. For example, McGuire makes a point of discussing the history of violence in the mid-1900s, illustrating much the way Joy James does (see below), the curiously shifting visibility or invisibility of violence, contingent on the construction or perception of the criminal actors and targets.

In general, white male privilege offers protection to white men (and white women by proxy), even or especially as perpetrators of violent crimes. At the same time, white men failed or refused to protect black women. Furthermore, the former often denied or prohibited black men from protecting their loved ones (black women and children) from specific kinds of violence. White men often punished black men by denying them the ability to protect black women. Much of these tensions fueled the fight for civil rights and social justice. The violence that permeated particular parts of the country became a central point of agitation and then organization of the Civil Rights Era and black women's liberation movement.

Joy James discusses the disproportionate amount of sexual violence committed by white men, and the way this statistical reality disrupts myths or controlling images about who has or receives "dangerous ways of looking":

> Today's statistics are illuminating. Currently, the FBI reports that more than 90 percent of rapes are intraracial; in interracial rape cases, the percentage of white male assaults on black women exceeds that of black male assaults on white women. One hundred years ago, the percentage of black male assaults on white women was even lower, given the racial segregation and the social restrictions on white women. While the percentage of white male assaults on black women was higher (as black women worked as domestic servants in white homes), white males had virtual immunity—as the caste that adjudicated, legislated, and enforced the laws—from prosecution for sexual violence against black women and near immunity from attacks on their female family members or on white women of the lower classes.[10]

Both James and McGuire highlight the illegibility of violence in ways that echo Nielsen's point, that society chooses to ignore some forms of violence, like offensive public speech. The differential and selective attention to violence illustrates whose bodies are considered threatening or vulnerable, disposable or valuable. Attention to alleged crimes has justified violence, while inattention to other forms of violence has allowed them to persist. Both approaches enable violence, and explain how dangerous *not* looking at violence can be; not looking or looking away from violence facilitates its presence in society. *Not* looking at violence may be just another "dangerous way of looking" at street harassment; in denying or pretending the problem does not exist, it injures real victims of such harassment and harm.

Street harassment not only sweeps women targets up into conversations—or verbal entanglements—they typically prefer not to have with harassers. It also pulls women into *visual* entanglements with men harassers. In noting that she does not desire men strangers invading her space, Samantha demonstrates her displeasure at the visually consuming, predatory, and/or rapacious feel of the male gaze of men harassers. Other respondents shared similar sentiments, expressing the lack of bodily autonomy they felt in the face of such scopophilia. Rather, they felt the persistent male gaze steadily compromised the degree to which they could experience bodily autonomy more fully and freely.

Samantha and others lamented their inability at, or the impossibility of, controlling the gaze of men harassers. This points to the ways street harassment controls women socially, through discourses of harassment (as another kind of dangerous discourse), as well as the always already "to-be-looked-at"-ness of women in public spaces.[11] Street harassment attempts to socially control women by dissuading them from engaging in "dangerous ways of speaking" during social interactions with men who harass. Street harassment intends to socially control women's presence (and absence) in society.

When the "dangerous discourses" produced by men harassers during street harassment dissuade women from entering public spaces. When women otherwise minimize their presence in public, street harassment operates as a controlling mechanism. It also makes a spectacle out of women who may wish to reject the surveillance and scrutiny of street harassment but may not know how to do so safely and effectively.

This complicates the idea of visual pleasure as a double-edged sword.[12] Scholars acknowledge and accommodate the possibility that people can enjoy being looked at, but what happens when they do not? What happens when these potential visual pleasures turn violent? What becomes of visual pleasure when it becomes a "dangerous way of looking" or being looked at?

Red, a middle-class bisexual black woman, shared experiences that partially address and answer the above questions. She noted the many ways that men attempt to harass her, including the following: whistling at her, honking a car horn, or "trying to get your attention by any means, whether it's a, 'Psst, psst,' or 'Hey, hey!'" Her description of street harassment exposes the imposition and insistence of such social behavior.

Several study participants expressed similar views, noting how men harassers prove an imposition or invasion. These terms reveal the ways that street harassment operates on a spectrum that normalizes rapacious behavior and how harassers attempt to colonize and control women's bodies. Men who harass may engage in behavior that denies women their subjectivity; harassment reflects any target being denied the ability to consent to the interaction. Admittedly, "consenting to harassment" is a paradoxical term. Yet, it gestures at the need for more public education around ways to engage in civil attention, or interactions that are benign or benevolent, pleasant even, as opposed to harmful, by way of intent and/or impact.

The efforts that currently support and facilitate this public education includes various websites devoted to sharing information about street harassment and its discontents. Existing and emergent grassroots efforts to document street harassment indicate that some people are recognizing, and attending to, the problem of street harassment. While the technology helps people visualize the geographies or web of violence, does it challenge the problem or create new ones? I turn next to explore this and other questions, such as this: "Is the technological surveillance connected to street harassment a 'dangerous way of looking'?"

The Technological Gaze: Dangerous Ways of Looking?

In an effort to document how extensively society weaves the web of violence, various technological interventions have been offered up or created for the purpose of graphically capturing these geographies of violence. As increasingly grassroots efforts continue to emerge, important questions also emerge about the efficacy of these technologies. For example, websites such as "Hollaback" and "Stop Street Harassment" exist to offer support for women who have experienced street harassment.[13] On the former website, targets or victims of street harassment are encouraged to take pictures of their harasser(s). Documenting the person who street harasses presumably operates in a "to catch a thief" (or criminal) sort of way; the photo could read like a preliminary mug shot of sorts.

While some might consider this approach an empowering move for women targets of street harassment, I find it worrisome on a few levels. The posting of pictures diverts or redirects the surveillance of women targets of harassment to men who harass. This may allow some women to appropriate the male gaze or employ the technological gaze (through smartphones, cameras, or similar devices) for their own potential empowerment. However, is making a spectacle of men who harass a way of "dismantling the master's house with the master's tools" or is it simply building new ones?

Because the technological gaze replicates the power of the male gaze in this operation, it ostensibly mimics the unwanted attention of harassment, redirecting it back to the men who harass from the women who get harassed. While this may seem subversive, the strategy arguably intensifies the surveillance of the women (as they often post a general location in which the harassment occurred). The problem of street harassment as a social problem is hardly undone through this tactic.

Posting a picture of a man who harasses, which then also records and posts the (geographical) point of the harassment (thereby indicating the site of the harassment, and thus, the location of the victim), allows the technological gaze to reveal as much about the women target/victim as the men who harass. Might having this information recorded online actually facilitate, rather than challenge, such harassment? In other words, could or do harassers utilize this technological tool of surveillance, intended to police their own behavior, *against* the very women photographing or "outing" them as men who harass?

Does knowing the locations where street harassment occurs suggest *more* or additional "dangerous ways of looking," not simply at people and social behavior, but at particular places or locations? Do we perpetuate "dangerous ways of looking" at such sites, in the suggestion, through "discourses of danger," that some locations are more dangerous than others? In mapping out where women report street harassment, do we consider the plethora of information not gathered, because it is not shared or reported on the site? Does this erase the spaces where street harassment occurs but women opt not to, or cannot, report it, perhaps because they are too shaken up or experience such a disturbance by the incidence that they do not turn to the technology first, but rather to attending to themselves? Do we ignore, or make more visible, the web of violence woven throughout society, when we create a space that ostensibly shows us *exactly* where women encounter street harassment, based on their own accounts?

When we are careful to link the various kinds of violence that women face, we can begin to appreciate how complicated this "hollaback" approach remains. Is there any evidence that women face retaliatory harassment after posting pictures of a harasser on the website? Do these women face other kinds of violence as a form of retribution for their own attempt at empowerment or even vindication? What does mapping out where women face harassment accomplish, beyond visualizing the extent to which women experience harassment?

Is this visualization of violence a preliminary step to documenting its occurrence more formally? Would this encourage, for example, the Department of Justice, or other related agencies, to collect data on street harassment? Would illustrating where violence against women occurs encourage others to intervene (if not prevent such violence)? Given all of the modes of surveillance, why do more people *not* intervene if and when street harassment occurs?

In some ways, these questions relate to my earlier point—that street harassment generally hides in plain sight, often appearing to be a conversation between strangers, not an uneven exchange of potentially offensive public speech from harasser to target. By hiding in plain sight, as it so often does, street harassment seldom signals or calls for attention, because it masks as everyday interaction, not violence.

In thinking about these issues of surveillance, spectacle, and the body, Holloway observes, "Legal interest in privacy and *the* body depend on an intimate, gendered, sexual spectacularity.[14] Her work shows the vulnerability and visibility attached to certain bodies. Vulnerability and visibility show up in the narratives and embodied realities for women who experience street harassment. Their private selves, lives, and bodies suddenly become "public texts." In other words, "My private identities are always and already public."[15]

Dangerous ways of looking at (black) women are as public texts, or always already objects, not subjects. "Dangerous ways of looking" at women reduce them to fragments, and facilitate their objectification and sexualization which often precipitates violence against women.[16] Conversely, some people might argue that worrying about men as a potential or actual threat is a "dangerous way of looking" at men.

As discussed in the chapter on "dangerous ways of seeing," "dangerous ways of looking" also shape people's perceptions of themselves and others. Some of the women in the sample spoke about how their appearance, their bodies, invited the gaze and street harassment. For example, their mere presence in public presented them as inviting the gaze. Many felt that this invitation was beyond their control, as their bodies were viewed through the lens of controlling images. As noted earlier, women targets of street harassment attempted to deflect men harasser's "dangerous ways of seeing" them, in an effort to avoid being harassed.

"[I]n the everyday indicative world, women and their bodies, certain bodies, in certain public framings, in certain public spaces, are always already transgressive—dangerous, and in danger."[17] As Mary Russo suggests, we attach meanings to bodies, and in turn must negotiate these meanings during social interactions. For women to enter urban public space with bodies read as endangered and dangerous begins to explain why women are treated in similar ways. Yet, the dominant discourse about embodiment of women in public spaces takes various forms depending not only upon gender, but race, class, sexuality, age, and other social locations. Thus, women's bodies come under differential kinds of scrutiny and surveillance, during street harassment, and in society in general (I discuss this later on, too).

Scholarship shows the extent to which women's bodies endure constant, if shape-shifting, surveillance, providing and satisfying the scopophilia of harassers and others. Many of the gendered narratives women learn involve avoiding "dangerous ways of looking" that invite the gaze. This reflects a "dangerous discourse" in shifting the burden to women. Nevertheless, many respondents commented on this in their interviews, as I discuss next.

Dress or Clothing as Dangerous Ways of Looking

As a girl I was kept under strict surveillance, since virtue and modesty were, by cultural equation, the same as family honor. As a teenager I was instructed on how to behave as a proper senorita. But it was a conflicting message girls got, since the Puerto Rican mothers also encouraged their daughters to look and act like women and to dress in clothes our Anglo friends and their mothers found too "mature" for our age.[18]

When asked about the potential conflicting messages they may have received throughout their lives, the women I spoke with revealed varying levels of awareness about their physical appearance with regards to clothing choice and noted the different strategies they employed to ensure feeling safe, comfortable, and sometimes cute in public spaces.

In their attempts to maintain the appearance of respectable femininity, some women intentionally altered their clothing when they traveled from their suburban residences or workplaces to the urban setting of the university they attended or to participate in some recreational (athletic, musical, artistic, cultural) event. Women with a heightened awareness of serving as a racialized, gendered sexualized spectacle in these urban settings often noted that they toned down their dress.

They took to wearing whatever minimized or neutralized the attention they grew to anticipate, often with anxiety and annoyance. Whether the women chose to wear longer skirts, no skirts at all (in order to hide/cover their legs), no pants (which highlighted the bow legs men so often sexualized them for), more professional clothing (to create artificial and illusive status differences between the women and men they perceive as lower or working class), and so forth.

Wrapped up in these choices of dress and clothing is women's awareness of themselves and their bodies as objects of visual consumption enjoyed by men, but also the agency that allows them to recognize, rather than dismiss, their feelings about being such a spectacle, and make choices that enable the women to remain comfortable and confident in the face of eliding the scrutiny that being such a spectacle can bring, or celebrating the attention that some women may actually desire in various urban public spaces.

Next, I consider the male gaze, its impact on women, and the various ways women invite, avert, or remain ambivalent about men "undressing women with their eyeballs." How do women respond to being subject to the surveillance, scrutiny, and evaluation entangled in serving as a spectacle?

The issue of visual consumption (and visual imposition or invasion), the phenomenon of reckless eyeballing, in which men casually, comfortably, and shamelessly ogle, observe, evaluate, and possibly imagine their targets in various states of undress, was all too familiar to several of the women in my sample. They shared feelings of vulnerability and frustration with the visual consumption by men. Women are expected to concern themselves with their appearance and how they look to others, including men harassers looking at them.

Here, "dangerous ways of looking" link to "discourses of danger" and "dangerous discourses" in that women feel responsible for (or are made to feel so regarding) their safety. A consistent theme across interview conversations related to women respondents discussing their appearance (clothing, behavior, etc.), in relation to their negotiation of street harassment in public spaces. Their narratives provide evidence of their awareness of the ways they imagined they *could* put themselves in harm's way or in the face of danger, depending on their appearance. They lamented and resented these considerations, while staunchly critiquing having to manage this responsibility.

Some scholars describe this sort of behavior as sexual terror stemming from rapacious threatening men,[19] while others discuss issues of sexual danger, the treatment of women as sex objects, and the disparaging treatment of women in general in a misogynistic and misogynoiristic society.[20] When seemingly benevolent, this treatment of women as sex objects may reflect men's intention at seduction; when malevolent, the result is often sexual street harassment. Nevertheless, the blurred line between seduction and sexual harassment left many women repulsed by the rapacious looks of men. Few others could think of few better social repellents and barriers to interactions than being visually consumed in a sexualized manner by male strangers on the street or other public spaces.

What follows is an exchange between Samantha (a white working-class heterosexual woman) and I:

> Samantha: "Sometimes it's just the staring thing [versus street remarks or comments]. And that just really annoys me, because I only want my significant other to look at me like *that*. You [these men] just don't have that right."
> Author: [requesting clarification] "What is *that*?"
> Samantha: "Um, the 'I want you; come and get me' kind of look. . . . That creepy 'I want you in my bed' smile."

Samantha's comments reveal the degree to which women's bodies become or are always already "public texts"[21] under constant surveillance for men's visual and sexual pleasure. Samantha captures the contemporary effect of an historical problem: men's "right to look" and women's denial of bodily autonomy and agency.

As public texts, women's bodies, especially black women's bodies, have historically and contemporarily been considered community property.[22] My study allowed women to speak out about the invasive looks or other detestable or undesirable behavior of men who harass. Speaking out about street harassment in these interviews parallels the ways that "African American women called on a tradition of testimony and truth-telling . . . in order to reclaim their bodies and their humanity."[23]

The reclamation of women's humanity remains an ongoing achievement or progress, given the plethora of ways women endure objectification and sexualization. Take, for example, another anecdote the respondent, Samantha, shared during the interview. She witnessed a man in a public service office freely and nonchalantly taking pictures of women's buttocks with his cell phone camera. This criminal behavior is a dangerous way of looking.

Afraid of the confrontational conversation she wished she had courage to have rather than simply imagine it unfolding, the respondent confessed that she wanted to interrogate and question the man about his objectifying actions. Instead, she chose to avoid having such an interaction with him. Samantha's comments convey the extent to which men's visual consumption of women may go unnoticed. Even when noticed, it often remains unchecked or unregulated, because of the potentially harsh reactions that may result.

Intervention of street harassment and other forms of violence are difficult moments because the person imagining the intervention cannot predict whether s/he will become the next target. Perhaps the person witnessing street harassment does not intervene precisely because s/he has already or repeatedly been a target of street harassment, and cannot handle potentially getting drawn into another person's harassment, along with her/his own. In this way, it is important to see reluctance to intervention as a possible form of self-protection, not a refusal to help or normalization of or indifference to street harassment.

Certainly, I am not faulting this respondent for her non-response. Instead, I am simply highlighting how little formal consequence exists for men who engage in dangerous ways of looking in public spaces and during street harassment: by visually consuming women in objectifying, dehumanizing, and sexualizing ways (that the women might be unaware of and/or object to otherwise).

By extension, how might women experiencing or witnessing such harassment feel the burden of obligation to assume responsibility for the men's behavior? How do they make sense of the rhetoric that says street harassment debatably results from the women's presumably provocative behavior that prompted such attention in the first place?

In general, men know that they can engage in these "dangerous ways of looking" at women, without facing many negative sanctions or formal punishment. Male privilege protects men's "right to look," and supports the kind of culture that normalizes such behavior. Only recently have increasingly legal measures been established to prevent the dubious practice of "upskirting," where people take pictures of women's underwear by snapping a photo underneath their skirts. These photographic practices of women's bodies in urban public spaces reflect violations of women's bodies for the visual pleasure of the person taking the picture(s). Upskirting constitutes yet another way in which women's bodies are consumed, in this case visually, without proper or adequate consent.

The "look" that Samantha described being disgusted by, along with these technological looks captured through "upskirting," becomes "dangerous ways of looking," perhaps arguably more so when situated in the context of rape culture. That men look at some women rapaciously links directly to the act of rape as a nonconsensual form of gender and sexual violence. It connects the visual and the physical acts of consuming women with or without our consent. It demands that we reconsider what right to look we have, and how we deny women the right to look, too. (The right to look in terms of clothing and appearance, and the right to be in public spaces without worry of danger, harm, or injury.)

Recently, a woman posted an image online of herself bare-breasted, with a sign that read, "This is still not an invitation to rape." The attendant article articulated this very point, and connects to street harassment. It underscores that women who show up in public should have the right to walk freely, without their bodies being viewed as an invitation for unsolicited attention. What would it mean for men harassers to ask a woman for permission first before speaking or looking at her in a particular way? What would it mean to give consent to such requests? Is this un/realistic or idealistic?

If people could shift the discourse to disrupt the "silence of violence," could they imagine encouraging even (maybe especially) complete strangers to solicit and/or offer ongoing consent in various aspects of their interactions (including the sexual *and* the social)? Speculatively, normalizing such practices might minimize the occurrence of street harassment while encouraging enthusiastic consent and respectful communication. What women describe experiences in the street might feel qualitatively different with these practices put in place consistently.

Moving from the rhetoric of "protection" to the practice of "permission" shifts the discourse and its impact on individuals. Through the seeking and granting or denying of consent, people would create space for the purpose of communicating more clearly their individual (dis)interests. In admirable attempts to clarify the blurred lines between hello and harassment, between visual pleasure for the harasser and for the target, people would simply be engaging in conversation without the element of harassment woven into the picture.

This notion of mutually consensual public conversation and visual consumption might appeal to women who face street harassment,[24] but consent might be just as difficult to acquire or enforce as the regulation of street harassment itself.[25] The women in my sample often noted how little control they had regarding the male gaze, and their inability to physically prohibit or avert the male gaze frustrated and annoyed most of them.

Attempts to avert the male gaze included dressing much more conservatively than they desired, so as to discourage any additional attention although a baseline of attention was anticipated but not always welcomed; remaining relatively absent from spaces of intense and obvious male scrutiny, evaluation, and entanglement; trying to avoid certain places known to be the site of previous and presumed potential further harassment or visual consumption;[26] and altering the paths that one takes in order to physically and socially circumvent the reckless eyeballing that felt to some like getting raped by men with their eyes.

Pamela, a white middle-class respondent, described her individual efforts to avert and avoid the male gaze. Firstly, she commented on the double standard in place that punishes women for wearing certain types of clothing: "It's just that you shouldn't have to live your life thinking, 'Oh, if I wear this today, I'm probably going to get some comments or some catcalls, but if I wear this [dress conservatively] I' . . . I don't want to have to do this. I mean, it's ridiculous." When asked how that makes her feel, the additional investment in maneuvering around and thinking about how to handle this dressing double standard, Pamela retorts, "Well, it pisses me off because I can't run in a sports bra but men can run in bum huggers and no shirt . . . And really, it's okay. That's okay because no one's going to make catcalls to them. . . . or make them feel uncomfortable. I just think that it's a double standard that I try to at least not uphold." Pamela exemplifies one of the more vocal opponents of these problematic gender expectations, as she reflects on but refuses to internalize these "discourses of danger." She issues these challenges by doing things she is encouraged or socialized not to do, which liberates her a bit from the controlling aspects of these discourses.

Continuing her comments on the regulation of women's appearance in terms of clothing, Pamela remarks with palpable frustration:

> There's definitely a policing and it's one of those things that I think in our society we tend to blame the victim and not the person who's causing the problem. Um, I know for me it's, I won't walk down the street at night alone obviously I have people tell me all the time that I shouldn't run in just a sports bra on even though it's 100 heat index outside and in some ways, I—I feel like I am

affected by the comments and that sort of thing but in other ways have really grown accustomed to it and put up with it and I definitely do think it causes stress, there's definitely stress involved when you're running down the street and someone just out of nowhere starts blowing the horn and starts screaming at you, and you're obviously going to react, to have to feel stress, to have an increase in your adrenaline, and physical reactions to it. . . . And I think that's what's really interesting to, to look at the long-term effects, physical effects, or stress invoked by street harassment.

While Pamela outlines what she believes are the physiological consequences of harassment, she also highlights how normalized the regulation of women's actions and bodies has become, and how the perpetrators of this policing go unregulated or unpunished. As with other women, Pamela expressed disappointment and frustration at the perpetual policing of women as victims rather than the men making running in a sports bra a recreational hazard.

Even when women are dressed casually, not necessarily athletically, they can attract the gaze, and potentially "dangerous ways of looking." Samantha noted,

Yeah, you know, there are times, especially in the summer when I'm walking to school and I have on short shorts and a tight, not tight, a fitted shirt and I will cross my book bag so that the strap looks like a seat belt and so that just makes my chest stick out even further than it already does, and so sometimes I feel like men see that as, "Woohoo," an invitation, "open for service," or something. "Open for business" or—so sometimes I do feel like it, but it's more of an unintentional thing; it's, "I wanna be cool; I don't want to be hot." Comfortable, but it's perceived in many ways.

In trying to staying cool and comfortable in often oppressive heat, Samantha ends up being perceived as "inviting," falling under the gaze of men harassers who find her "hot."

Similar to Pamela, Samantha tried to refute the pressures on women to appear a certain way in public. Curiously, this "way" is pleasing but not too inviting; it marks another "line" which women, not men, are expected to know how not to cross, but rather around which to tiptoe or dance. Samantha explained her behavior in this way:

I dress how I dress. I'm one of those people who, I don't care what other people think for the most part, except for the people I care about. Then I care about what they think and then it's still a sticky situation. Um, I'm going to dress the way I'm going to dress and if someone has a problem with it, that's their problem. . . . I made a point to go out at different times of day or there are times when I think, "Oh, I'll wear this cute skirt to school today," and then I think,

"Naw, I don't want to be walking down the street in that," so, I will sometimes change. Yes.

In cases where she does not want attention publicly, she does admit to or acknowledge dressing differently, to deflect the gaze. Given how much the women in this sample alone reported facing street harassment, it is important to point out that the various ways women appear, speak, or think will never fully protect them from violence, as long as people are perpetrating this violence.

Other respondents' comments and experiences supported the existence of these gendered double standards. Felicia, for example, inadvertently perpetuated the notion that a woman who dresses up perhaps deserves whatever adversarial conversations or comments she encounters presumably by way of her own doing and provocation, while women who dress down deserve to elide harassment.

As previously noted, accounting for women's appearance when they are harassed is a dangerous discourse because it risks perpetuating the idea that women should avoid "dangerous ways of looking" (dressing) in order to avoid harassment. As with rape, sexual assault, and other forms of violence, street harassment ceases when people stop perpetuating this behavior, not when women alter their appearance in public. Everyday violence and violence against women end when people stop harassing, raping, sexually assaulting, hurting, and harming others.

That many of the women respondents in my sample noted what they or other women accompanying them were wearing—or even that they observed among other women in public, yet they never attended to what the men who harass wore, attests to the pervasiveness of this problem. The dilemma in making these "dangerous discourses" visible is embedded in the question of undoing gender, in its damaging and dangerous dynamics and impacts, in the expectation and regulation around women's appearance in public, as opposed to a focus on the source of the problem: men who harass.

Despite attempts to avoid or minimize their to-be-looked-at-ness, many women shared narratives that suggested these efforts proved more futile than successful. Instead of altering their appearance, to manage or avoid their own "dangerous ways of looking," some respondents reported avoiding men's "dangerous ways of looking" by averting their gaze. I describe these tactics in the next section.

Avoiding "Dangerous Ways of Looking": Diverting and Deflecting Attention

For those women in the sample who generally expressed mild discomfort or unease in urban public spaces, reciprocating attention and engaging unfamiliar others in conversation remain out of the question. Instead, the women relied on an assortment of diversionary tactics to deflect the men's attention. Some of these tactics include the following: avoiding eye contact with the men; eliding social interaction by maintaining a certain social distance (because the women believed that proximity to the harasser served as their invitation to conversation); looking focused, mean, purposeful, hurried, harried, or otherwise uninviting.

Felicia, a middle-class heterosexual white woman, commented, "Like in certain places, typically I don't make eye contact, like in downtown, in the middle of the city, I don't make eye contact with people passing by. You know, you're in the city in the mix of things and"—I inquire, "You engage in civil inattention?" Felicia confirms, "Civil inattention. You're right . . . so I guess that would be a way that I would try to avoid harassment, is by not making eye contact." Felicia proudly shared this strategy for navigating what she perceived to or experienced as unsafe spaces. She attempted to avoid men's "dangerous ways of looking" at her by refusing to make eye contact with her.

> She offered this additional anecdote:
> It's funny. My mom came down one time, and she lives way out in the suburbs, and I don't know why she came down here, and I met her and we were walking through and it's midday and someone harassed her. It was funny because they were clearly harassing my mom and it was funny *because* they were harassing my mom. "What did that guy just say?" He muttered something under his breath, but you could tell he was clearly verbalizing something about her. And, um, what did I do? I was like, "Mom, did you say hello, say hi to him?" and she's like, "Yeah, what are you supposed to do when you pass someone on the street?" I said, "Don't make eye contact. Keep your head down. Go where you need to go." It's funny because where she lives, everybody knows everybody.

She concludes by telling me how her mother joked, "Oh yeah, Felicia won't make eye contact with anybody when she's downtown." For this respondent, obeying the rules of the civil attention ritual served as a source of comfort for her while traversing urban spaces implicitly filled with potentially dangerous, menacing, annoying, or threatening people. Although Felicia admitted that street harassment remains a rare occurrence for her, a few but intensely harassing incidents convinced her that disengagement from men strangers proved an initial step toward prohibiting conversation or at least dissuading unpleasant interactions with men strangers.

Sarah, a working-class white heterosexual woman in her twenties, conveyed similar sentiments when she spoke about how she dealt with the street harassment she encountered. Sarah drew differences between decidedly and purposefully making eye contact with unfamiliar others, and noted that in these cases, stranger interaction remains acceptable. Conversely, she argued that when people purposefully try not to make eye contact, or intentionally avert their eyes, dodging eye contact with others, and strangers make an effort to engage, that's harassment.

In Sarah's view, men ignored her efforts to avoid eye contact with them, and employed various strategies to verbally entangle her in conversation (despite her visual lack of enthusiasm in them). Consequently, she confessed, "I think what I do is accept eye contact from women much more than from men. Like if I'm walking down the street and I catch eye contact with a woman, I may smile at her, or we smile at each other, but I'm much less likely to do that with a man." In this way, denying others (men) eye contact remains a strategy for this and other respondents attempting to exercise some individual control of the situation.

Another respondent, Rita, a white middle-class respondent, noted that she similarly minimizes eye contact with others. Instead, she prefers to ignore those who harass her rather than engage them in any way. By disengaging with men who harass, Rita—in her perception—exercises control over the situation. Recognizing that men who harass her want some demonstrative reaction, she disengages to deny them that satisfaction. She adds, "I will ignore it or try to show any reaction like I didn't hear it because sometimes, I don't know what the other person really has in mind." The unpredictability of the harasser's action inhibits Rita's action, but partially on her own accord, as she actively decides not to entertain their entanglement efforts.

In terms of avoiding the gaze, Pamela shared this: "And, I think, for me in that way, it's that I find different ways to run or I avoid places where I know people are hanging out." While she noted that she does not avoid going out at night, she does make a point "at night, just be with someone, or a friend, or a group of people. That's something I've always been taught."

She continued, highlighting the extent to which she must consider contingencies, or engage in the emotional work[27] of ensuring that she *feels* safe, even if safety is illusive. "Well, I'll go out at night; I just don't walk places by myself, like I avoid walking in the street at night. I'm sure that it's for a number of reasons: it's dark; you can't see; someone may be hiding and jump out or yell or think you're a prostitute."

Upon hearing some of her anxieties, I tell Pamela about a then-recent incident where, in the early morning, I was getting into my car when a man pulled up alongside my vehicle and slowed down to the point that I got scared. He never did anything, never motioned toward me, but I told her that I wondered if he thought I was a prostitute (I was a graduate student at the time, heading to the university campus, likely to teach, write and/or do some combination of both activities that day). I recall questioning what I was wearing (contrasting my casual attire to the women I sometimes saw wearing short skirts, heels, and other items to signal their services or gesture at the work they do); I wondered what provoked his action and implicit perception of me.

While an isolated incident, in my personal experience, I wonder how often women must grapple with the inconvenience created by mistaken identity, in social situations where some men misread them as sexually available and accessible when such may not be the case. Even this example illustrates the trap of describing my appearance as putatively "different" from the women who purposefully rely on "dangerous ways of looking" to advertise that they are prostitutes, in ways that I do not. This dilemma of describing, much less managing, these dangerous ways of looking reflect the kinds of emotional labor that women engage in to make sense of street harassment and other forms of violence we navigate in our everyday lives.

While mostly explored in the context of the workplace, emotional work reflects the unpaid energies that people invest in keeping social situations smooth and seamless.[28] The problem stemming from emotional work involves its invisibility precisely because women assume the responsibility rather than experience another tenuous, potentially volatile situation. Instead, they appear more accommodating, gracious, et cetera than usual, or in Pamela's case, must make all of these additional considerations when contemplating leaving her (the) home, considerations most men do not similarly have to make.

The cumulative effect of these concerns, considerations, or anxieties would make the most resilient women think twice about when and where to walk in urban public spaces. Thinking twice, or thrice, about if and how to be in public 1) reflects a spatial injustice and speaks directly to the persistence of gender inequality in our society; 2) indicates a kind of self-protective work required of women to reduce their risk and ostensibly ensure their safety; 3) exposes the extent to which women must protect themselves, despite gendered discourses describing men's roles as the protector of women (or the failure/refusal of men to protect women, as suggested by traditional gender roles); and illustrates the emotional work that women engage in when navigating urban public spaces.

These considerations (thinking twice or thrice) create a kind of emotional work that remains largely unrecognized and invisible, but reveal the multiple consequences that street remarks and street harassment create for its (typically) women targets. Ironically, this intensifies or magnifies the problem of street harassment itself and the problem of spatial injustice in general. If women are unable to enjoy public life and spaces in ways similar to or that approximate the relative freedom that men enjoy in public, they experience this difference as a matter of spatial injustice.

That many women engage in emotional labor as a strategy for responding to or dealing directly with men who harass reflects another layer to spatial injustice, in that this engagement can be quite hazardous to women and women's safety. This engagement can be recognized as part of the "dangerous discourses" I discussed earlier, since women who talk back to men harassers can agitate them and experience intensified harassment or worse, as a kind of retaliation or retribution for talking back to men harassers.

Perhaps another "dangerous discourse" would include the presumption that all men are harassers and all women are targets of harassment. Another might be that women experience harassment in similar ways. The purpose of this book is to show the nuances of the negotiations and strategies that women employ when navigating public spaces. It is important to note that how women respond to street harassment often reflects their cumulative set of experiences not only with street harassment but various other forms of violence. It also reflects their embodied knowledge and potential resistance that develops from repeated exposure to such harassment.

This point elaborates on the concept of emotional labor. It shows that women who repeatedly face street harassment may find that performing emotional labor gets easier and/or harder over time. These divergent responses to street harassment reflect the plethora of considerations women must make to reduce their risk of harm during street harassment and in social life in general.

As one respondent, Red, noted, there is a constant calculation or assessment of safety, danger, and threat, in order to determine how best to deflect or dodge men's "dangerous ways of looking" and "dangerous discourses" during street harassment: "I try to stay aware at all times but I'll walk more quickly if it's dark or I'll try to walk with someone to the parking deck."

Rather than avoid places as a means of minimizing street harassment, Red insists, "I walk the same way every day. Whatever! I'm not going to make the journey longer for me." Instead of inconveniencing herself, Red travels intentionally but cautiously through urban public spaces. To navigate such spaces, she employs other strategies such as this:

I think the less eye contact you make, the less street harassment you get. If you look in their [the male harasser's] direction, they may be thinking, "Oh, she might be looking at me." I try to stay straight ahead and don't look at anybody around me. . . . I'm drowning people out around me, so I can't hear what they're saying. I'm focused. I'm ready to get to my destination without being harassed.

What strikes me as both amusing and sad about what Red said is that she sounds like she is preparing for a race, one that requires focus and concentration, to eliminate the possibility of distraction. I am left wondering how often Red can cross the finish line by reaching her destination without distraction, without facing street harassment. Refusing to compromise either comfort or her safety, Red similarly engages in emotional work, in this case sizing up certain spaces to ensure that she feel safe and unthreatened, and that she remain relatively unbothered as she moves around the city and throughout her life.

While Red suggests that she refuses to inconvenience herself by moving around spaces where she may anticipate (or previously experienced) street harassment, she arguably *is* inconveniencing herself by having to engage in the mental and emotional labor of keeping herself safe. If men did not harass her, she would not have to make these considerations on such a regular basis. That women are required to manage men's behavior reveals the extent of the emotional labor women perform.[29] Red resists the imposition of street harassment, but her point distracts from the men who harass. Ultimately, men should be held accountable and responsible for their actions.

Much of the discourse on rape culture suggests this approach to safety, which is why it constitutes a "dangerous discourse." It holds women targets, not men harassers, accountable or responsible for street harassment. As with rape and other forms of violence against women, women are taught risk-reduction strategies for minimizing harm or threat of violence. Conversely, some men are *not* taught to avoid rape or violence. They are *not* typically instructed to avoid harassing others, especially women. Instead, some men are often encouraged to perpetuate violence against women, as a way of performing masculinity, expressing dominance over women, and facilitating the bonding between men.[30]

Red's discussion illustrates the many considerations she makes to minimize social interactions with men strangers; these considerations constitute the emotional labor that women perform in order to manage risk and threat of interpersonal violence, such as street harassment. The decision-making processes that women must engage in also expose the extent to which women are targets of men's attention during street harassment, even as they desire the attention of other men, for the purposes of male bonding.[31]

While Amy, Red, and others contended that, in their opinion, just being female motivated men to give them attention, other respondents including Jenny and Snow felt that men harassed women as a way to strengthen homosocial bonds with other men. For example, Jenny made comments that supported this idea, as she also alluded to the homoerotic and homosocial nature of harassment. She suggested that, in some ways, harassment has very little to do with women, and in fact, seems much more to do with men, particularly when men harass in groups.

Snow, a white, working-class graduate student noted that harassment seems to her a ritual between men, or a form of male bonding that implicates women but has more to do with men forming a social/sexual connection amongst the men themselves. Perhaps it is that men avoid "dangerous ways of looking" at one another, and use women as a way to diffuse or deflect this attention.

The other interesting and notable part of Red's comment is the point she makes about the power of looking, as the person (object) being looked at, which destabilizes the power imbalance. Looking back at men harassers may appear to even out or equalize the gaze, or the notion of having the right to look. However, implicit in her comments is the suggestion of the "dangerous ways of looking" for or among *women* targets, not simply the men perpetrators, of street harassment. Based on her logic, women then can engage in "dangerous ways of looking." What makes this dangerous is that women lack the privileges and social power that most men can access, including the right to look.

Red's tactics for deflecting attention points to the compounded effect of power asymmetries that exist in interactions and institutions in our society. She equates eye contact with confrontation, and believes that avoiding eye contact reduces the charge of the confrontation. By looking at men who harass, women appear to be "encouraging" the attention of men during street harassment.

In American culture and society, the normative expectation during healthy interactions requires direct eye contact as an expression of respect. People who fail (or choose not) to make eye contact for any number of reasons are often regarded with suspicion. Thus, it is important to note that a woman's reluctance to make eye contact with a man during street harassment indicates a socially skewed interaction. It draws attention to the decisions women make to avoid eye contact, as a mechanism of self-protection, and as a possible strategy to preserve the performance of respectable femininity.

Notably, not making eye contact in a society that associates this behavior as an indication of trustworthiness and character is telling. A woman who looks away from a man could be mis/read as denying him some respect; she could also be viewed as being deferential or docile to him ("with downcast eyes").[32] It would be shortsighted to only see the avoidance of eye contact as a gesture of disrespect on the part of the woman to the man; in fact, we could argue that the avoidance of eye contact reflects (versus initiates) the man harasser's initial disrespect of his women targets. Furthermore, to solely view women's avoidance of eye contact as docility ignores the ways women purposefully and actively choose this avoidance strategy to minimize men's harassment.

A "dangerous way of looking" at eye contact avoidance then is as only a form of docility. Women targets of street harassment may acquire the spatial street knowledge (to become "streetwise"); again, this shows not only the emotional labor of dis/engaging men harassers so as to survive these urban public spaces socially, but also emotionally and physically. That the women maneuver these spaces in ways that are constantly considering and anticipating the threat of harm produced by men who harass (or during street harassment) exposes the centrality of men in women's lives, whether that is preferred or enjoyed by women.

Women's refusal to look at men harassers may be both an act of docility or deference, but it, as indicated by the respondent, albeit a *constrained* choice. Choosing not to make eye contact with harassers as a way of hopefully dissuading their harassment illustrates the various strategies women employ when in urban public spaces. Women must often consider the behavior of men, rather than solely being responsible for their own behavior.

For women targets, one of the most "dangerous ways of looking" at men harassers is directly, because that would equalize and humanize women in a moment where women are treated as unequal objects, not equal subjects, to men. Finally, these "dangerous ways of looking" (looking in the direction of or directly at harassers) also exposes the way women would once again be held accountable for men's bad behavior.

If a woman target of harassment looks at a man harasser or in his direction, she might be seen as "encouraging" his attention (his *harassment*, really) and "asking for it," in terms of any adverse attention he consequently provides. That this gesture would likely be interpreted as such, as not as a gesture of respectful engagement or recognition, again announces another double standard that punishes women for entertaining the idea of interacting with men harassers with civility. It is not surprising that women would be punished for appearing to encourage engagement with men strangers, as it compromises the women's appearance of respectability.

According to another "dangerous discourse," disreputable women remain undeserving of the protections afforded comparably respectable ones. Yet, the everyday violence that is street harassment reveals how frequently most, if not all, women targets of such violence are denied decency, respect, protection, and civility during the interaction. Instead, women suffer verbal assaults, and further injury from the numerous interpretations of how un/successfully she handles being harassed.

Men harassers face little social scrutiny. Seldom do they risk jeopardizing their respectability or integrity from their participation in or perpetuation of street harassment. The "dangerous discourses" that encourages this interactional incivility as a successful performance of masculinity endorses this everyday violence; it is this violence that impacts everyone, and not just the target or the harasser. Street harassment compromises the quality of all social life.

The above example illustrates the powerful intersection of discourses. That is, where "dangerous discourses" and "dangerous ways of looking" meet, women get caught in the proverbial middle of these crossroads. This reminds us that the power asymmetries in society privilege and protect men who participate in and produce "dangerous discourses" during street harassment (as street harassment), and seem to encourage men's "dangerous ways of looking" at women, for the benefit of men's visual pleasure, and as assertion in the power of looking for men. These power asymmetries typically neglect or intentionally fail to protect women targets of such harassment. They translate women's responses to street harassment into behavior that often further endangers women, when women's ways of responding to street harassment become alternate forms of "dangerous discourses" (speech and silence, both, or neither), and "dangerous ways of looking" (avoiding eye contact, averting their own gaze to discourage the male gaze, and etc.).

Power asymmetries can make women's strategic responses to street harassment seem less so (less strategic); These responses may appear performative, specifically in terms of respectable or emphasized femininity. Seldom do they show up as the often-resistant acts that they are, nor do they register as a rebellious kind of femininity that is being expressed. This performance reproduces gender and the power asymmetries described here, that transpire during street harassment and that are embedded in all aspects of social life.

Olivia supported the sentiments that averting the gaze or avoiding direct eye contact with men who harass discourages their harassment: "I can walk through the [area] and, and not one thing will be said to me. I act like I'm mad." She provides this example from an earlier part of our conversation:

> When my brother was here in June, he said he saw, when we were walking with my friend, so many guys trying to get eye contact with me but I try really hard not to make eye contact, to decrease the number of times. And when he and I were walking, because he didn't want to walk with me, and have people think that we were together, he said he watched the way I walked and said that when I'm on campus, I tend to have a very determined look on my face, very "don't approach me" and I did that to try to keep from having to discourage it (unwanted attention or harassment).

Olivia's comments reveal the extent to which she has to pretend to be focused or determined, rather than more oblivious to her own behavior and physical and social environments. This consideration and alteration of her behavior when navigating urban public spaces is a different way of understanding how women targets of harassment develop strategies for dealing with street harassment. Such calculations also reveal how gender spatiality, and spatial injustice really, play out such that women targets of harassment must cultivate their own interventions and strategies of survival. Doing so is their way of working to ensure their safety and well-being.

The paradox here, of course, is that women victims of violence often risk intensifying or escalating the violence directed at them, if they agitate their harassers; this level of attention and care (of the men's potentially escalating violent behavior) directed at the dynamics of harassment is yet another burden or layer of injustice in the interaction itself.

That women feel a sense of obligation (to themselves and others) to figure out or to try and anticipate how to handle street harassment reveals the degree to which women are expected to ensure and manage their own safety, even in the face of threats from men harassers. Furthermore, women are expected to appease or placate men harassers, for fear that the women may risk further insult, injury, harm, and/or worse (attendant) violence.

Women arguably also fear that placating men who harass further implicates the former in the interaction, as most people pose questions re-victimizing the target of harassment, "Why would you talk to a complete stranger, especially one who is harassing you?" and protecting the perpetrator harasser, by not asking, "Why would you harass any woman, much less a complete stranger?" "Why would you talk to a woman like that?"

That women feel a sense of discomfort in being harassed and then are expected to comfort the men harassers is ironic at best, and a kind of cruelty or variant violence (or approximate violence; a kind of side effect or even an expression of the gender and spatial injustice I'm discussing) at worst. So often, it appears as if the men expect women to interact with them as if the street harassment interaction is not only between equals, but equally enjoyable for all involved.

That men harassers do *not* see how their remarks and verbal interactions with women they street harass are injurious and emotionally laborious "dangerous discourses" constitutes more "dangerous ways of looking" at street harassment (or not looking, as is the case here). Not looking at and seeing the ways that women have to comfort men while made to feel discomfort by the same men, when in urban public spaces, reflects the "dangerous ways of looking" (when people choose not to see a problem that hides in plain sight, and the numerous impacts that street harassment imposes on its targets).

These "dangerous ways of looking" involve a looking away from the problem, along with a denial of the adverse impact that street harassment has on its targets. Denial of a problem that largely affects the majority of women is dangerous in the way that denial communicates the value (or lack thereof) of women's safety, and the right to have mobility, bodily autonomy and freedom from—not with—violence in this country.

The myriad "dangerous ways of looking" also speak to the complexity of street harassment as a social problem, primarily in the way that we look at street harassment as an everyday inconvenience, not a form of everyday violence. Street harassment may be predictable to the degree that it becomes routinized as an everyday interactional violence. Nevertheless, many women report on its unpredictability.

Street harassment can feel like a scary experience in and of itself. Women's reactions to being harassed can feel that much more fraught. Many are riddled with indecision and wrestle with the dilemma of a question, What is the best/ safest response to harassment? The unpredictable nature of the mis/behavior of men who harass make the negotiations with street harassment so nuanced, tenuous, and potentially dangerous. Men who harass may likely feel a sense of entitlement about the way they look at women.

Should women mirror the way men harass or look back at men who harass, the women may discover that they embody "dangerous ways of looking" (when they appropriate or mirror the male gaze intended for them as objects, not intended for them as subjects refusing to be looked at, or the to-be-looked-at-ness[33] of women's bodies in this society.) These layers of consideration must be taken into account, in conversations about spatial in/ justice and everyday violence.

Taking women and the problems of street harassment seriously reflect some ways we can collectively move toward a socially just society. Otherwise, women targets of street harassment may continue to feel the sting of social and spatial injustice in these ways: 1) the devaluation of their own lives, 2) a discrediting or an invalidation of their experiences with street harassment, and 3) a re-interpretation or re-framing of women's experiences as "exaggerations," escalations, or distortions of reality, as a means of denying women legitimacy, legibility, and authority of their realities.

If women's accounts of street harassment are not taken seriously, why would their attempts to navigate street harassment? As one respondent illustrated, confronting street harassment individually remained as challenging as doing so respectfully, and as skillfully and safely as possible. According to Red, any and all strategies for dealing with street harassment prove futile, in terms of efficaciousness. She casually observed, not with absolute defeat but mild matter-of-factness: "It really doesn't matter what you do. *Someone* is going to harass you." Her words point to the seeming inevitability of street harassment, and the perpetual performance of masculinity and femininity expected to play out during the interaction. Her comments highlight the importance of seeing street harassment as a social problem, and implicitly, of engaging in more public education around this issue.

While much of my research questions focused on how individual women dealt with street harassment, this book serves as a way of recognizing Red's point: street harassment must be understood as more than an occasional problem that impacts individual women perceived to "invite" such attention or engage in such interactions. By recognizing the broader context of rape culture (see earlier chapters), I attempted to show that street harassment serves as yet another expression of violence against women.

Red underscores the way that street harassment is normalized, routinized, and reproduced, when she says, "*Someone* is going to harass you." Just as more attention needs to be directed at helping perpetrators recognize themselves as part of the problem of rape culture, more attention needs to be paid to helping harassers see themselves as such. Perhaps, for men, the most dangerous way of looking is not looking at themselves (being reflexive and self-aware), and not seeing themselves as harassers.

The parallels between rape culture and street harassment play out in this public education, in that in many cases, men perpetrators rely on the "dangerous discourses" including the "just" in ways that are far from ideal: 1) rapists rely on the description of rape as "just sex" to create the appearance of a simple misunderstanding or a semantic debate about the differences between consensual sex and "just sex" (the latter of which the victims of sexual violence would likely describe as rape), and 2) harassers rely on the description of street harassment as "just a conversation" to create the appearance of a consensual conversation or equitable interaction amidst power asymmetries and social unevenness or lopsidedness.

Drawing attention to these parallels, to these dangerous discourses, draws attention to the problem of violence (street harassment and other forms) and the problems of the discourses produced within and around this violence. The only "just" in these discourses would place an emphasis on *just* sex or *just* words, where all individuals involved felt relative safety, freedom, and enjoyment, not risk of hostility in the form of retaliatory, or continued or accelerated violence.

Shifting Discourses from "Just Words" to *Just* Words?

For women who experience reckless eyeballing, in addition to the numerous forms of assaultive, offensive, injurious speech[34] from men who harass, they might desire increased regulation of men's sexual expressions and sexually implicit or explicit behavior. This would serve as an attempt to create a violent-free and less patriarchal and objectifying social world.

A kind of gender/sex police seems necessary to ensure that men who harass could be kept in check; this sort of regulation, admittedly, remains plagued with problems scholars have detailed at length.[35] These problems include the presumption that all men harass (they do not) and that all speech acts constitute harassment; they offer a generalized critique of the street harassment industry, but fail to crumble and disrupt the daily acts that constitute street harassment. In recognition of those limitations, a push toward greater parity in speech and in society would move us toward *just* words in a just world.

Instead, we have accounts of women who worry that men harassers think their behavior is benign and their words kind. Meanwhile, the women encounter them as "dangerous discourses," not "just words" nor *just* words. They worry that the words wrapped up in dangerous discourses will wound them socially, emotionally, if not physically (or put them in greater harm's way). For example, for Julie, facing excessive vulgarity and insults hurled her way in urban public spaces produces a kind of anxiety and uncertainty; she conveyed a perplexity about how to respond to some of the harsher comments men make to her.

An avid runner, Julie suggested that she encounters similar sorts of "drive-by harassment" when she runs and "can't get a good look at them" [the harassers], "because I often get harassed or yelled at when I'm jogging and they drive by in a car. . . . Usually, they'll yell, 'P—y,' yeah, or stuff like that." This kind of sexually offensive verbal attacks on this and other women points to the intense assaults women often face. As a related point, how do men harassers *expect* women to respond to these (offensive and vulgar to many) words? Notably, many of the words that men who harass say or shout to women reflect the extent to which misogyny is woven into colloquial language in this society.

Clearly, that men refer to women in these profane and unjust ways, an absence of civility and decency, of *just* words, is present. The ostensibly derogatory words remain reductive of women, collapsing their worth, or the way men harassers view them, to the singularity of a sexual object. The names men call women generally indicates how men harassers see women, and it says a lot about how men see themselves. These reflect more dangerous ways of seeing as previously discussed, which shape the dangerous ways men look at the women who they harass.

In the absence of formal regulation of men's street harassing behavior, women resort to individual strategies for dealing with these dangerous ways of seeing, looking, and speaking. Some women engaged in spatial practices that allowed them to do what they had to do during the day while minimizing street harassing encounters. Some would try to travel around groups of men, rather than pass directly by them, because the women believed that closer proximity to men inspired more, rather than less, of the men's attention.

Similarly, some of the women tried to occupy densely populated public spaces, particularly during daylight hours (to blend in, feel like part of the crowd, or otherwise share space with others). The onset of darkness marked a transition to heightened danger for women who frequently experienced harassment during the day. To them, the darkness offered anonymity to male harassers, by largely cloaking or concealing the men's identity (physical appearance and countenance). Darkness intensified some of the women's feelings of vulnerability in public space. While they may not have actually experienced more harassment at night, they felt more vulnerable at that time.

In some ways, this interpretation shows how women regulate their behavior to mitigate "dangerous ways of looking" from potential harassers. That women feel less safe in public at night speaks to "discourses of danger" that suggest women are safer inside, in the private sphere, than out at night or after dark. This notion clouds the threat of violence that women face in the home, and how that violence actually escalates at night, when men are likely to also be in the home.[36] Suggesting that women are safer inside than in public minimizes the threat to women everywhere, as it varies throughout the course of each and every day.

Some of the women in the sample challenged "dangerous ways of looking" by embodying subversive femininity. For these women, the male gaze and the hint of darkness (the sun setting at night) did not dissuade them from freely occupying and enjoying urban public spaces. For example, Jennifer, a bisexual middle-class white woman admitted:

> [I] would be less likely to talk to someone [at night] than during the day. [I also have] this kind of thing where I don't like to let fear prohibit me from doing things, so even if I have that like, even if something makes me nervous, I'll do it anyways just because I don't like that freedom taken away from me. It's like running at night.

Jennifer articulated an intentional subversion and resistance to traditional gender role expectations. She celebrated being able to break with or transgress gender rules—by running late at night—that otherwise might limit her participation in activities she finds enjoyable and relatively safe.

While an individualized and rebellious response to the social problem of spatial and sexual injustice, Jennifer's actions remain important. They challenge discourses of danger, or the false notions of women's safety, and they remind us of our agency and autonomy. They convey our potential to express embodied resistance to create ruptures to these gender rules.[37]

Running at night alone challenges the expectation articulated by some other respondents, that women should minimize their presence in public *particularly* at night. The idea that women need to "take back the night" is as important as recognizing that women deserve to feel safe at any point throughout the day or night. This idea is as important as encouraging men harassers to stop street harassment of women.

Women employ their own "dangerous ways of looking" to deflect undesired attention from men harassers. These dangerous ways of looking include disrupting the codes of femininity and breaking away from the performance of respectable femininity. For example, Jennifer noted that her "tomboyish" or imperfectly feminine gender expression influenced her experience with street harassment.

She hinted that, because of her "gruff looking" appearance, she was able to elide the kinds of regulating and policing effects that more traditionally feminine women might experience. Her more masculine and less put together appearance apparently buffered her from some of the harassment she believes she might encounter were she to look decidedly or conventionally more "girly."

Notably, relying on these "dangerous ways of looking" may in fact be dangerous to those who reject convention. That is, intentionally rejecting gender norms, or more casually failing to perform gender appropriately (respectably) can cause "gender trouble."[38] Women targets of street harassment from men may experience movement away from respectable femininity in multiple forms: men harassers may purposefully use harassment as a mechanism of social control, to regulate women's bodies, and their departure from these traditional gender expectations; or men may harass women because the women fail to embody or perform respectable femininity; and then the harassment itself calls into question a woman's "respectability," given that women are viewed as inviting harassment.

These layers then regulate women through discursive practices produced during street harassment, through the ideologies about gender conformity and respectable femininity, and through the act of street harassment as further impunity of a woman's "questionable" character (not the harasser). This discussion reveals the adverse impact that "dangerous ways of looking" has on women's lives.

It is no wonder that some women attempt to avoid "dangerous ways of looking" like they are inviting harassment, by following the codes of gender. Internalizing these codes, or becoming our own gender police, is no more liberating or less oppressive than having someone else policing our appearance, behavior, or movement throughout society, is it? What if women cannot embody femininity in ways that placate others? What kinds of gender trouble surface in those situations?

Recent discussions of hate crimes of transgender and genderqueer individuals suggests that, even if women present a more masculine appearance in order to deflect street harassment, they may actually be harassed or targeted more for their "dangerous ways of looking" gender nonconforming. This topic has not been investigated extensively, but emergent literature speaks to the importance of understanding and connecting the experiences of various marginalized or oppressed populations to one another, to clearly see how extensive the web of violence is woven throughout society.

Curiously, and counterintuitively, gender conformity does not guarantee women protection from harassment. For women, smiling is a form of emotional labor and a way to perform gender conformity. Thus, some women respondents resorted to smiling and other strategies they believed would placate and pacify the harasser, but soon found that smiling at strangers inspired further communication and convinced the men that the women were more interested than in actuality.

Unfortunately for both the men and the women, the men misread the smiling as a woman's signal encouraging further conversation. This proved unfortunate for the men who realized that the smile signified a more palatable, subtle delayed rejection; and unfortunate for the women who then had to deal with the intensified efforts of men who misread the smile as an invitation for more communication. Susie noted,

> It wasn't until I got to college, and I was talking to my dad, saying, "You know what, Dad? It's so sad that like dudes your age, they try to talk to me." And he was like, "Just keep walking and don't say anything to them." That's the only time I had this "parent pow-wow" with him about this stranger thing. Other than that, you always know not to talk to strangers. But just kind of taught myself, cause from my freshman year, I used to smile at them, and the next thing you know they're walking beside me.

In her attempts to circumvent accusations of being mean or unfriendly, Susie resorted to smiling as a means of easing through different social situations. Instead, she found herself having to fend off men who misinterpreted her smile as some sort of invitation for interaction. Other women noted that men *expected* them to be pleasant, to the point that the men almost demanded this pleasantry from women by insisting that the women smile. Julie said,

> One thing that really bothers me that happens a lot is when walking on the street, I'll pass a man and he'll say, "Smile, Smile. The day is not that bad." And they probably don't perceive what they're doing as harassment but I am instilled with a feminist consciousness that tells me, "Why do I have to smile for you?" I'm just walking down the street. I mean, I doubt that men get told that when they're walking the street, so it's very gender-specific because men don't get told, "Smile, life's not that bad."

Expressing her frustration at the gendered double standard that says women should smile, upon request and regardless of their true feelings, Julie highlights a level of regulation embedded in harassment. This emotional regulation of women's feelings, in addition to the regulation of women's spatial practices, particularly when populating urban public spaces, reflects the intensified surveillance and scrutiny women undergo. It highlights the extent to which some men, through discursive practices, attempt to control or shape women's emotional and social behavior.

In fact, when one harasser found that Susie failed to respond in the way he anticipated or hoped for, he told her so. Because Susie failed to reciprocate the man's interest in her, and instead fell silent in surprise at what she felt were sexually charged and inappropriate remarks, she found herself facing evaluation from this male stranger. The gender imbalance that exists serves as a reminder that some women feel neither entitled nor empowered to impose their opinion of men onto men.

Most of the women in my sample did not feel so emboldened as to confront men with the same sorts of evaluative comments as the men shared with the women. This partially reflects the freedom that most men enjoy with their speech, which contrasts with the constraint that many women feel with their words. As noted in an earlier chapter, Amy corroborated these findings when she spoke of the male privilege that men assert with women in public spaces, when the women do not respond to the men's attention in what the men deem appropriate.

Finally, Sarah noted her frustrations at the way men who harass attempted to regulate her behavior: "The times when I'm bothered by it but not to the extreme is where I think, whatever just happened, like if somebody says something, I think, 'Well, would they have actually said that if I was a man?' I kind of do that. 'Well, no, I know they wouldn't have done that if I were a man.' So, that *in itself* bothers me because I feel like I'm having to be treated differently because I'm a woman." When I asked Sarah how that difference made her feel, she explained,

> That it's not fair. I don't like it at all . . . And they can do that, and some people really do understand that they have no idea what they're doing and they don't realize that it's bothersome. I mean it is all about them exerting their power over you because you just have to, like take whatever they do and not react in any way; we're just supposed to walk away quietly and pretend we're not bothered by it, or that we feel good that we were told, "You have a nice butt," or something. I'm very glad that I have a nice butt.

In contrast to Sarah and other respondents, a few of the women in the study appreciated the male gaze and worked to invite such attention, at times anyway. Others had grown accustomed to men's attention. They worked neither to invite, nor avert, the male gaze. In fact, a few respondents remained admittedly indifferent to the attention of men strangers; they suggested that they neutralized the impact of the male gaze by simply ignoring men and their harassing behavior.

When asked if she finds ignoring men a useful strategy for dealing with street remarks and harassment, Red straightforwardly stated, "It is, for me, because generally it just takes less time. Ignore it and you can keep going. And also, the less interaction you have with it, the less you think about it after the fact. So . . . [it helps you] forget it." Later on in the interview, she reiterated, "Once you ignore them, they know: 'I'll just stop before it gets any worse.'" Another respondent, Felicia, notes, "You don't reciprocate. You just keep going, you know. And that's what we did [after the harassment], the normal thing that you would do if someone did that."

The strategy (of ignoring men who harass) risks potentially normalizing the behavior because it allows the harassment to occur without intervention or disruption; it feels like tolerating something, taking medicine, accommodating something that otherwise creates a disturbance in women's daily lives. Nevertheless, normalization aside, ignoring men's harassment meant that the undesired attention dissipated more quickly than otherwise might be the case.

The technique of ignoring men who harass also operates as a coping mechanism for women exhausted from the everyday violence of street harassment. Red's comments speak to how emotionally, mentally, and socially laborious the constant calculations of confronting street harassment remain; dealing with this everyday violence, or men strangers' unsolicited attention, evaluation, and comments proves exhaustive in its adverse impact on women.

CONCLUSIONS

Street harassment sours so many social interactions between strangers that might otherwise be light, fun, and friendly, not menacing, threatening, or the like. It runs the risk of ruining the spontaneity of urban public spaces. Street harassment likely taints consequent social exchanges for women who encounter street harassment regularly.

Several of the women in my study expressed ambivalence about much of the attention they received from men during moments of street harassment, though some reportedly enjoyed some of the attention that gets embedded in the process of street harassment. One queer-identified working class black woman, Parker, noted that she receives a lot of attention for her looks, but expressed some uncertainty about what motivates men to make her a spectacle. While she simply enjoyed dressing up and expressing herself visually/aesthetically (in terms of her dress, etc.), many men misinterpreted that creative expression of self as some kind of provocation, an invitation for their attention.

Many women in the sample reported this experience of being perceived as motivating and inviting men's attention. Whether because of their dress, skin color, attractiveness, gender expression, performance of femininity, or other factors, the women I spoke with frequently received unsolicited and unwanted attention. They regarded most of this attention as harassing and unnecessary to their lives.

In the end, women who wanted or were largely unbothered by the attention found the *insistence* of men's attention in the form of street harassment just that—harassing. In the women's accounts, the men seemed to rely on existing gendered power differentials to assert themselves; they openly, casually, and commonly expressed their thoughts about and desire for the women passersby. Thus, while some women may create a spectacle of themselves and generally enjoy attention, they found any persistent, intrusive, evaluative attention undesirable in comparison to the more friendly and casual comments or remarks, such as "That's a hot outfit."

Arguably, women who dress or move provocatively, in people's perception, are expected to assume responsibility for any adverse consequences such dress and movement might generate. Some respondents, including Felicia, communicated and corroborated this idea during their interview conversations with me.

The problem of street harassment is as persistent as the paradox of men offering to protect women while also injuring and harming them. How does patriarchal behavior of protection operate to protect women from men's patriarchal behavior of violence? Such a paradox, while slight, does not immediately reveal itself and instead makes men seem genuinely concerned for women's safety.

It is often men who support and perpetuate the patriarchy who make the protection of women necessary in the first place. Thus, this "look but do not touch" sentiment exists in the United States; women are frequently still viewed and understood as property (of men) in need of (men's) protection from various dangers (men).

As Butler notes, the language of "protection" is a paternalistic one at best, which captures its contradictory capacity. In the absence of "violence against women," what, in fact, would women need protection from? Shifting the thinking around, in order to interrogate these "discourses of danger," and ideologies around "protection," further clarifies where the problem exists (not in the failure to protect women, per se, but in harming and hurting women in the first place).

Enabling visual consumption but prohibiting physical or sexual contact or consumption privileges and facilitates voyeurism, and masks the ways that such scopophilic behavior communicates a patriarchal domination quite similar in tone to many men's physical and sexual consumption of different women. Consequently, allowing men to make a spectacle of women, but forbidding men to touch women constructs visual consumption as forgivable, even acceptable behavior, while marking physical touch as more clearly punishable.

By extension, men who harass may enjoy that expression of dominance over women; without recognizing street harassment as a problem, then men harassers can continue to do as they please with women in this regard. As an extension and reflection of the social currency and power that being men generally affords them in society, men who harass enjoy a freedom, while compromising that for women. Accommodating this behavior makes light of, and fails to see street harassment as everyday violence.

NOTES

1. Nicholas Mirzoeff. *The Right to Look: A Counterhistory of Visuality.* Durham, NC: Duke University Press, 2011.

2. See Richard Pérez-Peña. "Woman Linked to 1955 Emmett Till Murder Tells Historian Her Claims Were False." *New York Times.* January 27, 2017. Accessed on May 5, 2022. Available online: www.nytimes.com/2017/01/27/us/emmett-till-lynching-carolyn-bryant-donham.html.

3. Danielle McGuire. *At the Dark End of the Street: Black Women, Rape, and Resistance.* New York: Vintage, 2011: 51.

4. Danielle McGuire. 2011: 39.

5. Laura Mulvey. "Visual Pleasure and Narrative Cinema." *Screen* 16: 6–18, 1975.

6. Laura Mulvey. 1975: 836.

7. Joy James. *Resisting State Violence: Radicalism, Gender, and Race in U.S. Culture.* Minneapolis, MN: University of Minnesota Press, 1996; Danielle McGuire. *At the Dark End of the Street: Black Women, Rape, and Resistance.* New York: Vintage, 2011.

8. A nod here to pioneering psychologist and multiracial scholar, Maria P.P. Root. See *Love's Revolution: Interracial Marriage.* Philadelphia: Temple University Press, 2001.

9. Rosa-Linda Fregoso. "Toward a Planetary Civil Society" in *Mexicana Encounters: The Making of Social Identities on the Borderlands.* Edited by Rosa-Linda Fregoso. Pp. 1–29. Berkeley, CA: University of California Press, 2003a; Diana Taylor. *Disappearing Acts: Spectacles of Gender and Nationalism in Argentina's "Dirty War."* Durham, NC: Duke University Press, 1997; Melissa Wright. "The Private Parts of Public Value: The Regulation of Women Workers in China's Export-Processing Zones" in *Going Public: Feminism and the Shifting Boundaries of the Private Sphere.* Edited by Joan W. Scott and Debra Keates. Pp. 99–120. Urbana Champaign: University of Illinois Press, 2005.

10. Joy James. 1996.

11. Griselda Pollock. *Modernity and the Spaces of Femininity.* New York: Routledge, 1992.

12. Laura Mulvey. 1975.

13. See ihollaback.org; stopstreetharassment.org/.

14. Karla Holloway. *Private Bodies, Public Texts: Race, Gender, and a Cultural Bioethics.* Durham, NC: Duke, 2011: 14–15.

15. Karla Holloway. 2011: 18.

16. Jean Kilbourne. *Killing Us Softy 4: Advertising's Image of Women.* Film. Directed by Sut Jhally. Northampton, MA: Media Education Foundation, 2010.

17. Mary Russo. "Female Grotesque: Carnival and Theory" in *Writing on the Body: Embodiment and Feminist Theory.* Pp. 318–336. New York: Columbia University Press, 1997: 323.

18. Judith Ortiz Cofer. "The Myth of the Latin Woman" in *Women Writing Resistance: Essays on Latin America and the Caribbean.* Edited by Jennifer Browdy de Hernandez. Pp. 109–116. Cambridge, MA: South End Press, 2003: 110.

19. Linda Mahood and Barbara Littlewood. "Daughters in Danger: The Case of "Campus Sex Crimes'" in *Sexual Harassment: Contemporary Feminist Perspectives.* Edited by Alison M. Thomas and Celia Kitzinger. Pp. 172–187. Philadelphia: Open University Press, 1997.

20. Alison M. Thomas. "Men Behaving Badly? A Psychosocial Exploration of the Cultural Context of Sexual Harassment" in *Sexual Harassment: Contemporary Feminist Perspectives.* Edited by Alison M. Thomas and Celia Kitzinger. Philadelphia: Open University Press, 131–153, 1997. See also Moya Bailey. *Misogynoir Transformed: Black Women's Digital Resistance.* New York: New York University Press, 2021.

21. Karla Holloway. *Private Bodies, Public Texts: Race, Gender, and a Cultural Bioethics.* Durham, NC: Duke, 2011.

22. See Karla Holloway. 2011.

23. Danielle McGuire. *At the Dark End of the Street: Black Women, Rape, and Resistance.* New York: Vintage, 2011:30.

24. Jaclyn Friedman and Jessica Valenti. *Yes Means Yes!: Visions of Female Sexual Power and a World Without Rape.* Berkeley, CA: Seal Press, 2008.

25. Laura Nielsen. *License to Harass: Law, Hierarchy, and Offensive Public Speech.* Princeton, NJ: Princeton University Press, 2006.

26. Lilia Cortina and S. Arzu Wasti. "Profiles in Coping: Responses to Sexual Harassment Across Persons, Organizations, and Cultures." *Journal of Applied Psychology 90(1):* 182–192, 2005.

27. Arlie Hochschild. *The Managed Heart: Commercialization of Human Feeling.* Berkeley, CA: University of California Press, 2003/1983.

28. Arlie Hochschild. 2003/1983; Miliann Kang. *The Managed Hand: Race, Gender, and the Body in Beauty Service Work.* Berkeley, CA: University of California Press, 2010.

29. See Arlie Hochschild. 2003/1983.

30. See Elijah Anderson. *Code of the Street: Decency, Violence, and the Moral Life of the Inner City.* New York: W.W. Norton, 1999; Anderson, Elijah. *Streetwise: Race, Class, and Change in an Urban Community.* Chicago: University of Chicago Press, 1992.

31. Elijah Anderson. 1992.

32. See Martin Jay. *Downcast Eyes: The Denigration of Vision in Twentieth-Century French Thought*. Oakland, CA: University of California Press, 1993.

33. Griselda Pollock. *Modernity and the Spaces of Femininity*. New York: Routledge, 1992.

34. Judith Butler. *Excitable Speech: A Politics of the Performative*. New York: Routledge, 1997.

35. See Daphne Patai. *Heterophobia: Sexual Harassment and the Future of Feminism*. New York: Rowman & Littlefield, 2000.

36. See Emilie Buchwald, Pamela R. Fletcher, and Martha Roth (Eds.). *Transforming a Rape Culture*. Minneapolis, MN: Milkweed Editions, 2005; Laura L. O'Toole, Jessica R. Schiffman, and Rosemary Sullivan (Eds.). *Gender Violence: Interdisciplinary Perspectives (3rd Ed.)*. New York: NYU Press, 2020.

37. Judith Butler. 1997.

38. Judith Butler. 1997.

Conclusion

Throughout this work, I attempted to provide evidence of street harassment as a social problem, by offering evidence from the literature and excerpts from the narratives offered up by respondents who participated in my study. I discussed the limits in the extant literature, pointing to the relative absence of scholarly studies on street harassment.

My work aims to contribute to the existing literature, by drawing attention to the ways in which women negotiate street harassment. I described the plethora of ways that the women in my sample attempt to socially (and sometimes physically or geographically) move around this violence in their daily lives. Research participants shared their working definitions of street harassment and how they understand the social problem, as well some strategies for dealing with men who harass.

I situated street harassment with the context of rape culture and the web of violence that exists in this society, as a way of illustrating the expanse of the problem. I argued that the web of violence woven into this society accommodates street harassment and maintains rape culture. These problems go unrecognized and unregulated largely because of patriarchal power and the widespread refusal to see street harassment as a problem. Often, street harassment is *misrecognized* as civility, instead of a form of everyday violence that its victims endure.

To illustrate the trouble in not seeing street harassment as a problem, I show how and why street harassment "hides in plain sight." Violence against women does much the same, concealed by shame and guilt, veiled from public revelations, or by "the silence of violence." This work shows the many ways women targets of street harassment attempt to "survive the silence of violence."

In showing how they challenged the controlling images that circulate in society, or the "dangerous ways of seeing" among the men who harass, these women demonstrated both vulnerability and strength in strategically maneuvering through urban public spaces. They weighed their options situationally, but always consider(ed) a number of contingencies. In doing so, they revealed how "discourses of danger" work to discourage and dissuade women from being in public. Discourses of danger mask the violence that women may confront in private. By linking the two spaces, we gain a deeper understanding of the web of violence that exists in this society and within which street harassment remains situated.

The work of centering the voices of women proves important. However, the arguably more difficult and imperative challenge remains in remedying street harassment. Presenting an analysis of the "dangerous ways of speaking" and "dangerous ways of looking" related to street harassment illustrates the dilemma that women targets face in deciding if and how to respond to men who harass, as well as how to manage the various discourses designed to hold women accountable. Ultimately, this is a dangerous discourse, in the way that men who harass are not held responsible or accountable for their actions.

This work draws attention to street harassment as everyday violence. It highlights how often women face violence in public spaces, on the street, as well as other possible sites. This work calls for more sustained and collective efforts to be made to address and ameliorate the problem of street harassment, but also the problem of the expansive and persistent web of violence.

LIMITATIONS OF THE WORK

One of the limitations of my study pertains to who I chose to recruit for my study. I purposefully drew a sample of women, in order to understand how they employed agency and experienced vulnerability and courage in navigating street harassment. I drew from their narratives as a way of sharing the strategies that they used, in their efforts to mitigate or minimize any adverse impacts from street harassment. My hope is that the book offers up this information as a source of inspiration and empowerment, but also as a continued call to make all spaces safer, more inclusive, and more welcoming of everyone.

Possible Directions of Future Research

One direction that future research on this topic might take would involve interviews with men. The problem of street harassment resides with the people who perpetuate it, not the people who are pulled into it or adversely impacted by it. Interviewing men who harass has the potential to accomplish what much of feminist research aims for, in terms of heightening awareness or raising consciousness.

To this end, conducting research with men participants would provide them with the space to share their understanding of street harassment, including behaviors that they may not recognize as that. One such study reflects a potentially powerful intervention, as it could help men who harass to understand their behavior beyond what they might see as sociality and civility, but rather as hostility and harassment.

Men's participation in such research might offer support for existing gender ideologies and expectations about men and their performance of masculinity. To some of the discussion offered in an earlier chapter, men who harass would also have the space to share the ways in which they, too, may have experienced harassment, from authority figures, or other people in public spaces. Future research would continue to address the gap in the literature, and in society, that normalizes street harassment and accommodates its persistence.

Researchers might consider ways to creatively share their findings, making access to this information broadly available. Such a practice would be a part of academic feminism, while linking this work to the long-lasting efforts of the #MeToo Movement and others advocating for an equitable and just society. Studies that outline some policy or legislative changes would ideally offer up practical applications of the research, including specific solutions or interventions to street harassment as everyday violence.

References

Alcoff, Linda Martin and Laura Gray. "Survivor Discourse: Transgression or Recuperation" in *Signs: Journal of Women in Culture and Society 18(2)*: 260–290, 1993.

Alexander, Michelle. *The New Jim Crow: Mass Incarceration in the Age of Colorblindness*. New York: New Press, 2012.

Allison, Dorothy. *Two or Three Things I Know for Sure*. New York: Plume, 1995.

Anderson, Elijah. *The Cosmopolitan Canopy: Race and Civility in Everyday Life*. New York: W.W. Norton, 2010.

———. *Code of the Street: Decency, Violence, and the Moral Life of the Inner City*. New York: W.W. Norton, 1999.

———. *Streetwise: Race, Class, and Change in an Urban Community*. Chicago: University of Chicago Press, 1992.

Bailey, Moya. *Misogynoir Transformed: Black Women's Digital Resistance*. New York: New York University Press, 2021.

Bartky, Sandra Lee. "Foucault, Femininity, and the Modernization of Patriarchal Power" in *The Politics of Women's Bodies: Sexuality, Appearance, and Behavior* (2nd Ed). Edited by Rose Weitz. Pp. 25–45. New York: Oxford University Press, 2003.

Beaulieu, Sarah Pierson. *The Enliven Project*. Available online: theenlivenproject.com /category/sexual-violence/double-silence/ Accessed on March 30, 2022. Published 2014.

Beneke, Timothy. *Proving Manhood: Reflections on Men and Sexism*. Berkeley, CA: University of California Press, 1997.

Berger, Melody. *We Don't Need Another Wave: Dispatches from the Next Generation of Feminists*. New York: Seal Press, 2006.

Bernard, Jessie. The Future of Marriage. New Haven, CT: Yale University Press, 1982.

Blum, Linda. *At the Breast: Ideologies of Breastfeeding and Motherhood in the Contemporary United States*. Boston: Beacon Press, 1999.

Bonilla Silva, Eduardo. *Racism without Racists: Color-Blind Racism and the Persistence of Racial Inequality in America*. Lanham, MD: Rowman & Littlefield, 2017.

Bordo, Susan. "Feminism, Foucault, and the Politics of the Body" in *Feminist Theory and the Body: A Reader.* Edited by Janet Price and Margrit Shildrick. Pp. 246-257. New York: Routledge, 1999.

Bourgois, Phillippe. *In Search of Respect: Selling Crack in El Barrio.* Cambridge, MA: Cambridge University Press, 1995.

Bourdieu, Pierre, and Loic J. Wacquant. *An Invitation to Reflexive Sociology.* Chicago: University of Chicago Press, 1992.

Bowman, Cynthia Grant. "Street Harassment and the Informal Ghettoization of Women" in *Harvard Law Review 106(3)*: 517–581, January 1993.

Brookbank, Elizabeth. "Talking Back: Women in New York City Confront Street Harassment." Interview with Michele from the Street Harassment Project. *Off Our Backs.* Pp. 20–24, September–October 2002.

Brown, Brené. *Daring Greatly: How the Courage to Be Vulnerable Transforms the Way We Live, Love, Parent, and Lead.* New York: Avery, 2015.

———. *The Gifts of Imperfection: Letting Go of Who You Think You're Supposed to Be and Embrace Who You Are.* Center City, MN: Hazelden, 2010.

Brown, Ruth Nicole. *Hear Our Truths: The Creative Potential of Black Girlhood.* Champaign, IL: University of Illinois Press, 2013.

Buchanan, NiCole T. and Alayne J. Ormerod. "Racialized Sexual Harassment in the Lives of African American Women" in *Women and Therapy* 25(3/4): 105–121, December 31, 2002.

Buchwald, Emilie, Pamela R. Fletcher, and Martha Roth (Eds.). *Transforming a Rape Culture.* Minneapolis, MN: Milkweed Editions, 2005.

Butler, Judith. *Precarious Life: The Powers of Mourning and Violence.* New York: Verso, 2006.

———. *Excitable Speech: A Politics of the Performative.* New York: Routledge, 1997.

Castellanos, Rosario. "Language as an Instrument of Domination" in *Women Writing Resistance: Essays on Latin America and the Caribbean.* Edited by Jennifer Browdy de Hernandez. Pp. 73–78. Cambridge, MA: South End Press, 2003.

Centers for Disease Control (National Center for Injury Prevention and Control, Division of Violence Prevention). "Fast Facts: Preventing Intimate Partner Violence." Available online: www.cdc.gov/violenceprevention/intimatepartnerviolence/fastfact.html Accessed April 20, 2022. Page last reviewed: November 2, 2021.

Chesney-Lind, Meda and Nikki Jones (Eds.). *Fighting for Girls: New Perspectives on Gender and Violence.* Albany, NY: SUNY, 2010.

Cofer, Judith Ortiz. "The Myth of the Latin Woman" in *Women Writing Resistance: Essays on Latin America and the Caribbean.* Edited by Jennifer Browdy de Hernandez. Pp. 109–116. Cambridge, MA: South End Press, 2003.

Cohan, Audrey, Mary Ann Hergenrother, Yolanda M. Johnson, Laurie S. Mandel, and Janice Sawyer. *Sexual Harassment and Sexual Abuse: A Handbook for Teachers and Administrators.* Thousand Oaks, CA: Corwin Press, Inc., 1996.

Conboy, Katie, Nadia Median, and Sarah Stanbury (Eds). *Writing on the Body: Female Embodiment and Feminist Theory.* New York: Columbia University Press, 1997.

Connolly-Shaffer, Patricia. "Staging Cross-Border (Reading) Alliances: Feminist Polyvocal Testimonials at Work." Published Dissertation. Available online: conservancy.umn.edu/bitstream/141437/1/ConnollyShaffer_umn_0130E_13 269.pdf., 2012.

Collins, Patricia Hill. *Black Feminist Thought: Knowledge, Consciousness, and the Politics of Empowerment.* New York: Routledge, 2008.

———. *Black Sexual Politics: African Americans, Gender, and the New Racism.* New York: Routledge, 2005.

———. "Toward a New Vision." *Privilege: A Reader.* Edited by Michael S. Kimmel and Abby L. Ferber. Pp. 331–348. Cambridge, MA: Westview, 2003.

Cortina, Lilia and S. Arzu Wasti. "Profiles in Coping: Responses to Sexual Harassment Across Persons, Organizations, and Cultures." *Journal of Applied Psychology 90(1):* 182–192, 2005.

Cvetkovich, Ann. *An Archive of Feeling: Trauma, Sexuality, and Lesbian Public Cultures.* Durham, NC: Duke University Press, 2003.

Davis, Angela. *Women, Race, and Class.* New York: Random House, 1981.

DeFour, Darlene C. "The Interface of Racism and Sexism on College Campuses" in Michele Paludi's *Sexual Harassment on College Campuses: Abusing the Ivory Power.* Pp. 49–55. Albany, New York: State University of New York Press, 1996.

de Hernandez, Jennifer Browdy. *Women Writing Resistance: Essays on Latin America and the Caribbean.* Cambridge, MA: South End Press, 2003.

Duneier, Mitch. *Sidewalk.* New York: Farrar, Straus and Giroux, 1999.

Duneier, Mitch and Harvey Molotch. "Talking City Trouble: Explorations" in *Gender, Media, and Public Space.* Cresskill, NJ: Hampton Press, Inc., 1999.

Espiritu, Yen Le. "'We Don't Sleep Around Like White Girls Go': Family, Culture, and Gender in Filipina American Lives." *Signs 26(2):* 415–440, Winter 2001.

Fernandez, Ana Maria. "Violencia y Conyugalidad," *La Mujer y la Violencia Invisible.* Eds. Eva Giberti and Ana Maria Fernandez. Buenos Aires: Editorial Sudamericana, 1989.

Filipovic, Jill. "Offensive Feminism: The Conservative Gender Norms That Perpetuate Rape Culture, and How Feminists Can Fight Back." In *Yes Means Yes!: Visions of Female Sexual Power and a World Without Rape.* Edited by Jaclyn Friedman, 13- 28, 2008.

Foucault, Michel. *Discipline and Punish: The Birth of the Prison.* Translated from the French by Alan Sheridan. New York: Vintage Books, 1977.

Freedman, Eden Wales. *Reading Testimony, Witnessing Trauma: Confronting Race, Gender, and Violence in American Literature.* Jackson, MI: University of Mississippi Press, 2020.

Friedan, Betty. *The Feminine Mystique.* New York: Penguin Books, 2010.

Friedman, Jaclyn. *What You Really Really Want: The Smart Girl's Shame-Free Guide to Sex and Safety.* Berkeley, CA: Seal Press, 2011.

Friedman, Jaclyn and Jessica Valenti. *Yes Means Yes!: Visions of Female Sexual Power and a World Without Rape.* Berkeley, CA: Seal Press, 2008.

Fregoso, Rosa-Linda. "Toward a Planetary Civil Society" in *Mexicana Encounters: The Making of Social Identities on the Borderlands*. Edited by Rosa-Linda Fregoso. Pp. 1–29. Berkeley, CA: University of California Press, 2003a.

Fregoso, Rosa-Linda (Ed.). *Mexicana Encounters: The Making of Social Identities on the Borderlands*. Berkeley, CA: University of California Press, 2003b.

Gal, Susan. "A Semiotics of the Public/Private Distinction." *Differences: A Journal of Feminist Cultural Studies.* 13:1, 2002.

Gardner, Carol Brooks. *Passing By: Gender and Public Harassment*. Berkeley, CA: University of California Press, 1995.

Gay, William. "Supplanting Linguistic Violence" in *Gender Violence: Interdisciplinary Perspectives (2nd Ed.)*. Edited by Laura O'Toole, Jessica Schiffman, and Margie Kiter Edwards. Pp. 435–442. New York: NYU Press, 2007.

General Accounting Office Report GAO 20–654. "Workplace Sexual Harassment: Experts Suggest Expanding Data Collection to Improve Understanding of Prevalence and Costs." September 2020.

Glassner, Barry. *The Culture of Fear: Why Americans are Afraid of the Wrong Things*. New York: Basic Books, 2009.

Gray-Rosendale, Laura (Ed.). *Me Too, Feminist Theory, and Surviving Sexual Violence in the Academy.* Lanham, MD: Lexington Press, 2022.

———. *College Girl*. Albany, NY: SUNY Press, 2013.

Hadleigh-West, Maggie. *War Zone*. Video recording. A Film Fatale, Inc./Hank Levine Film. Northampton, MA: GmbH Production, 1998.

Halberstam, Jack. *Female Masculinity*. Durham, NC: Duke University Press, 2018.

Haraway, Donna. "The Persistence of Vision" in *Writing on the Body: Female Embodiment and Feminist Theory*. Edited by Katie Conboy, Nadia Medina, and *Sarah Stanbury.* Pp. 283–295. New York: Columbia University Press, 1997.

Harding, Kate. *Asking for It: The Alarming Rise of Rape Culture—and What We Can Do About It*. Boston, MA: Da Capo Lifetime Books, 2015.

Harper, Phillip Brian. "The Evidence of Felt Intuition: Minority Experience, Everyday Life, and Critical Speculative Knowledge," *GLQ: A Journal of Lesbian and Gay Studies* 6, no. 4 (2000): 641–57.

Harris-Perry, Melissa. *Sister Citizen: Shame, Stereotypes, and Black Women in America.* New Haven, CT: Yale University Press, 2011.

Higginbotham, Evelyn Brooks. "African-American Women's History and the Metalanguage of Race." *Signs 17(2)*: 251–274, Winter 1992.

Hobson, Janell. *Body as Evidence: Mediating Race, Globalizing Gender.* Albany, NY: SUNY, 2012.

Hochschild, Arlie. *The Managed Heart: Commercialization of Human Feeling.* Berkeley, CA: University of California Press, 2003/1983.

Hoffman, Kelly M., Sophie Trawalter, Jordan R. Axt, & M. Norman Oliver. "Racial Bias in Pain Assessment and Treatment Recommendations, and False Beliefs About Biological Differences Between Blacks and Whites." *Proceedings of the National Academy of Sciences of the United States of America*, *113*(16), 2016: 4296–4301. doi.org/10.1073/pnas.1516047113

Hollaback! Street Harassment (website). Available online: www.ihollaback .org. Accessed on November 1, 2019.

Hofstadter, Richard. "Reflections on Violence in the United States." Available online: thebaffler.com/ancestors/reflections-violence-united-states. Accessed on April 30, 2022. Published July 2015.

Holloway, Karla. *Private Bodies, Public Texts: Race, Gender, and a Cultural Bioethics*. Durham, NC: Duke, 2011.

hooks, bell. *Talking Back: Thinking Feminist, Thinking Black (2nd Ed.)*. New York: Routledge.

Hunter, Marcus Anthony and Zandria F. Robinson. *Chocolate Cities: The Black Map of American Life*. Oakland, CA: University of California Press, 2018.

Hunter, Margaret and Kathleen Soto. "Women of Color in Hip Hop: The Pornographic Gaze." *Race, Gender, and Class*. Volume 12 (1 and 2), 2009: 170–191.

James, Joy. *Resisting State Violence: Radicalism, Gender, and Race in U.S. Culture*. Minneapolis, MN: University of Minnesota Press, 1996.

Jay, Martin. *Downcast Eyes: The Denigration of Vision in Twentieth-Century French Thought*. Oakland, CA: University of California Press, 1993.

Jensen, Robert. *Getting Off: Pornography and the End of Masculinity*. Boston, MA: South End Press, 2007.

Jhally, Sut. *The Codes of Gender: Identity and Performance in Popular Culture*. Videorecording, 2008.

Jones, Nikki. "'It's About Being a Survivor . . . ': African American Girls, Gender, and the Context of Inner-City Violence" in *Fighting for Girls: New Perspectives on Gender and Violence*. Edited by Meda Chesney-Lind and Nikki Jones. Pp. 203 -218. Albany, NY: SUNY, 2010.

———. *Between Good and Ghetto: African American Girls and Inner-City Violence*. Piscataway, NJ: Rutgers University Press, 2008.

Kalof, L., Eby, K. K., Matheson, J. L., & Kroska, R. J. "The Influence of Race and Gender on Student Self-Reports of Sexual Harassment by College Professors. *Gender & Society, 15*, 282–302, 2001.

Kang, Miliann. *The Managed Hand: Race, Gender, and the Body in Beauty Service Work*. Berkeley, CA: University of California Press, 2010.

Kaufmann, Michael. "The Construction of Masculinity and the Triad of Men's Violence" in *Beyond Patriarchy: Essays on Pleasure, Power, and Change*. New York: Oxford University Press, 1987.

Kearl, Holly. *50 Stories of Stopping Street Harassers*. New York: Praeger, 2013.

Kearl, Holly. *Stop Street Harassment: Making Public Places Safe and Welcoming for Women*. New York: Praeger, 2010a.

Kearl, Holly. "Street Harassment: A Real Problem that Requires Legal Regulation," *Huffington Post*, March 12, 2010b.

Kent, Tara E. "The Confluence of Race and Gender in Women's Sexual Harassment Experiences" in *Gender Violence: Interdisciplinary Perspectives (2nd Ed.)*. Edited by Laura O'Toole, Jessica Schiffman, and Margie Kiter Edwards. New York: NYU Press, 2007: 172–180.

Kilbourne, Jean. *Killing Us Softy 4: Advertising's Image of Women.* Film. Directed by Sut Jhally. Northampton, MA: Media Education Foundation, 2010.

Kimmel, Michael. *Privilege: A Reader.* Edited by Michael S. Kimmel and Abby L. Ferber. Pp. 331–348. Cambridge, MA: Westview, 2003.

Kottak, Conrad Phillip and Kathryn Kozaitis. *On Being Different.* New York: McGraw Hill, 2006.

Lamb, Sharon. *The Secret Lives of Girls: What Good Girls Really Do—Sex Play, Aggression, and Their Guilt.* New York: Free Press, 2002.

Lamb, Sharon (Ed.). *New Versions of Victims: Feminists Struggle with the Concept.* New York: New York University Press, 1999.

Leap, Terry L. & Smeltzer, Larry R. "Racial Remarks in the Workplace: Humor or Harassment." *Harvard Business Review.* 62(6), 74–78, 1984.

Lempert, Lora Bex. "The Line in the Sand: Definitional Dialogues in Abusive Relationships." *Studies in Symbolic Interaction,* 18, 1995.

Leo, Jana (2010). *Rape New York.* New York: The Feminist Press of CUNY.

Lerum, Kari. "Sexuality, Power, and Camaraderie in Service Work." *Gender and Society 18(6):* 756–77, 2004.

Lorde, Audre. *The Cancer Journals.* San Francisco: Aunt Lute, 1980.

Lucal, Betsy. "What It Means to Be Gendered Me: Life on the Boundaries of a Dichotomous Gender System." *Gender and Society 13(6):* 781–797, 1999.

McGuire, Danielle. *At the Dark End of the Street: Black Women, Rape, and Resistance.* New York: Vintage, 2011.

McIntosh, Peggy. "White Privilege and Male Privilege: A Personal Account of Coming to See Correspondences through Work in Women's Studies." 1988.

Mahood, Linda and Barbara Littlewood. "Daughters in Danger: The Case of "Campus Sex Crimes'" in *Sexual Harassment: Contemporary Feminist Perspectives.* Edited by Alison M. Thomas and Celia Kitzinger. Pp. 172–187. Philadelphia: Open University Press, 1997.

MeToo Movement. Website. Available online: metoomvmt.org/get-to-know-us/tarana -burke-founder/. Accessed on April 25, 2022.

Miller, Chanel. *Know My Name: A Memoir.* New York: Penguin, 2020.

Miller, Jean Baker. *Toward a New Psychology of Women (2nd Ed.).* Boston: Beacon Press, 2012.

Mills, Sara. *Discourse.* New York: Routledge, 1997.

Mirzoeff, Nicholas. *The Right to Look: A Counterhistory of Visuality.* Durham, NC: Duke University Press, 2011.

Moraga, Cherrie. "La Guera" in *This Bridge Called My Back.* Pp. 27–34. New York: Kitchen Table: Women of Color Press, 1983.

Mulvey, Laura. "Visual Pleasure and Narrative Cinema." *Screen* 16:6–18, 1975.

Myers, Kristin. Racetalk: Racism Hiding in Plain Sight. New York: Rowman & Littlefield Publishers, 2005.

National Center on Domestic Violence. "Violence Against Trans and Non -Binary People" at the following website: vawnet.org/sc/serving-trans-and -non-binary-survivors-domestic-and-sexual-violence/violence-against-trans -and Accessed on April 21, 2022.

National Institute of Justice, "Most Victims Know Their Attacker." Available here: nij.ojp.gov/topics/articles/most-victims-know-their-attacker. Accessed on April 20, 2022. Published on September 30, 2008.

New York Civil Liberties Union (ACLU of New York). "Stop-and-Frisk Data." Available online: www.nyclu.org/en/stop-and-frisk-data. Accessed on April 20, 2022.

Nielsen, Laura. *License to Harass: Law, Hierarchy, and Offensive Public Speech*. Princeton, NJ: Princeton University Press, 2006.

O'Toole, Laura L., Jessica R. Schiffman, and Rosemary Sullivan (Eds.). *Gender Violence: Interdisciplinary Perspectives (3rd Ed.)*. New York: NYU Press, 2020.

O'Toole, Laura, Jessica Schiffman, and Margie Kiter Edwards (Eds.). *Gender Violence: Interdisciplinary Perspectives (2nd Ed.)*. New York: NYU Press, 2007.

Ochoa, Maria and Ige, Barbara K. *Shout Out: Women of Color Respond to Violence*. New York: Seal Press, 2008.

Paludi, Michele. *Sexual Harassment on College Campuses: Abusing the Ivory Power*. Albany, NY: State University of New York Press, 1996.

Patai, Daphne. *Heterophobia: Sexual Harassment and the Future of Feminism*. New York: Rowman & Littlefield, 2000.

Pérez-Peña, Richard "Woman Linked to 1955 Emmett Till Murder Tells Historian Her Claims Were False." *New York Times*. January 27, 2017. Accessed on May 5, 2022. Available online: www.nytimes.com/2017/01/27/us/emmett-till-lynching-carolyn-bryant-donham.html

Pierce-Baker, Charlotte. *Surviving the Silence: Black Women's Stories of Rape*. New York: W.W. Norton and Company, 1998.

Pollock, Griselda. *Modernity and the Spaces of Femininity*. New York: Routledge, 1992.

Reddy, Chandran. Freedom with Violence: Race, Sexuality, and the US State. Durham, NC: Duke University Press, 2011.

Roberson, Amaya Naomi. "Homeland Insecurity: The Terror of Street Harassment" in *Off Our Backs*. July-August 2003:66–68, 2003.

Root, Maria P.P. *Love's Revolution: Interracial Marriage*. Philadelphia: Temple University Press, 2001.

Ryder, Judith. "'I Don't Know If You Consider That as Violence . . .': Using Attachment Theory to Understand Girls' Perspectives on Violence" in *Fighting for Girls: New Perspectives on Gender and Violence*. Edited by Meda Chesney-Lind and Nikki Jones. Pp. 129–148. Albany, NY: SUNY, 2010.

Russo, Mary. "Female Grotesque: Carnival and Theory" in *Writing on the Body: Female Embodiment and Feminist Theory*. Pp. 318–336. New York: Columbia University Press, 1997.

Sethi, Rachna. "'Out of Place' Women: Exploring Gendered Spatiality in Delhi." *Journal of Postcolonial Writing*, Vol 54(3): 398–420. Special Issue: Delhi: New Writings on the Megacity, 2018.

Sheffield, Carole J "Sexual Terrorism" in *Gender Violence: Interdisciplinary Perspectives (2nd Ed.)*. Edited by Laura O'Toole, Jessica Schiffman, and Margie Kiter Edwards. Pp. 111–130. New York: NYU Press, 2007.

Smith, Joanne, Meghan Huppuch, and Mandy Van Deven. *Hey Shorty! A Guide* to Combating Sexual Harassment and Violence in Schools and on the Street. New York: The Feminist Press at CUNY, 2011.

Springer, Kimberly. "Divas, Evil Black Bitches, and Bitter Black Women: African American Women in Postfeminist and Post-Civil-Rights Popular Culture" in *Interrogating Postfeminism: Gender and the Politics of Popular Culture*. Edited by Yvonne Tasker and Diane Negra. Durham, NC; Duke University Press, 2007. 10.1215/9780822390411–011

Stephens, Dionne P. and Layli D. Phillips 2004. "Freaks, Gold Diggers, Divas, and Dykes: The Sociohistorical Development of Adolescent African American Women's Sexual Scripts." *Sexuality and Culture* 7, 3–49 (2003). doi.org /10.1007/BF03159848

Sue, Derald. *Microagressions in Everyday Life: Race, Gender, and Sexual Orientation.* New York: Wiley, 2010.

Sutton, Barbara. *Bodies in Crisis: Culture, Violence, and Women's Resistance in Neoliberal Argentina.* Piscataway, NJ: Rutgers University Press, 2010.

Tasker, Yvonne and Diane Negra (Eds.) *Interrogating Postfeminism: Gender and the Politics of Popular Culture.* Durham, NC; Duke University Press, 2007.

Taylor, Diana. *Disappearing Acts: Spectacles of Gender and Nationalism in Argentina's "Dirty War."* Durham, NC: Duke University Press, 1997.

Taylor, Jill McLean, Carol Gilligan, and Amy M. Sullivan. *Between Voice and Silence: Women and Girls, Race and Relationship.* Cambridge, MA: Harvard, 1995.

The Latina Feminist Group. *Telling to Live: Latina Feminist Testimonios.* Durham, NC: Duke University Press, 2001.

Thomas, Alison M. "Men Behaving Badly? A Psychosocial Exploration of the Cultural Context of Sexual Harassment" in *Sexual Harassment: Contemporary Feminist Perspectives.* Edited by Alison M. Thomas and Celia Kitzinger. Pp. 131–153. Philadelphia: Open University Press, 1997.

Thomas, Alison M. and Celia Kitzinger (Eds.). *Sexual Harassment: Contemporary Feminist Perspectives.* Philadelphia: Open University Press, 1997.

Tolman, Deborah L. *Dilemmas of Desire: Teenage Girls Talk about Sexuality.* Cambridge, MA: Harvard University Press, 2002.

Tong, Rosemarie. *Feminist Thought.* New York: Routledge, 2017.

Upsetting Rape Culture (Website). Available online: upsettingrapeculture.com / Accessed on October 2018.

Valenti, Jessica. "Purely Rape: The Myth of Sexual Purity and How It Reinforces Rape Culture." In *Yes Means Yes!: Visions of Female Sexual Power and a World Without Rape.* Edited by Jaclyn Friedman, 2008: 299–304.

White, Aaronette. *Ain't I a Feminist?: African American Men Speak Out on Fatherhood, Friendship, Forgiveness, and Freedom.* Albany, NY: SUNY 2008.

Wirth, Louis. *On Cities and Social Life.* Chicago: University of Chicago Press, 1956.

Wingfield, Adia Harvey. *Doing Business with Beauty: Black Women, Hair Salons, and the Racial Enclave Economy.* New York: Rowman & Littlefield, 2008.

———. "The Modern Mammy and the Angry Black Man: African American Professionals' Experiences with Gendered Racism in the Workplace." *Race, Gender & Class* 14(1/2): 196–212.

Winter, Nicholas. *Dangerous Frames: How Ideas about Race and Gender Shape Public Opinion.* Chicago: University of Chicago Press, 2008.

Wright, Melissa. "The Private Parts of Public Value: The Regulation of Women Workers in China's Export-Processing Zones" in *Going Public: Feminism and the Shifting Boundaries of the Private Sphere.* Edited by Joan W. Scott and Debra Keates. Pp. 99–120. Urbana Champaign: University of Illinois Press, 2005.

Zeilinger, Julie. *A Little F'ed Up: Why Feminism Is Not a Dirty Word.* New York: Seal Press, 2012.

Index

curved space/s, 53, 108–9, 113–15, 139

D

danger, 14–16, 30, 32, 49, 52–54, 56,
62, 64, 66–67, 70n41, 73, 75–81, 83,
88, 90–93, 101–15, 119, 123, 125–
29, 131–34, 137–38, 141, 144–55,
158–60, 163–66, 166n20, 171–201,
205, 209–10
dignity, 91, 119
disappearing women, 115–16
discourses, slippery, 11, 35, 37
discursive practice, 74, 87, 129–30,
134, 201, 203
discomfort, with harassment 2, 24, 41,
147, 188, 196
docility, 77, 96, 130–32, 139–
40, 149, 162
dominance, 4, 76, 91, 192, 206
"drive-by" harassment, 146, 199

E

education, 21, 50, 113, 140,
178, 197–98
embodied resistance, 149, 200
emotional labor, 2, 15, 147, 161, 190–
94, 196, 202;
performing, 191;
smiling as, 2, 143, 146, 150,
182, 189, 202
evaluative comments, or remarks, 30,
93, 96, 144, 154, 173, 203, 205
"excitable speech," 24
exploitation, sexual, 117, 164
eye contact, 25–26, 150–52, 188–89,
191, 193–95

F

felt intuition, 6, 82
"female masculinity," 94
femininity, 9, 76–78, 80, 85, 90, 92,
94–96, 104, 110, 127, 129, 130–33,
137, 140, 144, 146–49, 160–61, 181,
193, 195, 197, 200–201, 205;

emphasized femininity,
95, 148, 195;
hegemonic femininity, 78, 90–91,
94–96, 149
feminist standpoint epistemology, 75

G

gaze:
averting the gaze, 195;
the male gaze, 15–16, 27, 79, 82,
151, 171–81, 185–89, 1193,
195, 197, 200, 203
gender conformity, 201–2
gender ideologies, 5, 211
gender nonconforming, 201
gender performance, performance
of masculinity and femininity,
85, 92, 205
gender(ed) spatiality, 196
"gender trouble," 201
Girls for Gender Equity, 20, 50

H

hate crimes, 201
hazards of harassment, 147,
158, 186, 191
hegemonic masculinity, 58, 76, 125,
147, 156, 164
"Hollaback!," 59, 178–79
human rights, 49, 118–19
hypersexualization of women, 27,
30, 81, 87

I

injury, 24, 53, 57, 68n25, 106, 173,
184, 194–96
injurious speech, 198
injustice, 13, 15, 20, 36, 57, 59, 64–65,
124, 131, 134–35, 139–40, 145, 149,
157, 190–91, 196–97, 200;
spatial, 20, 140, 190–91, 196–97
intensified harassment, 157, 175
interactional vandalism, 33, 36–40, 78,
97n7, 138, 173

About the Author

Melinda A. Mills is associate professor of women's and gender studies, sociology, and anthropology at Castleton University in Vermont. Dr. Mills is the author of the award-winning book, *The Borders of Race: Patrolling "Multiracial" Identities*, as well as *The Colors of Love: Multiracial People in Interracial Relationships* (NYU Press) and *Racial Mixture and Musical Mash-Ups in the Life and Art of Bruno* Mars (Lexington Books).